Disruptive Business

To my parents, Sabina and Herman Manu

Disruptive Business

Desire, Innovation and the
Re-design of Business

ALEXANDER MANU

Routledge
Taylor & Francis Group

LONDON AND NEW YORK

First published in paperback 2024

First published 2010 by Gower Publishing

Published 2016 by Routledge
4 Park Square, Milton Park, Abingdon, Oxon OX14 4RN

and by Routledge
605 Third Avenue, New York, NY 10158

Routledge is an imprint of the Taylor & Francis Group, an informa business

© 2010, 2016, 2024 Alexander Manu

The right of Alexander Manu to be identified as author of this work has been asserted in accordance with sections 77 and 78 of the Copyright, Designs and Patents Act 1988.

Publisher's Note
The publisher has gone to great lengths to ensure the quality of this reprint but points out that some imperfections in the original copies may be apparent.

British Library Cataloguing in Publication Data
Manu, Alexander, 1954-
  Disruptive business : desire, innovation and the re-design
  of business.
  1. Organizational change. 2. Creative ability in business.
  I. Title
  658.4'06-dc22

Library of Congress Cataloging-in-Publication Data
Manu, Alexander, 1954-
  Disruptive business : desire, innovation and the re-design of business / by Alexander Manu.
    p. cm.
  Includes bibliographical references and index.
  ISBN 978-0-566-09240-4 (hbk)
  1. Technological innovations--Management. 2. Diffusion of innovations. I. Title.
  HD45.M329 2010
  658.4'063--dc22

2010000634

ISBN: 978-0-566-09240-4 (hbk)
ISBN: 978-1-03-283841-0 (pbk)
ISBN: 978-1-315-57762-3 (ebk)

DOI: 10.4324/9781315577623

Contents

List of Figures

Acknowledgements

I am grateful to the many individuals that have helped me learn about the unique dilemmas their organizations are facing, and allowed me a small measure of participation in solving them. To Margaret McKellar, Jon Affleck at Unilever, Geoff Craig at Maple Leaf Foods Canada, Pia Erkinheimo and Minna Takala at Nokia Group in Espoo, Finland, my thanks for their insights and trust.

I am indebted to Jeanne Liedtka and Sami Viitamäki for their enthusiasm, passion and generous contribution of knowledge, ideas and time to this book. Mark Outhwaite conducted the original research in the transformation of IBM from 1995 through to 2005; his attention to detail and his continuously probing nature, have greatly helped my framing and articulation of the changes that took place.

My colleagues and partners at Innospa International deserve special recognition: warm thanks to Tuula Antola, for her energy, humanity, insight and sisterly love in moments of profound change, and to Matthew Jones for his friendship, reflective nature, constant intellectual sparring, and his significant contribution to the framing of desire, want and need as innovation drivers.

Jonathan Norman at Gower Publishing, has embraced this book from the beginning and has made the process a pleasure; to him and to Bryan Campbell, who has edited the material with expediency and accuracy, and Kevin Selmes who has designed a superb book in record time, my many thanks for a flawless collaboration.

Finally, my gratitude to my family, Sophie, Sasha, Booboo and my father Herman Manu; their continued moral support and guidance allow my spirit to stay young and curious, as it should.

Panazol, Haute-Vienne, Limousin
March 2010

Prologue

Look around you. Look carefully for a few minutes, at everything that surrounds you in this very moment. Absorb everything. Now imagine the world you see, *without fire*. When is the last time you thought about the role fire plays in our life? Probably never. And here is the opening: *You are the product of fire!* Your life, in everything you know, learned, do, and desire to do, is the outcome of a discovery made 1.9 million years ago by one of your early ancestors.

This is a book about how you transformed that discovery into innovation, and how innovation has transformed you. About innovation as behaviour, innovation as culture, and the hopes and outcomes of everyday life.

Fire was not an innovation; fire was a discovery. But the realized possibility of that discovery has changed the course of our history on this planet forever. The way we are, the way we want to be, and what we desire to become. A discovery has inspired in us possibility beyond the reach of all other animals. We are more. We will become more. We will transform fire into *us,* and transcend, moments at a time, our animal condition. By using fire to transform us, *we became the innovation.*

Fire. Welcome to the story of your life. And welcome to our economic system, our culture, and our business.

Introduction

Everything we know, do and desire is the outcome of fire.

Fire represents the first moment in history, when civilization transformed itself; the transformational part came when humans discovered that fire can be put to beneficial uses, which vastly changed their behaviour and with that, their expectations. What is interesting to note is that fire already existed in the surrounding environment, but it was not being put to a beneficial use. People came across it, and looked at it, but it had no 'media' for humanity because we did not use it for anything. It only became an 'innovation' when one day, a human figured out how to preserve it and then someone else – probably thousands of years later – figured out how to *start* a fire. At first we used it for its obvious physical properties of heat and light, and before long we used it for another major transformation: as a source of energy. Disruptive innovations such as fire and electricity are not fully manifest in the moment 'the new' is introduced by discovery; the disruption occurs only when human motivation embraces 'the new' as a technology and allows it to enhance and expand everyday life. Innovation is a bridge to a better self. All discoveries that become technologies through our use are temporary bridges into the future. They are temporary because they lead somewhere, to a place yet to be defined, by an individual yet to define the destination.

And so, to the first redefinition: *Innovation is not a process, but an outcome.* When you treat innovation as an outcome, the role of a business organization becomes to create the tools, objects and services through which people can manifest what they want, who they are and who they want to become. In this view, all innovation is aspirational. The role of business is to create *media* for you to become something else, a better self. If transformation is the key to growth, then the tools of transformation – or the *media* for transformation – are what a company creates. This applies to everything from soap to computers and iPhones. Any company that knows what its true job is, creates essentially products for transformation. And transformation takes us away from our life of habit, into a new ambiguous territory, with new measures and new expectations, or what might come next. Transformation takes us to a place of ambiguity, a place where the old measures do not apply. This is why ambiguity scares: our lives are very much about habits. Once we have a fixed paradigm of what tomorrow will be like, we are unlikely to change much. So if you want to participate in life, and be part of the perpetual transformation offered by innovation, you need to be able to absorb everything that is new. If you look at the world twice you will perpetually see what's new, and how you need to continually transform yourself and your organization because of what is new today.

When you look at a newspaper headline or hear about a new behaviour that people are engaging in, step back and look again, without jumping to judgment. See it twice, and look at it from a point of view outside of your daily habit. You can dismiss Facebook as a fad, or something that 'kids do', but if you look at it again, you will understand that Facebook is basically a broadcast station for every human that uses it, and a media for transformation. When you look at these tools as proof of transformation, you see them in a different way, and then life in society and your role in it becomes something new.

This understanding of life as a dynamic is not something that companies typically plan for, because, after all, strategic plans are made today, from the perspective afforded by the moment, and from assumptions that, at times, simply move the date five years from now. The dynamic quality of life has to be better accounted for in corporate strategy. And to do so we must treat innovation as the dynamic behaviour by which transformation manifests itself. Innovation is humanity transformed by fire, electricity, the movable press, books, mechanical gears, digital devices, steel, sugar, coffee and oil. Innovation is a human activity; that moment in which behaviour is changed by fire, or electricity, or digital data.

As we use an invention, our goals change and our motivation changes, making further innovations necessary. In today's business world, innovation is tricky. In my work for large corporations I realized that great ideas typically get disregarded, and are not implemented because of a lack of understanding of *where innovation fits*. Many organizations treat innovation as 'a process to be managed', rather than 'an outcome that creates culture and changes people's lives'. Treating innovation as a process reduces it, its practitioners and results, to the basic elements of any process. But as this book will attempt to demonstrate, innovation is not a process but an outcome. There are many processes that result in innovation outcomes, and they will be explored in the section that follows.

In this book I organized the content in nine sections. This introduction is not an attempt to summarize each section, but rather intended to give you a taste of some of the milestones you will find on this journey.

Perspectives for a Conversation about Innovation

Innovation is in a crisis of identity. There are multiple roots for this crisis, which are explored at length in the first section. In my opinion some have to do with mislabeling what innovation is while some have to do with the opportunities, and threats, posed by crowd sourced massive innovation, an immediate reality that calls for the redefinition of what 'innovation' is, in the context of an empowered and participatory user. At the level of the corporation, the new reality calls for a new focus, new incentives, new tools, and a renewed scope for the efforts designed to bring about innovation outcomes. They also need precision in the language surrounding innovation – from its definition to its vocabulary of action – so all stakeholders are on the same page.

As I make the case many times in this book – and the risk of repeating this often might be mitigated by the importance I attach to its understanding – innovation is an outcome, not a process. Organizations fancy the latter because *processes can be managed*, and this is what organizations are good at. This hides the lack of expertise – and mindset – in creating and managing a culture of innovativeness, and an organizational ecology populated by innovation 'connoisseurs' rather than innovation managers. The management of the outcome is much different than the management of the process, and this is where definitions are important: innovation is an outcome achieved by a multiplicity of processes, some including imagination, creativity or simply repetitive tasks.

The redefinition of innovation as a *human behaviour outcome*, a dynamic in constant change, requires the shaping of new responses in business and the economy. I will make the case in the chapters that follow, that organizations must treat innovation as the moment in which human behavior is being changed by a particular invention, discovery or event, which in this work is referred to as an *innovation object*.

The past understanding of what innovation 'is', was generally connected with a breakthrough in technology – some new tool being employed in some new way. This understanding limits the potential of innovation as bound by the tools employed, instead of the imagination employing them. The latent imagination triggered by an innovation outcome is the true goal of innovation. It is not what *'I can do with this now?'* but *'what can I become doing this in the future?'* The tool is not a response, but a question. *Every innovation is a question.* The truly important innovations are a series of questions.

A few definitions: Innovation is an outcome, a new behaviour, a new way of doing things. Disruption is a behavior – an outcome involving a media and a user – changed by invention. Invention is a moment of discovery or creation of something new. Disruptive Business means the sum of new behaviours and their support models. Innovation is a moment of use, a manifest behaviour that engages *an innovation object* into new uses, and modifies the habitual conditions of the present.

This position challenges the current understanding of innovation, and some of the labels applied to innovation typologies, such as the label 'disruptive innovation'. In general, the current discourse around innovation addresses competently the technology side of an invention, at the expense of the motivational side of the user, the human motivation which leads in the behaviour of use. *Humans are the ultimate medium through which technology manifests itself.*

Fire was not a disruptive innovation; it became so only when *human motivation* made it part of everyday life actions and allowed it to modify life in all aspects. I make the case in Chapter 1 that *the disruption is the human being.* Innovation outcomes are answers to goals residing in us, in human motivation, and our motivation starts in desire. We are bound to desire; to perpetually seek media for a better self. To perpetually seek innovation. And from desire we have changed, improved, and reshaped human life.

And here I propose another challenge to the current understanding of innovation : Innovation is rooted in Desire, not need. Desire is the motivation for behaviour. Desire leads to goals, and goals lead to motivation, the internal condition that gives rise to what do we want to do, based on our goals, what can *we do* – based on the norms of behaviour – and what *we will do* – the actions that we voluntarily decide to undertake. Motivation is the ethos of goal orientated behavior, and a company's ability to understand motivation, directly contributes to the success of their products and services in the marketplace. *As desire is constant, innovation is constant.* In this dynamic, innovation is *the constant state of being human,* and business – the activity and the organizations that supply innovation outcomes – is the *variable.*

The role of any business is thus the Organized Capability of creating and distributing media for the manifestation of behaviour. 'Media' in this context is a term covering technologies, objects and services through which people manifest in the present what they want, who they are, what they want to become.

How do we get to innovation? The process of innovation is Design. Design makes 'media' suitable for behaviour. Innovation as an outcome needs a process to achieve that outcome, and that process is design.

The process that best describes the capabilities needed to arrive at innovation outcomes – which include attention to motivation, goals and desires, resulting in a new behaviour – is the design process, because it is best at connecting technology, user preferences, our wants, psychology and ergonomics with what a piece of equipment can produce, and what the system can effectively distribute.

We can not talk about innovation as a stand alone; we can only talk about 'Innovation Behaviour'. The two are intertwined. *The study of innovation is the study of innovation behaviour.* As such, it is the study of what behaviour is a reaction to: desires, goals and motivations. Behaviour is the reaction in response to a stimuli from the environment. By design – or at times, by accident – a stimuli is provided. Innovation behaviour is the response.

Innovation is a Behaviour Outcome

For many thousands of years, humans innovated out of a competitive spirit. We had to, as we needed to survive and we were in competition with other animals. Once we discovered fire, we could start manipulating it to create tools, and the first tools we created allowed us to advantageously compete against the other animals in the gathering of food, in the construction of shelter, and so on. Most of the tools and environments we have initially created for a few thousand years after we started using fire, were the result of a competitive drive. Until one day, about 8000 years ago,[1] when someone turned copper into a pendant, an object for personal adornment. And object beyond competition. A pre-competitive object of desire. Jewelry. An object about a new destination.

We are now 8000 years later, and some companies have the same competitive mentality, as if this pendant was never made. They assume that in order to change and transform anything, they need to find a benchmark against which transformation needs to be measured. Innovation for competitive advantage encourages an Innovation Problem Framework – give me a problem to solve as the starting point. This results in a process in which the limits for what can be achieved are most of the time already defined by the problem definition. This model is no longer sufficient or desirable. This type of innovation does not create a strategic advantage, but mitigates a weak position. While our first innovations were competitive, humanity moved quickly to pre–competitive innovation. The concept of comfort is one of these innovations. A moment in time when we found ourselves wanting a pillow. Pillows have nothing to do with 'need', or with 'competitive drive'.

A pillow is obviously not about competing, so it must be about something else. The problem a pillow solves does not reside in our capacity to merely survive; it resides in our desire for the quality of that survival.

The cultural diffusion and use of pillows in most geographic areas of the globe, and the industry that the pillow as a product has created, is essentially a manifest surrender to the simplest of life's desires: the desire for pleasure. The primary motivators in life are very few and rudimentary: a search for sweetness, for smoothness, for shiny things and for pleasure. These are very basic and human and they lie at the root of industry as we know

---

1   A copper pendant was found in what is now northern Iraq that dates to 8700 BC. Rayner W. Hesse (2007). *Rayner W. Hesse*. Greenwood Publishing Group. p. 56. ISBN 0313335079.

it today. Pillows, then, are not just pillows. The pillow is an outcome, not a process, and the pillow appeared in our lives because we were searching for a smooth, soft place to rest our heads. This is a statement about *who we want to become,* and it is profoundly human – I can not think of any other animal that makes pillows. As a mindset for innovation, the concept of 'beyond competition' starts with *questions* rather than problems: How can I live in comfort? How can I feel pleasure? How can I keep warm? Let us look at coffee is another example of an innovation behaviour beyond competition. Coffee is the second largest commodity on the planet, and for a reason. The first is oil, and we understand why oil is a commodity, but can anyone explain why coffee is a commodity? It makes you realize that we are in search of something, because coffee is not food: it is directed to pleasure. In the end, we would not have an economy if we did not have hope, and we would not have an economy if we did not have a quest for pleasure, or the desire to become something else.

This book will propose the model of Pre-Competitive Innovation as a strategic tool. Pre-Competitive Innovation starts with Innovation Questions rather than Innovation Problems. We will present a view of the new context in which we innovate today and argue that the necessary condition for success is an understanding of the root cause of change: Human Desire. Pre-Competitive Innovation is the capability of redefining and reformatting products, services and systems that realign people's desires, goals and motivations with the potential of new technology and the capabilities of organizations.

It is not about the technology, but about having the courage to design new structures and organizational patterns that address the possibilities that accompany new technologies and new knowledge. In this framework, innovation is about the creation of culture. Emergent behaviour patterns – the seeds of innovation – start with very simple acts that get multiplied on a collective scale. Your friend just posted a video on YouTube; he sends you a link and your appetite is awakened, you too want to post a video. You too want to contribute content. When the interest, time and passions of a multiplicity of people converge upon a single domain of action – YouTube in this example – we have an Innovation Object. Innovation objects are the magnets of human ingenuity at any given time, uniting their focus and energy, and resulting in new innovation behaviours. Electricity was such an innovation object, so was the steam engine, the printing press and more recently, digital media.

The future of any innovation object is a measure of its capability to create the experience most conducive to emerge our latent behaviour, and the desires that shape who we are in our best representation. This is why innovation objects are good predictors of things to come in technology in society, in behaviour, in culture and in the economic system. However, as Chapter 2 will show, unfolding the future is not about the signals we find in technology; it is about the signals we find in our behaviours.

Dealing with habit and ambiguity. Individuals and organizations expert at identifying latent behaviours, and the shape of the technology experience that will allow them to emerge, are indispensable to an innovation enterprise. The enemy of change – in the organizational or personal context – is habit. Habit as a system is a set of imposed constraints on a set of variables. The combination of variables and constraints in our environment defines our range of actions in the environment. The dynamics of behaviour form a system in permanent change and adaptation. Any new variable introduced in this system – be that fire, the cell phone, the iPod, or the printing press – is subjected to the same benchmarking constraints as all the variables already present in the system. It is measured on scales that do not fit it. The new variable is seen as beneficial if it provides the answer to the question *'what is the problem for which the new variable is a solution?'* How does the cellular phone as an example, change, help or impede what I have always done? Signals are not at the periphery of your present operational reality. Signals are in our midst. The weakness of individuals and organizations to recognize the meaning and the potential of signals – be they in emerging technologies or emergent behaviour – is a result of the limits of their self imposed boundaries, as dictated by the habitual environment in which the individuals and their organizations operate. The weakness comes from treating signals as 'novelties' with potentially little impact on the present. The capability to map a signal in its earliest stages, accelerates our understanding of the possibilities resident in it, and allows for the appropriate course of action to be chosen. This is the shortest definition of foresight.

Shaping the Future. Instead of relying on the reported needs of an established market, innovation at the strategic, pre-competitive level draws insight and direction from detecting signals in the environment. Applying imagination and intuition to an incisive reading of the current forces that influence your business – and even those forces that seemingly do not – is a capability of the foresight innovator. The ability to detect and interpret emergent signals, translating insight into foresight into action, combined with the courage to risk habit by creating new precedents is the job of the strategic innovator. Formulating questions that motivate exploration, fostering courageous, empathetic and diligent leadership are all necessary aspects of the foresight approach to innovation. To achieve this, it is first necessary to recognize and separate ourselves from the problem-mitigation approach to innovation, and to understand that breakthrough innovations cannot be substantiated by reference to past precedents. An appropriate course of action will maximize the opportunity – or minimize the threat –for both the individual and the organization. To maximize the resident opportunity, we must first recognize the *different nature* of a new variable.

What is *different* between a cell phone and a landline location based phone? Not in the device itself, *but in our attitude, goals and expectations from it? What is different in us and how will THIS change OUR nature?*

A question-based framework has no loyalty to the status quo. This approach embraces a new variable as an opportunity to explore new possibilities. A business operating in the question framework asks, 'What new benefits and behaviours could be released by, through, and because of *this* signal? What organizational capability is required to deliver such benefits and enable such behaviours?' The responses to these questions move an organization forward into a foresight pre-competitive space. Thus, a pre-competitive innovation process merges the exploratory nature of a question-based innovation process with the traditional problem-oriented, responsive process.

The New Context

Chapter 3 provides a new perspective of current behavioural disruptions which are relevant to the continuity of business, as well as a set of practical methodologies for business design, aimed at creating innovation outcomes of value to users.

The New Context is the Environment that provides the stimulus for innovation behaviour. The development of this context is not necessarily of our choosing, but rather a convergence of multiple agents, referred to later in the text as 'tactical agents', in as much as they are integral to the evolution of this environment characterized as the result of multiple parties, sometimes unrelated, working toward the same goals, and in the same technology spaces.

The new context in much of the industrialized world is what the UN's International Telecommunications Union[2] has termed 'The Internet of Things' – a place in which every person, object and space is both a link and a holder of information. These are spaces where digital data resides on embedded or on mobile devices, can be transmitted and received, and can be managed. With the proliferation of the tools, the infrastructure and the behaviours now made possible, it is fair to term the new context as a mobile society. The mobile society is the sum of the lifestyles of its participants, and the participants are in a constant state of searching for media to navigate it, for media to engage with from play to work, learning to knowledge, entertainment and leisure. Thus the challenge of the mobile society for organizations is *not about technology, but about strategy*.

At this point we must deal with a few labels: if we mislabel something then we place it on the wrong shelf, in the wrong folder, in the wrong category. There is no 'Disruptive Innovation'. This label has misstated the nature of innovation. What is disruptive is technologies and emergent behaviours. When behaviour engages technology in an innovation outcome, we have a *disruptive business model*.

Our understanding is further impaired once we *mislabel actions*. This is what happened recently with Social Media. I do not know of any media that is *not social*. That is an important thing because if you frame opinions or questions in the wrong way, by using the wrong label (social media, new media...) then the whole discussion becomes irrelevant. All media is social; humans exist because of other people, so our condition is one of plurality. Everything I use – which is *every media* I use – from my shirts, to my shoes, to my car, to my pendant made of copper 8000 years ago, they are all social media.

For anyone involved in communications – be that brand communication, marketing, news, or other forms of consumable and time sensitive content – the strategic challenge includes the understanding of the nature of mobile digital media: this is not 'just another channel'! *Mediums are not channels: mediums are modes of individual action*. Chapter 3 further details a few of the immediate changes that are required in order to respond to these challenges, as well as the principal themes of this new context: Empowerment, Participation and Engagement.

Empowerment refers to means available for the transformation, collaboration and sharing of content on an unprecedented scale made possible by the nature of digital data content which is re-mixable, easy to transform, mush, be acted upon. This empowerment invites Participation, as individuals capable of digital data transmission and reception – now a majority in the industrialized world – are *enabled as participants* in the *creation and direction* of the mobile society. Once this enablement becomes a behavior, the individual makes the voluntary choice to actively engage in its manifestation, by creating and consuming content which he or she finds meaningful. This engagement deepens their connection with the issues of meaning, making them a personal cause and a further behaviour to be acted upon. This is the *innovation behaviour cycle* at work. For the actors empowered for participatory engagement – the Millennial generation born after 1980 –

2   The Internet of Things: Executive Summary. (November 2005) ITU Internet Reports 2005. Geneva: International Telecommunications Union.

everything is possible. Freedom is not just a conceptual term, but an acted upon percept. They feel it, they crave it, they use it.

The empowerment and participatory behaviour that are the essence of people's engagement with YouTube, are not a technological innovation: *They are manifestations of innovation as a behaviour outcome* and the trigger for a innovation behaviour cycle that forms a new continuum reshaping value, creating new transactions and changing the meaning and metrics of the economic system. As we manifest these behaviours, new social interactions take place which lead as outputs in the engagement with new forms of exchange, which in turn, create new behaviours. Chapter 3 defines this as the *dynamic system ecology of behaviour*. This dynamic makes rethinking innovation an imperative.

Rethinking Innovation

When behaviour engages technology in an innovation outcome, we have new sets of actions taking place, actions that involve transaction points where value is exchanged against either other type of value – money – or against time spent in the performance of the actions. *This human activity is the human economy.* This exchange creates a *disruptive business model.* This disruption might have been planned or accidental, but it is a disruption never the less, as it is a new variable affecting the money supply (total amount of money available in the economy at a given time).

In the big picture of the economy, and as a simplistic example, consider this: the $24 billion Google pulls in revenue every year must come from someone else's bottom line. And Google is not alone. A plethora of new businesses are diverting streams from the revenue lines of former incumbents in almost every economic sector, either directly – by competing against incumbents – or indirectly, by providing new products and services the users now consider of value for the current context, rendering obsolete an increasing number of behaviours and their media: fax machines, encyclopedias, classified advertisements in newspapers, modems, floppy disks, recorded music – and possibly its industry, rules and star making system – print directory advertising, landline telephones, analogue television sets, analogue radio, to name just the few and the obvious. These are all products of culture as *innovation behaviour* which is nothing more and nothing less than another way of looking at the components of culture at any given time. As the behaviour changes, culture changes, and it becomes obvious in my view, that a rethinking of the role and capabilities of business needs to take place along with the rethinking of innovation.

People are only interested in new things for a short time. The future of any human activity depends on the extent to which it can create an *economic exchange*. Otherwise it has no value. Value is implicit in the media we use, only if you, or I are willing to exchange things against it; it only exists if it can create some action. One can not 'start a business'. One can only start a company; business is the result of some actions, the variable of multiple converging factors. In some cases, the only action possible is the exchange of money, in other cases I can allow people to come to my Facebook page in exchange for information mutually valuable to both parties.

The future of anything is connected to the economic exchange it generates. In the Innovation Behaviour Mapping Tool (Figure I.1), this connection is illustrated by the

ACTION which in turn creates the BUSINESS ACTIVITY. Simply put, *Motivation + Media = Behaviour = The Economy.*

If the 'media' holds no action potential – and thus potential value – to society, and the groups it represents, then nobody is going to use it for long. The key to a sustainable innovation behaviour product or service, is the ability to determine, in a dynamic and synchronic way, what is the value of the 'thing' as media to its users. The *dynamic* dimension means that you will give your user the media that provide a compelling experience time and time again, by tuning the Action components – either the Relationship or the Satisfaction modes – to provide a stimuli that is rooted in the context valuable to the user.[3] Rooted in whatever is the 'New Context' of the individual. The *synchronic* dimension means that behaviour cycles, once completed, demand new compelling experiences to sustain the business; these experiences are altered by the context just created by the previous behaviour cycle. As exemplified earlier with the use of fire, once we know it exists, we demand more.

Our desires, goals and motivations change, and this is where we can now find what generates a business. Synchronicity is launching the iPhone at the precise moment when every Apple user was ready to engage in the behaviour of using it.

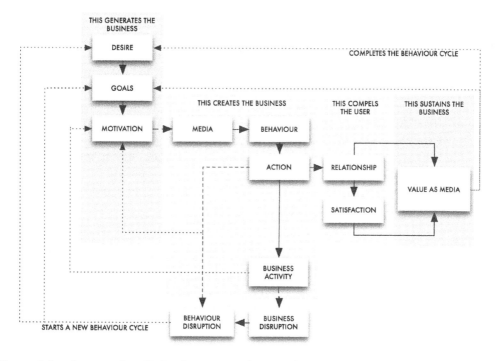

Figure I.1   Innovation Behaviour Mapping Tool

---

3   As an exercise in the use of the Innovation Behaviour Mapping Tool illustrated in Figure I.1, place the following in the 'Media' box and play with the variables: Global Warming, Catholic Church, *Halo* (the video game), the iPhone, Shopping Malls, Amazon, the Blackberry, the printed magazine, the printed newspaper, and even Peace in the Middle East... What you will be after is the maintenance of the Action leading to the Relationship, that will bring about the Satisfaction and thus sustain the 'Value as Media' of the issue in question.

The Innovation Behaviour Mapping Tool is a matrix that helps determine when a particular media – idea (or a brand), a product or a service – needs renewal in the form of new stimuli. When asking 'what is the value of any media for its users', we must look at where it all starts: everything starts in desire, which establishes goals, which establish motivation. Motivation needs a media, of any sort, and if motivations and media are a match, then you engage in behavior. Behaviour involves Action. Action involves a Relationship; and relationship involves Satisfaction as a simple and only metric. This combination of satisfaction and relationship *creates value*. From desire, through goals and motivations, to value as media. Look at the iPhone: every single new application creates new value as media for the iPhone. The product is a mere platform for new forms of value.

Chapter 4 makes the case that the ultimate capability of a business organization is *the knowledge of initiating, managing, and monetizing the creation of culture*. This knowledge includes the skills of pinpointing the source of successful innovation outcomes: they are answers to *conscious or subconscious goals residing in human motivation, and motivation starts in desire*. In a post-industrial, globally competitive economy, the role of the business organization is no longer in *serving the marke*t, but it is about making – or transforming – markets.

The challenge is no longer about adding value, but about creating value. When employing innovation as strategy, organizations need to be less concerned about what people *are doing now,* and more concerned about *what people are about to do*. The field of any true business opportunity is in *the future*. And any step taken toward a designed future requires agility as a measure of the organization's ability. Measures of agility are the ability to act on intelligence received from the field, and from the periphery of the business, the ability to unlearn legacy processes, the ability to reshape legacy processes, legacy supply chains, legacy beliefs in one's business and the dynamic ability to reframe and rethink tools and metrics. Reframing and rethinking the metrics has to be not only a dynamic, but also a synchronic capability, aligned with the *constant human desire for a better experience of life*.

Purpose in Innovation: Creating Culture

Innovation is both a noun and a verb. Innovation is judged by its performance, experience, look, and feel. This is where the verb comes in, in the compelling experience quality of the noun. As a verb, innovation also works like this: from the motivation and desire towards the outcome. For some organizations this simple path may be ambiguous, so we need to define a few rules of engagement, a few steps that could be objectively measured, incorporating the constructive with the restrictive. A new ecology of creativity characterized by Innovativeness, a mindset of ideas leading to innovation as a lived experience. Innovation is defining, *one moment in time, the best circumstances for the way you experience life*.

This new mindset requires a new *spirit*: 'how I think of myself as an organization? How do I want to be seen by my user group? What values do I represent for them?' Spirit is a set of values, which creates its own sets of rules and herein lies another challenge for managers: the management of ideas is different from the management of facts. Facts are objectively measured, while ideas are ambiguous. Chapters 5, 7 and Chapter 9 deal with how to accomplish this at both the tactical and the strategic levels. Innovation producing activities start by defining a pre-competitive *innovation challenge*, a challenge that does not start with an identified 'need', but with the discovery of emerging behaviors and emerging technologies and the mapping of new opportunities at the intersection of the two.

Chapter 5 proposes the conceptual model of innovation as a relationship experience: Motivation leads to Behavior; Behavior leads to Action; Action leads to Relationship; Relationship leads to satisfying the goal (maintain, enhance, actualize); The satisfaction of these conditions creates Value (media for me) and the design of business models stars by defining how the value proposition is a dynamic media for its users.

The Role of Desire in Innovation

'We desire nothing because its good, but it is good only because we desire it'.[4] Same can be said about our media: we desire nothing because it is 'media'; *it is media because we desire it!*

To create this media that has dynamic value for users – media that constantly supplies what users are looking for in the 'now' – we must understand human goals and motivations for action, because human behaviour is goal directed. Desire gives *expression* to these (as in 'we let it all out'), and at that point they become *articulated goals* (which sometimes we find it easy to label as 'wants') while *need* – the media we use to satisfy both – is just a temporary *manifestation*. Expression, articulation, manifestation: the pillars of the economic system, of everything we produce, consume and cherish.

The understanding of human desire is thus a precondition. Chapter 6 groups desires in three categories: Basic Desires for the nourishment of the body; Motivating Desires and Ultimate Desires. In the first category we find our desire for Smooth, Soft, Shiny, Sweet, Fragrant, Intoxicating, Beauty and Pleasure. In the second, our desires to participate, to leave a mark, to maintain, to enhance, to actualize, and to propagate the self. In the third, the ultimate desires of Knowledge, Understanding and Hope. Human life in its totality is framed – consciously or unconsciously – around strategies designed to experience some, or all of these desires, because we permanently seek higher and higher media for the satisfaction of our goals. And participation in the economic system, as a producer of goods and services, or as their user, is mastered in a direct relationship with the understanding of these conditions.

The Ecology of Innovativeness

A New Mindset for Innovativeness: where can we find the competence and ability to innovate behaviour outcomes? In the corporate ecosystem most likely to encourage the free flow of ideas capable to generate new revenue models. The challenge is that of creating a culture in which platforms for the exploration of possibility are encouraged, funded, and free of the day to day metrics of the organization, balancing risk, ambiguity, courage and imagination with a pragmatic business ambition in a timely manner.

---

4   George Santayana paraphrasing Spinoza in '*The Sense of Beauty*' C. Scribner's Sons, 1896, P.18

While Chapter 5 deals extensively with the spirit required for creating a culture of innovativeness in organizations, Chapter 7 aims to define and exemplify – through a few practical tools – the mindset needed to carry the tasks to completion. In an ecology of innovativeness, 'spirit' gives us the meaning; the 'mindset' provides and manages the tools.

Companies need to create a Place of Possibility, a place where everyone feels empowered to explore and to share ideas, and where there is no fear of consequences. A place that empowers inquisitive minds to imagine the future, and think beyond the legacy of the past. A Place of Possibility introduces a new strategic vision, delivers compelling experiences that target the imagination and thus the creative potential; transforms a strategic goal into a shared story. This place of possibility is a bridge between pleasure and purpose, and a necessary dialogue and collaboration platform. Its primary objective – and that of the groups operating within it is to ensure that your organization recognizes and benefits from the next strategic shift, no matter what its origin. The first task is Framing the Innovation Challenge with the strategic objective of integrating, unleashing and accelerate the sensitivity, imagination and capability of innovativeness into the core business functions of the organization.

Massive Innovation: Contemplating a New Framework for Collective Collaboration

As a timely and powerful example of an innovation challenge, Sami Viitamäki contributes in Chapter 8 a methodology for a new framework for collective collaboration. Leading businesses have already for decades built and utilized networks and collectives external to their organization for increasing innovativeness, fueling growth and maximizing efficiency. At present, this opportunity is in the hands of virtually any business, as companies worldwide are engaging online communities and integrating external, voluntary and autonomous workforces, into their operations and decision-making processes.

Traditional frameworks for marketing, management and operations, fail to address the unique nature of these systems, for they are built for another era – an era of top-down processes and communications, of institutions used to possessing control of their environments, and of annual marketing plans that didn't need monthly, weekly or even daily adjustment. Effective business development and marketing at present requires constant collaboration with external entities. What is more, collaboration with communities and individuals empowered with the collective knowledge of the web, requires a new framework for planning and managing collaboration – one that reflects the fundamental changes in the environment and in people's behavior.

The FLIRT model presented in this chapter is a framework that identifies the key issues, and the drivers of collective collaboration for commercial purposes. The model enables the utilization of the power of the globally connected community, by fully exploiting the opportunities of modern digital networks and tools. The model has proven its applicability as a comprehensive handbook for planning and managing collaboration in a business setting, and is also a recognized academic contribution to the field.

Beyond Strategic Thinking: Strategy as Experienced and Embodied

Change is a necessary part of the human condition. In business, we mark these moments of change as successful innovations. Why are some innovations successful? What is the driving force behind the cultures that produce them? And why is design thinking of growing importance in business today? This book will present a view of the new context in which we innovate today and argue that the necessary condition for success is an understanding of the root cause of change: Desire.

Strategic thinking, no matter how well done, contained in mission statements, no matter how skillfully communicated, is rarely sufficient to motivate and sustain significant strategic change. That is the premise of Jeanne Liedtka's contribution. Drawing upon new developments across fields as diverse as cognitive science, philosophy, psychology, and the fine arts, Jeanne argues here that powerful strategies are driven by desire rather than by goals; they are *experienced*, rather than merely *thought*. Liedtka further elaborates on the differing aims, assumptions, and mechanisms that such a shift entails in practice, and concludes with how approaches to planning need to change to accommodate this reality.

What Game are You Playing?

Sometime in September 2009, when this book was almost in its final draft, I was part of a working session on innovation acceleration with a diverse team of experts from a leading communications provider. Even to an untrained eye, it was obvious that the atmosphere in the room was tense – one could blame it on the weather I suppose, as a low cloud ceiling was crying cold rain, the kind of unmerciful cold, these little drops that penetrate you right to the skin and spell out what you always want to avoid facing: Summer is almost gone and a long Winter is coming. But the tension was thicker than usual, especially coming from this group, the same people that just a year before seemed pumped and optimistic with new prospects. Their particular 'Winter' was a market cap drop from 101 Billion Euros at the end of fiscal 2007, to slightly more than 39 Billion Euros by mid 2009. Now, that is a significant drop of 62 billions in shareholder equity! One could easily – and conveniently – blame this loss as an effect of the reshaping of the economy after the financial crash of 2008. However, in the same time period, one of their closest competitors doubled its market cap, now (December of 2009) standing at a respectable $192 Billion dollars. So something was not right. And it was not the supply chain management – reportedly one of the best, if not the best, in the world – and not the lean and mean manufacturing processes, and not the clever tools and metrics measuring the performance of every piece of machinery and of every individual. What was not right was the 'value' the company's products were providing as media for its users. As simple as that, or as complicated as you now want to consider it.

But back to the meeting; the diversity of the team was also of note in the context of this perceived tension: there were representatives from corporate strategy, marketing, future technology, human resources, software development, hardware, user experience, industrial design, supply chain management, and innovation leadership. I am naturally using very vague function descriptors here in order to protect both the participants as well as the company in question. The subject of the meeting was an update on the current innovation climate in the industry, as a benchmark for what the company might be planning to do in the near future. My role was to display and define relevant developments in fields related to the core competence of the company, and connect these as a pre-requisite to strategies that were bound to affect the sustainable success of the company in a market space it once dominated.

As I started my presentation I noticed an immediate reaction; the mood turned from tense to sober, and on the same faces one could detect outright *anger*. Facial expressions ranged from 'who does this guy thinks he is?' to 'why are we listening to this?' to 'finally, someone tells it like it is!'. After I finished my introductory remarks, it was the turn of a group leader to present current efforts in innovation management. He chose to continue with a PowerPoint presentation, obviously prepared prior to my arrival. The first slide simply read:

'It is NOT Game Over!'

The rest of the presentation seemed like a blur to me , as how can one recover from such a beginning? And what will be the point? Where can we go from here? It is not game over? What game are YOU playing?

Read on.

1 *Perspectives for a Conversation about Innovation*

My position is that innovation is not a process, but an outcome. More precisely; innovation is the moment in which human behaviour as outcome, is being changed by a particular invention, discovery or event, which in this work is referred to as an *innovation object*. This position challenges the current understanding of innovation, as well as the current ecology in which innovation operates in organizations; its management, methods, tools, language, focus and metrics.

Naturally, the challenge extends to some of the labels currently applied to innovation typologies, such as 'disruptive innovation', seen today as a label addressing purely the technological side of an invention, rather than the more complex motivational and behavioural side. It is my position that a disruption is not manifest in the moment a new technology is introduced. The disruption is manifest only when human motivation embraces the technology, and allows it to modify – enhance in a beneficial way – everyday life. *The disruption is the human being.* Our acceptance and appropriation of new technologies, creates the business disruption, seen here as a disruption of the current habit.

Innovation objects invite innovation questions, and I am an advocate of framing such questions[1] every time we encounter technologies at the threshold of emerging as behaviours. Innovation objects require a different capability to carry through on their promises, because the nature of the promises changes with the very existence of the invention or discovery. When seeing the iPhone for the first time one can ask 'What can this do?', but the strategic questions we must ask are 'What else can this be?', 'What would we become through using it?' To be clear, the focus is not on what technology can do, but on what *we can do with it*. So here is the framing perspective for this conversation:

1. Invention is the Moment of Creating or Discovering Something New

We don't know yet if the 'new' is 'useful', so *new* in this context is a statement and not a measure. This discovery is a disruption of our habit; if we are *attracted* by its potential – this is where value comes from a new discovery – we cannot look at the world the same

---

1   Manu, A. 2007. *The Imagination Challenge: Strategic Foresight and Innovation in the Global Economy.* Berkeley: New Riders. 5–8.

way. Once we no longer ignore that fire exists, we must construct our lives differently, and we must think of the future in a different way.

2. Innovation is the Moment of Using that Discovery

Innovation is the moment in which behaviour, as outcome, is being changed by invention. Innovation is then a human activity, which resides in our motivations, and manifests itself as behaviour, once we have defined that something new is the *right media for this manifestation.* Once we have discovered fire, we have built civilization around it, and with it we have found in fire multiple answers to the question *'how is this media for me?'* Behaviour as outcome has been changed by discovery. From that moment on, fire became an innovation object; as we use it, our goals change, our motivation changes and we need new tools and technology to make it manifest new behaviour, as we are called to revisit all our assumptions and wants. We can now desire more, want more, and will need more devices to accomplish these new goals. This is the economic system at work. We humans, are 'the Business', and naturally, we are the Disruptive Business of the title of this book. It is our desires, wants and needs that created and sustain the economic system, commerce, science and technology. Culture.

Your need for toothpaste and toothbrushes starts with your want to be part of a civilized society. And this want is rooted in the desire to achieve, to be greater than yourself, to become. It is our shared history as humans that we desire to be more than we are. We desire to learn, to know and to understand, to create images of our existence, to leave our mark. And on this journey, we transform desires into wants, and wants into needs, transforming the staples of our everyday life; into roads, automobiles, subways, airplanes and ships, carrying the oil to feed all these wants and needs.

Questions are Wants

I believe that to be is to want – and that wanting is the critical condition of being human. In the pages that follow, I will look at the ways in which our desire for experiences inspires and shapes our wants. To want is to both recognize and desire new conditions. Beneath this desire is a value judgment – an implicit personal assigning of meaning to change – a tacit embracing and ranking of different states of existence. Against what criteria do we make these judgments? Is it because we hope for *purpose* that we feel the urge to pursue one destination more than another? Or is it merely the belief in the destination that ensures that the journey will continue? *Wanting is the pursuit of possibility, and implicitly assigns meaning to change.* Beneath this is a tacit belief in different states of being. Perhaps because we mortal beings can imagine ourselves as different from what we currently are, we feel a responsibility to become something more, to connect in order to understand ourselves through others, to pursue a destination. It is important to recognize the role of imagination in this pursuit. If we could not imagine a different way of being, then we could not feel guilt, or hope. We would not say 'I remember when the world was …' and so never dream 'I imagine a world where …'

To be is to *want to become.* We want to become, and for that we need *to have.* But what do we want to become? The latent destination of what we are, the thing that resides in us and is brought to the surface by new artifacts, technology or services – the possibility that was brought in us by fire.

In creating the platforms that inform hope for a new life, we need to identify the factors that change our definition of possibility. Tools are a good example; our tools are conditions of our existence in as much as they undeniably create the conditions to empower our imagination – new platforms for possibility and new destinations for becoming. Tools are momentary manifestations of our most recent best guess of this destination, and every choice we make is a best guess towards building a future self. Civilization is a journey towards creating the conditions we want. This is why humans are in constant need for 'Media' – the tools that bridge the 'what is' and the 'what may be'. It is also why all human tools are ephemeral and prone to obsolescence. It is our wants that obsolesce our needs expressed by tools.

Tools are only temporary passports to our destination and not our reason or purpose for travelling in the first place. Our reason and purpose is the objective of becoming. It is thus wrong to reduce tools to being extensions of human ability. They are not. *They are the expression of the human will to achieve.* They are extensions of the will to become. But at which point do we transform these tools into more than extensions of our will? When we create anew, through new experiences, new moments, or new manifestations of ourselves. And what does this all mean for your business?

It means that a business has the organized and planned capability of creating the conditions for the manifestation of behaviour (see Figure 1.1). Your business creates and markets the tools, objects and services through which people manifest what they want, who they are, and what they want to become. Your business creates the media for the manifestation of behaviour. Successful companies create indispensable media; from detergents to instant coffee, from your trusted mobile phone to banking services, from subway trains to the newspaper you read while you ride them.

Successful companies also have the foresight to understand what behaviour we are likely to make manifest next, given the right tools. YouTube. Facebook. Twitter.

An organization exists to deliver the capability of a particular technology to a desired behaviour. *The process of making this media suitable for behaviour is design* (see Figure 1.2). There is no hierarchy, but rather a time line from felt – understood and expressed – desire, to articulated want, to supplied need. In short, desire creates wants, which in turn create needs.

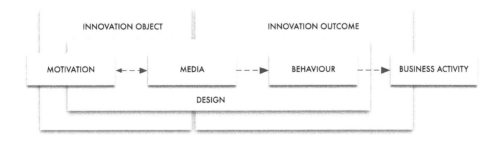

Figure 1.1   Motivation + Media = Behaviour = Business

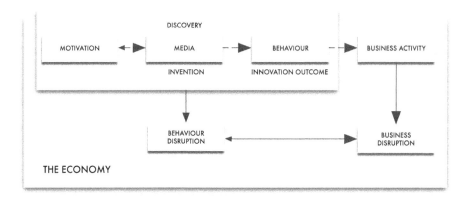

Figure 1.2   The Motivation Media Behaviour Economy

The equation 'desire > want > need' is often ignored in consumer studies, and it may now be the most important piece of the puzzle in delivering innovation outcomes, as it concerns the very nature of *what is an innovation.*

Innovation is rooted in desire, not need: the desire to become better through experiences of knowledge, education, literacy, tools, systems and services, all provisions for the achievement of our higher goals. An organization's capability to meet this desire, directly contributes to the success of their products and services in the marketplace.

- I desire to live in comfort: I need Copper.
- I desire to cook my food: I need Iron, I need Electricity.
- I desire safety and security in the structures I build: I need Steel.
- I desire lightweight tools for everyday life: I need Aluminium.
- I desire to adorn my body: I need Gold and Precious Stones.
- I desire convenience: I need Kellogg Co.
- I desire soft shirts and sheets: I need Whirlpool.
- I desire health and a soft skin: I need Procter & Gamble.
- I desire a warm home, clean clothes, comfort: I need General Electric.
- I desire to know and to understand: I need Google.
- I desire to be entertained: I need the Walt Disney Co.
- I desire to participate: I need Twitter, I need Facebook.
- I desire to leave a mark: I need YouTube.

All these things *are desired by humans*, all are media for the satisfaction of conscious or subconscious goals, and the economic system and the market are the outgrowth and reflection of that. How can a product or service create value? *By being media for the satisfaction of people's motivating goals.*

As desire is constant, innovation is also a constant and, according to Joseph Arbuckle of Phoenix Partnerships in Toronto, business is the variable. A business is a continuum of variable capabilities, constantly supplying the media we need in the present. The tools, services and experiences, that make us happy NOW. Apple Corporation is such enterprise and the example of business as the variable. Apple consistently delivers on the definition of innovation as a behaviour outcome, by creating culture, not products. The iPhone is not an innovation in technology; it is an innovation in the ways of engagement with technology, for new, desired, and beneficial outcomes, ways to make us happy. *We want the best of every experience.* A statement simple in its request, but complicated in its delivery – and creating along the way the tools, machines, industries, networks and systems that now form the complex of life on Earth.

The current best innovation outcomes and the business models that deliver them – Google, Apple, YouTube – are driven by desire, not in the hedonistic sense, but in the higher motivational theory[2] sense of the 'desires to know and to understand'. This is the current ethos of business and of innovation – and the explanation for the success of products and services that never solved 'a problem'. In his *Theory of Human Motivation*, Abraham Maslow calls us 'a perpetually wanting animal'. We are bound to desire. To perpetually seek media for a better self. To perpetually seek innovation.

Innovation is Media for Becoming

HOW IS THIS MEDIA FOR ME?

Consider this proposition before moving forward; that the single question, and the most relevant question we ask of everything is: *'How is this media for me?'* We ask of Dove soaps, Navteq maps, Knorr soups, Facebook, YouTube, Twitter, Starbucks, the iPhone, Google Earth, and Ford automobiles the same question: How can I actualize myself through you? How can *you* satisfy my motivating goals? How can *this* mediate my relationship with life, my environment, my friends, my work? *'How is this media for me?'* is the question that prompts the activity which creates the economy.

How can I have my voice heard through this? How can I have my ideas understood through this? Successful products, services and organizations have all provided the answer to this singular question. Conversely, if a technology, service or organization can not satisfy its role as a media for people's motivations, they will invariably disappear.

The success or failure of any thing (technology, service, concept, etc.) is directly related to its capability to be media for the satisfaction of our motivating goals. When something ceases to be media for people's motivations, it is replaced by the artifacts/technologies that represent a better media for the satisfaction of same.

Every object, service and space *is an answer*. A chair is the answer to the question: 'How do I suspend the human body above the ground in a comfortable position?' A mobile phone is the answer to the question: 'How do I keep in constant communication with the *ones I care about?'* In the moment a product or service appears – people use it – it contains elements from all the categories labelled in the Innovation Map illustrated in Figure 1.3. It has value as media, it creates an experience that includes a relationship, that leads to either satisfaction or disatisfaction. It involves action and behaviour. It includes a media – the product or the people and spaces of a service – it is rooted in motivations that stem from goals, which we set from desire.

Every object, service or system meets the conditions 1–6 in the moment of use, but does not necessarily meet conditions 7, 8 that lead to 9, *the value of the thing as media.* As expectations change, conditions 1, 2 and 3 change, with the result of a new

2   Maslow, A.H. 1943. A theory of human motivation. Originally published in *Psychological Review*. 50, 370–96.

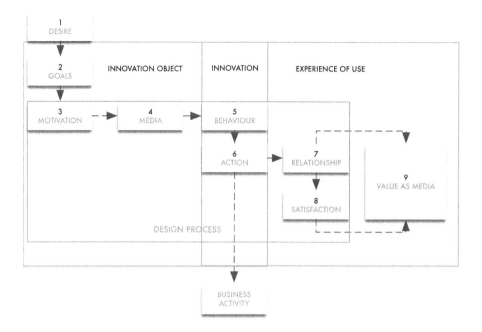

Figure 1.3   The Innovation Map

media (4) being required. The need for innovation comes from the changing nature of Desires, Goals and Motivation (1, 2 and 3). This is why we perpetually seek media for a better self, and perpetually seek innovation. New goals add new features on existing media, very much like the birth of a new baby might require the expansion of your house by one room. Decreased experience (7 + 8) might result in redesigning the media (4). This innovation map can be used both in planning the design process for an innovation outcome, as well as for the diagnostic of low performing innovations and insights into where specific innovations are in the behaviour cycle.

As discussed in the next section, foresight as a business capability examines how conditions 1, 2 and 3 are changed by 4, 5 and 6. The existence and use of 4 (Facebook in this example, see Figure 1.4) reshapes 1, 2 and 3, which starts a new behaviour cycle resulting in the seeking of a new innovation.

Looking at the World Twice

The proposition that innovation is a behaviour outcome is informed in part by my strategic foresight work for large organizations, and also by my academic practice at the Rotman School of Management, and the Ontario College of Art and Design in Toronto. What I hope to achieve here, is to have you learn to look at the world twice. When seeing a newspaper headline, when hearing about a new behaviour people engage in, when learning about a new way of doing things, step back. Look again, without jumping to judgment. See it twice, and look at it from a point of view outside your daily habit. See it from a position of understanding its future possibility.

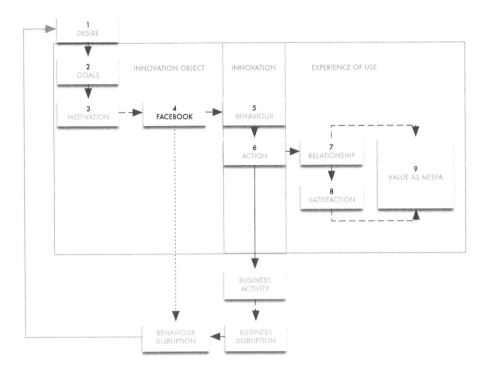

Figure 1.4   The Innovation and Behaviour Cycle Map of Facebook

I would like you to indulge the notion that the future may shape itself in the way we want it to. The way you and I can dream it to be. The way YOU want to make it. I ask that you allow yourself to return to the childlike state of being able to explore new ideas, without passing judgment, without once saying *'this is impossible!'* Give yourself this gift of being ready to absorb all as possible. David Hume wrote: 'The supposition that the future resembles the past is not founded on arguments of any kind, but is derived entirely from habit.'[3] My request is that you suspend habit for the next little while, so you can enjoy, explore and discover a few new ideas about the potential future of your business.

There is danger in assessing the future from the perspective of the present, and from the habits of everyday life. It is from habit that intelligent people make the silliest predictions. A few reminders will include:

'I think there is a world market for maybe five computers.'
(Thomas Watson, former CEO of IBM, 1977)

'There is absolutely no reason anyone would want a computer in their home.'
(Ken Olsen, founder of Digital Equipment Corporation, 1975)

'640K ought to be enough for anybody.'
(Bill Gates, 1982)

---

3   Hume, D. 1888. *A Treatise of Human Nature.* Oxford: Clarendon Press. 134.

These statements were not 'wrong' for the times in which they were made. For their respective places in time, they were absolutely right. But, as a vision of the future, *they are absolutely wrong*. So I urge you to keep your deep desire, your playful side, at the top of your mind while reading this book.

Three elements intertwine to shape the future, and the role you play – as an individual or as an organization – and their understanding and mastery is equal to the role you might play in shaping that future. The three elements that shape the future are *motivation, technology* and *business capability*. When these are aligned, we have services, we have products, we have a life in which all these services and products represent direct benefits to users, and to ourselves as makers. In a schematic way, you may look at behaviour, technology and capability as three independent timelines. Motivation usually leads – we all *want* something. Technology follows, providing the solution to that want, at times, technology leads, creating a product or service, and then finding a want, an application for it. Organizational capability usually lags, the ability of an organized business entity to deliver on people's wants with efficiency and effectiveness, takes trial and error, process design and redesign, all taking time as well as financial and human resources.

An often used example that illustrates this is Napster. The motivation behind the Napster behaviour – peer-to-peer file-sharing – was in place before the service appeared in 1999. People had both MP3 files, and the desire to share them, bypassing the established recording music channels. What was lacking was a meeting place for all the parties interested in manifesting this behaviour, and a business capability able to deliver file sharing in a secure and reliable way. The organizational capability did not exist yet, because the signal of the peer-to-peer file sharing behaviour was not seen as a sufficient threat by industry incumbents, to prompt the investment of time and resources, in the development of large scale capabilities leading to a service that could be monetized. Napster – and the associated behaviour – was seen by the record companies, the radio stations, the device makers, the music retailers, as something at the periphery of their business, an activity that 'might go away'. But it did not go away – anything but.

Napster was an early demonstration of the empowerment and participatory nature of new communication technologies, and the power of this engagement to change habit and manifest new behaviours. Figure 1.2 illustrates both the business disruption and the behaviour disruption. Figure 1.1 shows how Apple Corporation saw it; that Napster was a statement that users were dedicating their personal computers to music, to personal memories, to video. Apple introduced iTunes in January of 2001, nine months before the launch of its first iPod in October the same year. Apple Corporation made the media of peer-to-peer file sharing (MP3) suitable mass behaviour *by design*.

SEEING FIRE FROM HABIT AND FEELING FIRE FROM PASSION

Humanity before the discovery of fire, was a completely different place than humanity after the understanding of the benefits of fire (see Figure 1.5). *Discovery can be a very abrupt ending for habit.* The 'after' has nothing to do with the 'before', and this is hard for large organizations to cope with. But it is life. You cannot raise a child with any lessons learned about pregnancy.

When observing a phenomena and experiencing it for the first time, we are immediately searching for a theory. What does this mean? Where does this belong in the order of the things I know, and learned? Where does it fit in my existing framework as an organization? We are looking for meaning; we are comparing the components of the frameworks we operate in, with something new, and something we do not fully understand. But to understand it, we must compare it *with* something. In this process we are comparing the resolution of this new thing that we don't completely understand – its shape, size, impact – against our value system, our biases, our memories. Measured against our habit, it is natural then to conclude that '*nobody is going to use this*' because 'I don't need it'. We are rarely able to see beyond the boundary of rationality. Which is why we need *passion* when trying to understand the new. We must open up with passion to the possibilities that something new holds. Passion is not a rational mode of existence. You do not fall in love from the brain, ever. Look briefly at the fire you just discovered, then close your eyes. *Feel the heat. Understand its possibilities.*

Once humanity was able to control fire – producing it at will, and maintaining it – we changed *how* and *what* we consumed as food. We changed our immediate habitat into a warmer place, which allowed us to explore life in colder climates, and expand our territorial reach. We became masters at managing crops, using fire as a tool for land management and later, as fuel for the means employed to extract and fabricate metals, and harden our clay pots. Fire became light, and illuminated our quest for knowledge in the dark. The most powerful experience, is the experience of knowledge. Once we had embarked upon the journey of growth through fire, we created the world as we desired it, tool by tool, engine by engine, one rocket at a time.

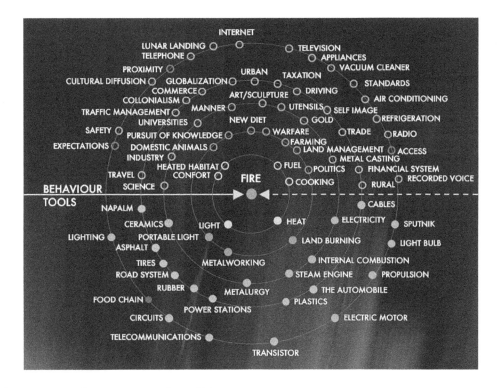

Figure 1.5   Fire as Innovation Object

There is little we can bring from our past – before this discovery was made – on this journey, little that can be of use. Cooked meat has no relationship with raw meat; it is not just a transformation of our eating habits, but a different plateau of experience. Same thing can be said about electricity, the steam engine, the discovery and use of the World Wide Web. The web browser revolution took over the Planet in exactly two years, and nothing would be the same again. So you cannot look at what the world used to be *before the browser* and the Internet, for any lessons on what the world will be like *after* the maximization of this behaviour.

EMERGENCE

The signals of all the future behaviours it creates, or will influence, are present in the moment of the discovery and introduction of any new technology. In your current practice, do you see signals of emerging behaviour? What would be their possibility to create new opportunities? What do you see as a signal with significant growth opportunity right now? In technology? In education? In culture? Where is, in your organization, the capability of transforming emergent behaviour and technology, into a new business opportunity, a new economic driver, and a new business model? Do you personally know anyone with this responsibility in your organization?

The reality is that most of the people you know are preoccupied with execution – for some reason, some very smart people have proclaimed execution to be the key capability of the competitive organization. Execution is one of the keys, for sure, if a strategic direction is in place, and if we know where we are going as an organization.

So who is in charge of keeping watch at the periphery of your business, noticing and interpreting the signals of emergence, transforming them into meaning for the organization? Philosophers used to do this for kings, as interpreting behaviour is more an art than a science, using insight and intuition, interpretation and unlearning. The art is in knowing how far and what to look for, how quickly you can redefine the path from the core of your business, to what has been the periphery. How quickly can you move from being a computer maker, to a mobile device leader, a music distributor and a cultural aggregator.

Apple Corporation,[4] is an example of the permanent redefining of what is 'core'. Is this an example of insight, or is it strategic foresight? Insight informs where to look, foresight paints a picture of what you may find when you get there, and what to do with it.

THE FUTURE: YOUR MOTIVATION, YOUR BEHAVIOUR, YOUR ACTIONS

What is the connection between needs–wants–desire, and how expectations change with our ability to participate in the shaping of culture in an interactive way? What new expectations arise from the ability to create, manage and distribute our own content, from the ability to collaborate on Wikipedia and broadcast to our own audience on Twitter? Are these the same expectations as we would have had five years ago, or did something profoundly change? And how is this affecting your business? We will explore

---

4   As I use the Apple Corporation as an example quite a bit, I want to make it clear that this is not a bias – I am a user of their products and services – but it is a pragmatic choice supported by the financial performance of Apple as a business. At the time of this writing in the summer of 2009, a comparative review of the financial performance of Apple against any number of businesses in a variety of market segments was positively favourable to the latter. Try it out for yourself at http://www34.wolframalpha.com/input/?i=Apple+

these questions together, in the next chapters. For now, here is my definition of the *future as a concept* in the context of business:

Motivation is the internal condition that gives rise to what we want to do, based on our goals, what can we do – *behaviour* – and what we will do – *action*. Behaviour is influenced and reacts to culture and its artifacts, to attitude, emotion, ethics, authority and persuasion. Action is what we actually *do*.

The future is the changes *we make* to the present through our *motivation, behaviour* and *action*.

The future as a concept is different from the future as a timeline. Without changes, new behaviours and new actions, the future is just the *present on a different calendar date*, next week, next month, next year. The future as concept means things that have not happened yet. The future involves actions. *Future products, services and experiences will only be what we want to reveal next about ourselves.*

AMBIGUITY AS A BUSINESS FUNCTION

When discussing the future, some might prefer to view it as a set of probable outcomes, and not as a specific set of circumstances that have inevitability, and that will come to pass. Believing that the future is a set of possibilities, cocoons executives in the comfortable zone of inaction – one cannot plan for multiple sets of possibility, so one waits until a tangible manifestation of the future threatens the competitive landscape of the organization (see Figure 1.6), and only then is the executive moved to act.

What are the sets of possible outcomes for the consumer electronics industry, following the invention of the transistor? Are we dealing indeed with sets of outcomes and randomness, or can we imaginatively use foresight to create a cohesive strategy, one that deals with the miniaturization of components and devices, lower costs, lower heat, resulting in the use of new case materials, portability resulting in the need for portable power, battery developments, etc. Sure, you might think this is now hindsight, and this is why it seems so obvious. So find some other example around you, and try to map the future it will create. This is not prediction, *this is thinking*. Sets of possible outcomes? What are they in the case of a technology called MP3? Is the MP3 compression technology, and the players that transform data into sound, just another of the possible outcomes, or the

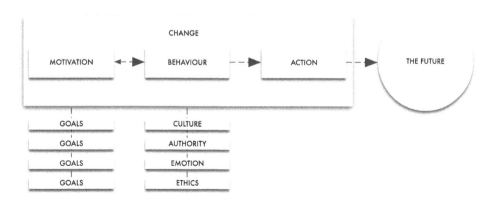

Figure 1.6   Planning the Future

logical pathway when one starts thinking, debating and shaping the future of recorded music?

Let's accept for the purposes of this discussion, that the future is not a set of possibilities, but a pathway of ambiguous outcomes – ambiguous in the sense that we do not know precisely their shape, but we can intuitively see the general outlines. Five years from now people will continue to eat soup. We just don't know which kind of soup. On the other hand, five years from now people will use something to communicate to one another. We don't have a clue what. Or we can choose to design it.

What must the responsible organization do? Who in your organization is in charge of dealing with ambiguity? I assume that you cannot name anyone at this time, as most functions in your organization have been crafted to serve a specific purpose, a purpose that has a name, *can* be measured, and *can* be audited. A purpose that fits the current business landscape of your organization. The future? Surely someone at 'headquarters' is looking after that. The reality is that no one at headquarters is looking after that, as no one likes dealing with ambiguity as a business function. Everyone likes dealing with precise frameworks, with measurable outcomes. This is what we learn in school. Ambiguity we learn in life, and at home. Human life is about ambiguity, about making choices based on the insightful interpretation of ambiguous signals. *She loves me. She loves me not.* We move mountains, if we need too, on the basis of ever changing ambiguous signals.

The interesting thing about ambiguity is that it is a dominant of your life, not an exception. Why is it that the same individual who masters ambiguity daily for personal survival, cannot be trusted to do the same in the organization? I don't have the answer, but the question is worth asking. Until we can find ways to shape organizations around the core human competence of dealing with ambiguity as a life function, we need to separate the management of everyday tasks, from the management of innovation outcomes.

FUTURE AND FORESIGHT IN BUSINESS

The ambiguous nature of innovation is expressed in this question, asked of Michael Faraday, the inventor of the electric motor, by the then prime minister of England: '*What use is electricity for?*' What do you possibly answer? How electricity would transform the world? Would the answer be even believable – if you reply 'imagine a day in which nothing around you will be possible without the direct or indirect use of an electric motor.' Here's what Faraday answered: '*Sir, there is every possibility that you will soon be able to tax it*'. Faraday's answer revolved not around the physical merits of the technology in question, but in its social, cultural and economic relevance, in the very near term ('*soon*') for the prime minister and his government.

How do we get to 'soon' from where we are today? Can you describe your life ten years from now? Did you ever ask yourself: 'Who am I, in ten years from now?' Do you think that successful people and organizations have a plan, and they know what they are going to be ten years from now? People who have consequence have become so not by accident, they have designed it that way. So, if you have a vision of yourself ten years from now, it is a destination that can prompt you to action today. You can work towards that destination and design the tools you need to reach it, step by step, starting from today. Foresight is not about the future; foresight is about *getting to the future*. Predicting the future of a signal of emergence is then not an exercise in connecting complex social, economic and political dots, but one of motivation centred questioning: *If this technology happens, what will people want to do with it?* (very much the same as *'what use is electricity for?'*).

Instead of relying on the reported needs of an established market, innovation at the strategic, pre-competitive level draws insight and direction from detecting signals in the social, economic and cultural environment. Applying imagination and intuition to an incisive reading of the current forces that influence your business (and even those forces that seemingly do not) is a capability of the strategic-level innovator. Beyond the ability to detect and interpret signals, a strategic innovator has an appetite for risk and the courage to set a precedent where none exists, translating insight into foresight, and foresight into action.

Foresight allows you to deploy energy towards the satisfaction of conditions not yet present to the senses. You are in charge of making them present; you are in charge of designing the game *and* the rules. The exercise is ambiguous because we are not used to writing our own rules. And we are not used to employing the imagination as a tool for business.

Think 50 years ago, 1959. What was going on then that is different from today? Desktop computers didn't exist, Bob Dylan didn't exist, neither did the Beatles, space travel nor email. Mobile phones used by the masses were, at most, a science fiction fantasy. The information society and the digital revolution were not even talked about. Our lifestyle was completely different. Our hopes for the future were different. In 1965 Stanley Kubrick made the movie *'2001: A Space Odyssey'*. According to his vision, by 2001, humanity had mastered space travel to the point of resource extraction on the Moon and beyond. We are now in 2010, and we have mastered many other skills, but not resource extraction on the Moon.

Put yourself in a situation in 2019, you just got home from your office. What does your world look like? How did you get home? What is your work environment? How does your home look? How do you do your laundry? Is there anything in your current ecology of objects, relationships, services and emerging trends that might give you a signal of what your life would be like ten years from now?

Approaching new information as a signal of future possibility, formulating deep questions that motivate exploration and suit an organization's goals, and fostering courageous, empathetic and diligent leadership, are all necessary aspects of a Pre-Competitive approach to innovation. To achieve this, it is essential to separate yourself from the problem-mitigation approach to innovation, and to understand that breakthrough innovations cannot be substantiated by reference to past precedents. The old habits and concepts that we bring to our notion of what innovation is, and can be, must be put aside if we are to move boldly forward in our explorations of what could be possible, both for our businesses and for ourselves.

Pre-Competitive Innovation is the capability of redefining and reformatting products, services and systems that realign people's needs and wants, with the potential of new technology, and the capabilities of organizations. It is not about the technology, but about having the courage to design new structures and organizational patterns, that address the possibilities that accompany new technologies and new knowledge. In this framework, *innovation is about the creation of culture*.

'Sir, there is every possibility that you will soon be able to tax it.'

2 *Innovation is a Behaviour Outcome*

This may be unlike other business books you have read, because it is full of ambiguity, in a field in which frameworks and structures are what you know, and what you expect. We need this ambiguity to operate with the freedom of mind that allows us to go to places that otherwise we would never see. I write and think from the perspective of a practitioner; I am involved in strategic foresight for companies that are in the midst of change. Change comes in many shapes, and our mandate is to define strategies that enable large organizations to understand and plan for what will be next. The practice is closely tied to sense making, and mapping emergent signals in behaviour, looking for phenomena and describing their disruptive potential for business. For your business today, and for your business tomorrow.

For a large organization, change does not present itself as a problem; that will be easy. Change presents as a dilemma; it requires that choices be made between a number of directions the company could take to continue to exist effectively. *The ultimate capability of a business is the knowledge of managing and monetizing the creation of culture.* And as change is constant, organizations need to redesign themselves permanently, and redefine their role in culture, by looking at their business in cultural terms.

What is important in distinguishing between problems and dilemmas, is that processes cannot generally solve the latter; you cannot engineer your way out of a dilemma. And successful organizations know that. During a recent search for documents on the Internet, I stumbled on an internal memo generated by staff working for a global leader in the software industry. The memo dealt with questions and answers scripted for the CEO and the Chairman of the organization, in connection with an annual meeting with employees. The key question was: '*What is your vision for the company in ten years, and what is it in 20 years?*' Three answers:

1. Continuing to invest in making big, strategic bets and doing innovative work;
2. Bringing in talent that ensures we have necessary abilities to seize opportunities;
3. Maintaining the dynamic environment.

In the pages that follow I will deal with some of these topics – the big strategic bet, how to define a new destination for your products and services, how to redesign your business around the talents of the digital generation, how to create and maintain a dynamic environment of innovativeness. Organizations involved in voluntary or involuntary business dilemmas, need a set of useful mind tools for the alignment of motivation, behaviour, technology and business capability. This alignment is what we call *strategic foresight*.

MOTIVATION, BEHAVIOUR AND BUSINESS CAPABILITY

Let us deal first with the main challenge: to understand that innovation is a noun; innovation is an outcome, not a process. More specifically, as suggested before, *innovation is a behaviour outcome*. Since it is not a process, it is not controllable, manageable or measurable by the traditional means of the organization. Innovation is the 'wow' moment of discovering the pleasure of using the iPhone.

The second challenge flows from the understanding of innovation as a behaviour outcome: what makes people behave the way they do. How can an organization innovate behaviour outcomes? Well, what do you think Procter & Gamble does every day? With the mission to 'improve the lives of the world consumers, now and for generations to come,' P&G's Gillette is not making safety razors, but delivering on the goal, *'The best a man can get'*. Pantene is not producing just shampoo, but *'developing formulas that help women achieve the healthy, beautiful hair they desire'*.[1] Any company supplying the staples of everyday life must have a certain expertise in human motivation.

Motivation is another name for the wants that inhabit us, sometimes without us having a name for them yet. *'I never knew I needed this!'* is the typical exclamation when faced with a technology we did not anticipate being useful to us daily, as was the case with the World Wide Web (WWW), or the Swiffer, and many more examples that will exhaust the pages of this book. When motivation meets a stimulus – the WWW browser as an example – it triggers a response, an action. This action is a latent behaviour now made manifest. In business terms: manifest behaviour makes you money now, latent behaviour will make you money in the future.

How many businesses think they will make money in the future – seen here as one to three years away – the same way they make money today? And how responsible is it to plan strategy only by looking at tangible behaviours, existing demographics and segmenting, instead of assuming that a fair amount of ambiguous change will take place?

Let us spend a minute on the difference between manifest and latent behaviour. Manifest behaviour is what we can observe; and from this observation we can define the needs for improving a product or a service, and from this, in turn, we can create a solution and a new a business opportunity. The resulting product or service will be in the competitive domain – all our competitors have the same opportunity to observe the manifest behaviour, and notice the same problem – and so will be the business opportunity. By the time we roll out our new and improved solution to the observed problem, chances are that our competitors will do the same thing.

Motivation to Behaviour. Latent behaviour on the other hand, is a behaviour that does not yet have a media for its manifestation. It is an action *you might be engaged in*, if given the right tool, and if the tool in question allows one to achieve one's goals. And this is how we get to motivation; we are all motivated by our goals, the goals we set for ourselves, as people or organizations. *Goals are the motivation for the behaviour leading to the actions carried out towards their achievement.*

What motivates human beings? Are we different from one another? Do we have different dreams about our future? How different? How are your motivations different than mine? Companies that understand what motivates people, are the companies that you want to

---

1   Available at http://www.pgeverydaysolutions.com/pgeds/articles-tips/Unlock-the-potential-of-nature-for-your-hair [accessed: 22 August 2009].

stay close to. Most companies in the business of consumer packaged goods understand the ultimate desires of their consumers; it is not about the practical need to be clean, it is about the goals of being clean, healthy, appreciated. The desire to be part of society.

Can my son Sasha consider himself as part of society if he is not on Facebook everyday? Is Facebook an option for him, or is it a media for his participation in the culture of his peer group? If the answer is not obvious to your business development team, then we have a problem. If you want to understand how change manifests itself in the present, you have to be on YouTube a few times a day. Why? Because this is where the eyes are now. With the eyes goes the brain, and the attention of your demographic is diverted from the consumption of goods and services, to the participation in the phenomena of YouTube, as both users and creators. More about this and your business later. If you want to understand where *the moment* is, and where new expectations start, you need to understand what motivates people's behaviour. So it is motivation first, behaviour later. It is strategy before tactics. Gaining insights around 'What people are about to do', leads to strategy; observing and reacting to what people are doing now, leads to tactics.

YouTube behaviour serves as a perfect example of the ambiguity of change, which is the cause of the dilemmas mentioned at the beginning of this chapter. Ambiguous change is just a moniker – a friendlier label – for a disruptive business model. YouTube is a disruptive business because it changes the context for both user, and the industry incumbents, in the moment it becomes an innovation object. As users get attracted to the object, the attraction changes the personal context of the user; changes the context of the brands the user is engaged with; changes the context of the value chain and the supply chain that provide the means of engagement between brands and users. What seemed at first glance to be an insignificant and trivial application of technology – a web site where one can upload video and download video, made or uploaded by others – has triggered a massive change of context. YouTube, the website, is not an innovation, *YouTube is a business disruption*; its creators observed what technology can, and where human motivation is and has always been, and they provided a platform that aligns human motivation – to be seen, to be heard, to make a difference – with the technology to do so seamlessly. A new business capability. And the creation of a new behaviour.

Motivation, behaviour, technology and business capability are rarely aligned; it is either that technology performs functions that are not understood by users – and thus deemed as 'not needed' – or business capability is not in place to respond to the manifest behaviour of people who are ready to upload, or download, their own video content for strangers to look at. This is where strategic foresight practitioners paint a picture of possibility, describing what will happen if behaviour, technology and business capability were aligned.

As discussed earlier, strategic foresight will ask the question, 'If this technology happens, what will people want to do with it?' The answers to this question will allow you to paint a picture of possibility. Once you have that picture you can create a business model, a blueprint of 'WHY' you could be making money. From there, you can define any number of business plans, outlines of the 'how' you make the money. The 'why' you make the money means: '*Do you understand the value of this thing?*' The only way to monetize a technological invention is to understand its value in social and cultural terms. This is when invention is transformed into innovation behaviour. When innovation as outcome supplies people with what they need, in the very moment of that need, *innovation becomes media for its users*.

Foresight uses insight into human motivation – why people do what they do – and what releases latent behaviour, and further, how can this *behaviour be monetized*. This needs to clear: *technology cannot be monetized!* Technology by itself *is not a business model*. It is not the telephone; it is you making a phone call. It is your desire to be in touch, to tell people you are OK, to show your life's memories on Flickr and share your opinions on YouTube, it is those motivations translated into behaviour and action that can be monetized. Foresight does not analyse everything from the logic of monetization, because when one does that, one can miss where the value resides. Foresight looks at *motivation as the source of value creation*, and value is always where the action is. Today's value is where the eyes are. When thirteen hours of content are uploaded to YouTube every minute[2] that simply means that thirteen *hours a minute – somebody is not watching your brand's message on TV*. And the 'somebody' is not just the minority anymore, but millions of viewers who are not watching your commercial, are not exposed to your message, and potentially, not having the time to use your product or service.

Let's recognize that video captures the visceral, dynamic quality in life and shares it with the world. This has driven YouTube's exponential growth in the last two years. Again, 13 hours of video are uploaded to YouTube every minute. That's the equivalent of Hollywood releasing more than 57,000 full-length movies every week. Hundreds of millions of people come to YouTube every month to search, discover and share this content with their friends.[3]

Chad Hurley, co-founder of YouTube

Innovation Objects

We have developed civilization around compelling *innovation objects* that converge with particular focus the attention, and activity, of culture at specific periods in time – culture being inclusive here of society, technology, industry and the economic system. For a long period, fire was such object; the printing press, the steam engine, electricity, all followed and overlapped over the course of the past 5,000 years, creating the world as we experience it today. It is the position of this book that *mobile digital data* and its use – particularly in the creation of a new, mobile society – is the converging innovation object of today. And the subject of this book because of it.

It is important to differentiate here between data, digital data, and *mobile digital data*. The innovation object is the fact that data is now mobile *and* digital. Mobile digital data could be transferred from one user to another, from multiple users to one, and from one to multiple. This creates an interconnectivity that is supportive of the human condition of plurality, of humans existing in social groups. This connectivity enhances our opportunities to communicate and collaborate, to exchange ideas, to learn and to know. The desires to know and to understand underline most of our actions, because to participate in plurality – to exist with others – means to assign the same meaning to things that are part of the social landscape. And to assign the same meaning means knowing all the variables, and understanding how they connect. Knowledge leads to communities grouped around social objects, the stories we share and care about, the issues that bind us.

2   Available at http://www.*YouTube*.com/press_room_entry?entry=QcVLqR7qnAM [accessed: 22 August 2009].

3   Available at http://www.*YouTube*.com/press_room_entry?entry=QcVLqR7qnAM [accessed: 22 August 2009].

For a given group of people, these are the common shared objects of interest, the subjects of our stories, our discussions, the things we celebrate and create interpretations of, or in other ways manifest one's relationship to. This is why *social objects* also play the role of innovation objects.

Social objects connect us as a community, we celebrate them, and we connect through them. In turn, social objects benefit from our ability to connect; the intensity of the object is greater as connectivity becomes the norm of everyday life. Intensity in this case refers to the *radiating power of the social object*. The death of Michael Jackson in June 2009 would have been a newsworthy event, captivating the airwaves for the appropriate amount of time in the news cycle, until the next story. It became a social object through the empowerment of YouTube. As of this writing (August 2009), there were, just on YouTube, over 355,000 tribute videos. The crowd acts as both content creator and content consumer; crowds are empowered to create, distribute and manage their own content, as well as consume the content created by others. This activity is the economy. *This activity is an innovation outcome*.

Because We Can!

On 22 May 2007, Howard and Shelly Place, of Buckinghamshire, United Kingdom, did what parents do *when they can*; they videotaped their two sons, two-year-old Harry and eight-month-old Charlie, during a typical interaction that a two-year-old has with an eight-month-old. Two kids doing what kids do. Two parents doing what parents have always done, recording by the means available, the moment for future memories. But the means available now include sharing these memories, voluntarily, with the entire world by the medium of YouTube. And so, Howard and Shelly watched their recording, found it funny and decided to post their video on line. They titled this recording 'Charlie bit my finger'. (According to NBC, the number one video clip of all time at the time of writing.[4])

They uploaded it on YouTube because if they found it funny, maybe somebody else will find it funny. And as of this writing, 124 million unique viewers watched the original 'Charlie bit my finger' video. In short order, Charlie became a phenomenon; thousands of remixed videos, thousands of re-enactments, thousand of remixed reenactments, and thousands of blog entries and embedded video. Over 8,670 videos uploaded only in relationship with the original 'Charlie bit my finger'.[5] And yes, a combined total of over 1 billion viewers. One billion viewers that, just as Howard and Shelly Place of Buckinghamshire, found the clip funny.

I believe that great leaders think like Howard and Shelly Place: *if I like this, if I found value in this, other people like me will like it too*. And now WE CAN ACT on what we think, now WE CAN upload at will content on YouTube. For Howard and Shelly Place there were no development gates, and no gatekeepers. They had no 'go' or 'no go' decisions made by others; they, the two creators, were in full control of the content creation, content management and distribution, at all times. This was strategy felt and experienced. It felt

---

4   http://www.nbc.com/Most_Outrageous_Moments/ on 4 July 2009.

5   Available at http://www.*YouTube*.com/results?search_query=charlie+bit+my+finger&search_type=&aq=f [accessed: 22 August 2009].

right, in their gut. And it was from there that they pushed the button to 'upload'. And if your question is *'why do people do this?'* the only immediate answer is: *Because They Can!*

YouTube is a relevant cultural moment, and it needs to be analysed from the point of view of the signal it represents, a signal of disruptive behaviour (see Figure 2.1). What does the signal mean? And, where is behaviour moving because YouTube exists?

When you stop asking the question 'why' and start asking 'what do people need to do this?', then you engage into building an innovation producing enterprise, an enterprise attuned to the world of its customers and users, the kind of enterprise that creates innovation objects, which in turn create other innovation objects. 'Charlie bit my finger', is both an innovation object and a social object; it attracts us as a group and it compels us, for individual reasons, to participate by creating further content.

A YouTube search of 'Charlie bit my finger' reveals a number of interesting developments. The first layer of hits includes copies of the original video. The second layer includes remixes, in which people lip-sync to the sound of the boy's voice and the baby cooing. Others provide their own voices in exact, word-for-word (and coo-for-coo) re-enactments. There are also remixes, in which people set samples of the voices to music and repeat them rhythmically. And then there are remixed-re-enactments, songs, blogs and embedded videos within blogs. The raw, unrehearsed home video, has created a culture around it, with meaning for millions.

Every one of the remixers or re-enactors of Charlie's original script identifies as a participant on the same platform for collaboration. What is the question to which 'Charlie bit my finger' is the answer? The question is: 'How can I participate in the shaping of the present?' What is the latency revealed by 'Charlie bit my finger'? One of our primary goals as humans is to participate and to leave a mark. Charlie is a compelling platform for participation. Can we design new business models out of this understanding? *Yes we can!*

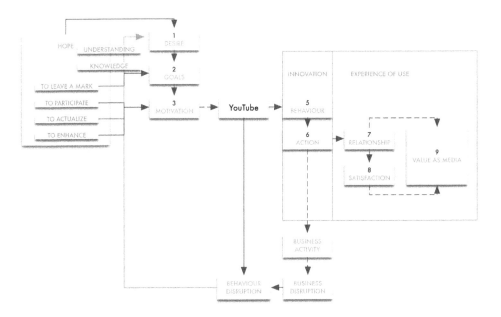

Figure 2.1   YouTube Map of Innovation, Motivation and Behaviour

If I am Apple Corporation, and I am trying to create value for the users of my iPhone technology platform, can I ignore the participatory reality of 'Charlie bit my finger'? Should I develop applications for the iPhone from habit, the same way I developed applications in the past, using a proprietary operating system, and closing all the gates for an open collaboration with my users? No. I get it; crowd sourcing.

I will make the crowds my partner, and I will open the doors wide, by creating tools (SDK – Software Development Kit), and by making them available and affordable; I will strive to set anyone up to become a developer of applications for my App Store. I will transform the crowd into my audience, and my audience into my business partner. What is the risk of doing this? Lower than the *risk of not doing it.* So I will give the crowd agency and the tools to transform my world, and their world in turn.

Media, Behaviour, Action: Humans empowered to change through Fire. The essence of the Apple App Store business model., as illustrated in Figure 2.2.

My colleague and collaborator Joseph Arbuckle developed the concept and practice of Values Based Innovation which is focused on the interdependence of the individual and his/her world, as one interactive system; there is no individual without a world and there is no world without an individual who creates it, and who is in turn shaped by it. Values based innovation brings new passion and power, imagination and insight to the development of self, and the production of our world both as a creative individuals and collaborative innovators.

In Arbuckle's view there is no self without a world and no world without a self – they are an interactive mutually creating/transforming system.

By now the App Store made history, with over 2 billion applications uploaded in the first year of operation. And over 85,000 applications created by users. Can this be a model for crowd sourcing innovativeness, and for the business model of the innovation creating enterprise (ICE) in other market spaces? I believe this is, at a minimum, is a

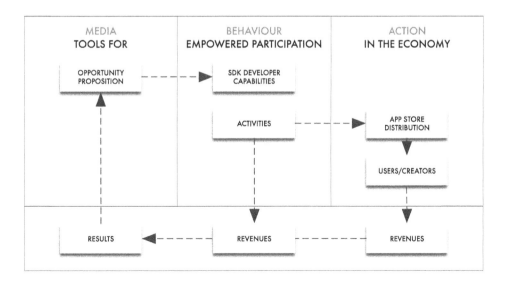

Figure 2.2   App Store Business Model

strong signal that the model can be exported to other domains. The model is described and illustrated later on in this book (Chapter 5) as well as expanded to other business domains, in the contribution of Sami Viitamäki (Chapter 8 'Massive Innovativeness', which gives numerous examples of corporations which have defined the strategic extent of user generated collaboration, and the tactical tools for doing it.

Signals of Disruption

'Charlie bit my finger' is a signal of redefined expectations. The ability to create and upload content is reshaping the culture from the point of view of the consumer. The reality of this moment is made possible by digital data being embraced as an innovation object. A technology for some, an attitude for others, and a life choice for many more. The ability to create, manage and distribute your own content. Is the engagement with your users – as with YouTube as an example of Web 2.0 – an option for your organization today?

Behaviour, technology, capability and the will to engage, are the elements that together shape the future. 'Charlie bit my finger' and the idea of the collaboration and engagement behaviours and platforms it represents, are redefining our expectations in multiple domains:

- Engagement expectations – the way we engage with society;
- Expectations towards brands;
- Expectations of participation in everyday life; and
- Expectations about the future.

I have termed this redefinition of expectations 'Everything 2.0'.[6] In the same way as the ability to create, distribute and manage on the Web is called Web 2.0, when we can manage, distribute and create content for everything in our lives, we have Everything 2.0. What happens when everything becomes 2.0? What happens to corporations? What happens to the old ways of doing business, the value chain, and the business model? I mentioned in the opening chapter that *'Future products, services and experiences will only be what we want to reveal next about ourselves'*. This is about us; it is about you. Who are we is the first question we need to understand in exploring what we are about to reveal. You may ask, what does 'reveal' mean? It means Facebook. Facebook did not exist just a few years ago; today millions of people are revealing a lot about themselves on social networking sites. This is a signal of something about to happen, and this emerging behaviour is manifest in many other domains, reshaping culture and the economy.

21 March 2007. On that date Paul McCartney signed a record deal with Starbucks Corporation. Starbucks does not make records. Starbucks sells coffee. Fifteen years ago it would have been unthinkable to sign a record deal with anything but a record company; why can he do it today? Because he is empowered, because Starbucks is empowered, because everything is in place; his motivation meets the technology, meets the business capability of Starbucks to act as a delivery point and market space.

---

6   Manu, A. 2008. *Everything 2.0: Redesign your Business Through Foresight and Brand Innovation, DVD Video.* New Riders. Part of the Voices That Matter series. First Edition.

So the questions we need to ask are: *What does this mean to me?* To my business, to my life, to my way of organizing my knowledge? Is this good for my organization? Is this something that will change us? And should it change us? This single example of Paul McCartney signing a record deal, is a signal of something that is happening in a profound way in many different organizations, changing forever the way we deal with life.

2 February 2008. Hip-hop artist Will.i.am produced a song in three days. The song, called '*Yes We Can*', set to music a speech by then presidential candidate Barack Obama, and included many guest artists. The video attracted 30 million viewers in three weeks. Such a feat could not have been accomplished just a few years ago. With the traditional record-label contractual requirements of the past, creating and distributing in one week, a work that reaches such an enormous audience, would have been impossible. It was possible today, with the empowerment provided by certain technologies, as well as the empowerment of his talent and that of his friends. Subject. Verb. Object.

'I called my friends, and they called their friends, and in a matter of two days we made the song and video,' Will.i.am says on his website. Because he can.

'Charlie bit my finger,' Paul McCartney and Will.i.am are signals. These signals have meaning, they represent something. The issue is, how do we map their meaning, and what do we learn from it for the future? What questions are these signals answers to?

What do you see when you see a signal like this? What questions do you ask?

SEEING AND QUESTIONING SIGNALS

Signals are not about what you see in their current manifestation, but about what they are about to become. So I do not look at Twitter and ask 'what does Twitter do?' I ask '*what will Twitter make us?*' '*What will be become by using Twitter?*'

What you need to do in order to see signals is to forget everything you know. Unlearn the way the world used to work. Stop asking rational questions. Unlearn every single thing, but not forever; for an hour, for the time you want to dedicate yourself to understanding the new possibility. Or for the two hours you want to watch a movie – you do this all the time. You suspend belief, you suspend rationality; you are in the temporary play space created by the narrative of the movie.

Signals and meaning. When we treat everything we see as a set of questions, signals start to have meaning. Take a look at a water bottle. What do you see? It depends on what you know, and what you know will depend on the questions you ask about the water bottle. The more questions you ask, the more you will see. Where is the water coming from? What process was used to bottle it? What material was used to make the bottle? If I want to make a bottle shape, what process is best suited for this material? The same holds true for any object that is around you in this very moment. The more questions you ask and have answers to, the more you will see about the world that surrounds you.

Now let us apply this questioning to the iPhone (any smart phone will serve for the purposes of this argument). What do you see? Is what you see in the first encounter enough for you to decide what this object holds, in terms of benefits and future potential? Because if you answer *yes* to this question, and start planning your next competitive strategy based on the first impression, and without asking the right questions, well ....

When looking at this object, you should not focus on what is in front of your eyes, the obvious icons of the existing applications, but instead, you need to look at what is not there, in the black space of the screen, in the infinite space in which new applications will reside. We don't know how many applications, we also don't know for what purpose, and this makes the iPhone ambiguous – is it a threat or an opportunity for my business? – as well as a classic disruptive business example. What would be possible? We can only answer this question from our imagination, as we have no frames of reference for what we cannot yet see on the device.

What questions did you ask when the iPhone was introduced in January 2007? Most people and organizations did not see it as a threat to their business, because they treated the device as a phone. Well, the iPhone was never just a mobile phone; it is a mobile digital data platform. What will it hold? The answers are coming out right now, at a rate of thousands of applications per day. At the extreme, we know what it will hold. *Everything we, the users, deem necessary as media for our existence.* This device is not a telephone; it is a culture. And more so, the iPhone is an Innovation Object.

Unfolding Opportunity

You are in a room, surrounded by familiar and unfamiliar things. Some may represent what you want most in life; health, wealth and happiness. Some may represent the things that could most endanger your life, and the lives of the ones you hold dear; disease, conflict, and disaster. These things surround you, but *you cannot see them,* the room is barely lit, and you can only sense a few of the objects. But everything is there, in plain sight, right in front of you. Why can't you see? How don't you see when your eyes are wide open? Maybe special goggles would help, ones that will bring those hazy shapes just outside your vision into focus.

The pages that follow are about how to build a set of those goggles, allowing you to see and interpret what is there, and how to employ knowledge to participate in the creation of new meaning.

The required capability to detect and make sense out of emergent signals, is a challenge for a number of reasons. We have learned and perfected a range of responses to change that is not conducive to imaginative pursuits, and in this range we have discouraged and lost our ability to play, learning to pursue the discovery of meaning with logic, but not with imagination. While there are plenty of schools that teach the limits of rational behaviour, there are very few, if any, that teach the way in which we can access and nurture our imagination. We can meet this challenge of seeing the possibilities of what is in plain sight, through the recovery of our imagination. This recovery begins with *unlearning,* with addressing the apparition of the 'new' through the eyes of someone *seeing everything for the first time*. This is an attitude that allows for the discovery and framing of powerful questions, exploring our imagination[7] without expectation or inhibition.

The apparition of the 'new' in the midst of habit is asking us to react, to take notice, *to take a stance*. Where do we go from here? If fire is this apparition, where do we go from here? Do we extinguish it out of fear – after all, it disrupts the status quo, it has dangers

---

7   Imagination: the ability to form images and ideas in the mind, especially of things never seen or never experienced directly. (Encarta® World English Dictionary © 1999 Microsoft Corporation).

within it, and we are not sure at all of the opportunities it might represent. But we can sense they are there; they just need to be discovered. When first looking at fire, we ask *what we can use it for* based on our past experiences; what can we make more beneficial to us, of what we already know? This is what we act on first, on what we know. Acting on the immediate is tactical. The tactical approach uses hindsight and insight; hindsight is the ability to evaluate the new within the context of associated behaviours, and insight is the ability to recognize these behaviours as signals of latent human needs.[8] This is usually where innovativeness goes first, improving pre-existing artifacts, pre-existing tools and systems. But the real maximization of the opportunity fire represents to dramatically benefit and change our life, comes when we use foresight. Foresight is the ability to translate the understanding brought by insight into a strategic opportunity.

Every discovery takes place in the context, and in relationship with, existing coordinates. These coordinates are giving meaning to our discoveries, as we measure them against what we know, what has been habit in our lives. Remove those coordinates from analysis and we are left with a field of new possibility. This is what imaginative foresight does; *it imagines the possibility beyond.*

When we imagine opportunities beyond the visible, having the courage to imagine a new way of life. A risky proposition for sure, as what we may find is a way of life that is drastically different than anything we knew so far, a way of life demanding of us profound changes, the construction of entirely new systems of living, and the building of new dependencies and relationships. This is why change in the moment of invention is hard. It requires unlearning the old habits and embracing possibility, with all its risks and rewards.

The maximization of an invention moment (Figure 2.3) – the discovery of a new technology – occurs when you understand how deep you have to dig into human nature. How deeply you have to dig into yourself. Then you can maximize the latent behaviours that will be released by a new technology; and once an invention becomes part of everyday habit and usage, when behaviour and technology are thus aligned, it achieves the status of innovation. Something of use and benefit to a plurality, something valuable in an obvious way and hence, marketable.

Imagining opportunity beyond the visible is the strategic aspect of foresight and requires a different mindset. The mindset in which you apply the invention to pre-existing conditions is a tactical mindset. But when you look at how to maximize for the future, you need a strategic mindset and you need imagination. The question, 'What could be possible?' is full of promise, but also full of ambiguity, and lacks the comfortable metrics we are used to. It calls for new metrics, new benchmarks and the redesign of the value chain.

---

8   Manu, A. 2007. *The Imagination Challenge: Strategic Foresight and Innovation in the Global Economy*. Berkeley: New Riders, 26.

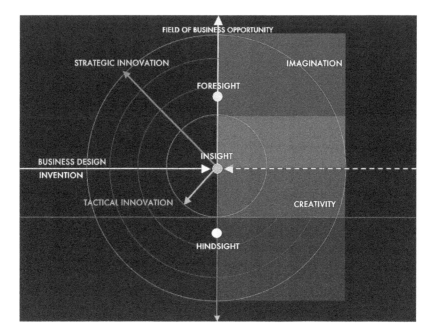

Figure 2.3   Hindsight Insight Foresight and Business Disruptions

From Dial, Talk, and Listen, to 'What Do You Want Me To Be?'

In 1973, Motorola engineers[9] presented to the Federal Communications Commission (FCC) the prototype of a new invention, the DynaTAC portable phone system, and soon after, the FCC announced that it would hold hearings on allocating spectrum for a new communication service called cellular.

The DynaTAC name was shorthand for the capabilities of the device – Dynamic Adaptive Total Area Coverage – as well as the capability of the system to track a caller's movements through a series of overlapping cells, and switch the incoming call to the cell nearest to the user, while automatically linking the call to the wire line network. This is a signal in plain sight. Everyone can see the technology employed, and the behaviour required to employ it. A radio with a keypad, a microphone, an earpiece, a small LED screen, and a battery; a device that allows the user to dial a number, talk and listen. Doing it all while being mobile, and free of a hard wire connection. To dial a number, talk and listen were not new behaviours; what was new was *doing this while walking*, or driving, anywhere within the range of a transmitting cell tower.

The FCC approved the DynaTAC 8000X radiophone in the Fall of 1983, and this marked the introduction of the first commercial[10] portable cell phone. The era of the Mobile Society has begun. But who saw then what was to come – mobile phones as an *innovation object* – and the transformations that the behaviour of mobility will bring about? Anyone who employed thinking, as a tool, should have seen what was to come.

---

9   Available at http://www.motorola.com/staticfiles/Business/Corporate/US-EN/history/feature-cell-phone-development. html. [accessed: 21 August 2009].

10   The stress here is on 'commercial use' as there were a number of radiophones in use by the military at the time.

Hindsight into the development of any technology would have informed at least the basic developments that were coming. So, lets look at them one by one.

On the technology side, the battery life will get longer and the battery will get smaller. The screen size will increase – just by looking at display technologies under development in the mid 1970s, one would have been safe in making this prediction – the display capability will increase to the point of high-resolution graphics being the norm. The network will spread its coverage. The cost of the unit will reduce once mass acceptance prompts mass production. The keypad will be multifunctional; adding characters to digits, and with this the ability to type. A full QWERTY keypad was not out of the question. On the behavioural side, dialing, talking and listening, will be expanded to taking notes, storing addresses, and once the display starts getting bigger and resolution improves, looking at pictures. And all of this just from hindsight, and from thinking about the *precise* attribute of the mobile phone as innovation object.

There are four signal attributes[11] of an innovation object: *precise, undeniable, intuitive* and *sensed*. Figure 2.4 maps what was precise at the launch of the DynaTAC.

Precise: The dimensions of the opportunity are exact, accurate, and detailed. What we know from hindsight is that the precise phase of an innovation object usually aggregates and obsolesces predecessors. Can we make the foresight call, in 1983, that telecommunication companies should revisit their business models? Can we make the call that broadcasters of radio and TV signals might want to revisit their models as well; or call the *New York Times*, and suggest to that reputable newspaper that the future of the advertising based revenue model is now, at a minimum, ambiguous? Well, it all depends on what questions we ask of what we see in front of our eyes. Any reasonable debate about the future possibilities of the radiophone will start with the next attribute.

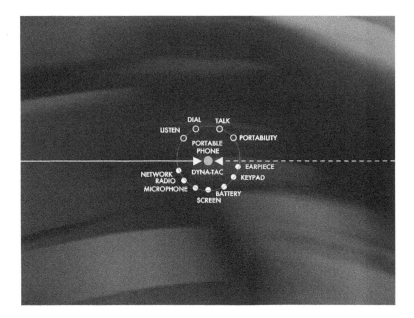

Figure 2.4   Mobile Phone Introduction 1

11   Manu, A. 2007. *The Imagination Challenge: Strategic Foresight and Innovation in the Global Economy*. Berkeley: New Riders, 21.

Undeniable: What is undeniable in the opportunity of a maximized cell network and maximized mobile behaviour? What cannot be ignored and holds the potential for high impact? We can use a bit of insight and, as soon as the market starts growing and adoption rates keep consistent over time, we need to start asking: *What does this mobile phone reveal about the behaviour of humans?* Where would it go from here? Figures 2.4 and 2.5 show what was precise and undeniable in 1983, once the FCC approved the commercial introduction of the system.

Insight will inform us that there is a reasonable expectation for the maximization of each of the technologies present, as well as an increased expectation by users that the unit will 'do more', as in Figure 2.6. This means that text will become 'to do' lists, schedules, calendars, address books. This also means the behaviour of being 'ON' all the time; within reach, with the freedom to be anywhere, while at the same time 'here', on the other end of a phone call.

In 1991 the system reached six million users in the United States alone. Is this its maximum market? What if we remove the coordinates of habit, coordinates from which we analyse and measure everything? What if we start thinking boldly about a new way of life, a life in which the mobile phone is *not an option*, but an appendage to actions of everyday life? What strategic opportunity do we see? This is the *intuitive attribute* of an innovation object.

Intuitive: The opportunity can be defined, but it has multiple manifestations. In the course of time, other innovation objects that develop synchronically with the mobile phone (see Figure 2.7), will impact and affect both technology and behaviour. We cannot look at the mobile system in isolation, but must look at other technologies that might use spectrum. Or might use data. So we need to ask the question: what else *will be mobile if it can*? And if we kept up with the news – even if just by scanning the periphery of what is relevant to a business involved in voice and data transmission – we have to know, by

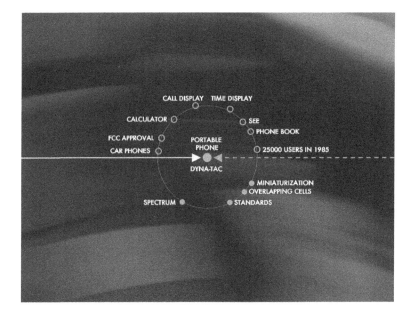

Figure 2.5   Mobile Phone as Innovation Object 1

1991, that a certain Tim Berners-Lee had a working prototype of a new system capable of linking documents over the Internet. Hypertext and the birth of the World Wide Web have to impact the map of possibility for the mobile phone as illustrated in Figure 2.7. The Internet will become wireless, and digital data will open up the appetite for digital data consumption on my once dial-talk-and-listen 'radiophone'.

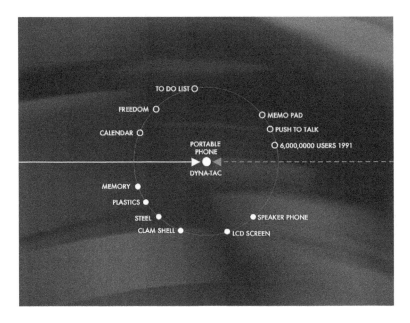

Figure 2.6   Mobile Phone as Innovation Object 2

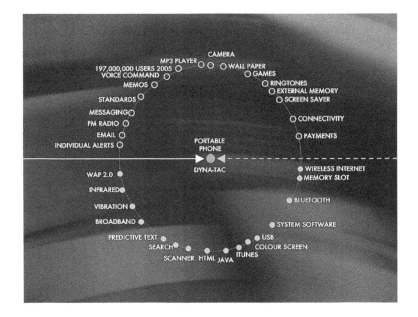

Figure 2.7   Mobile Phone as Innovation Object 3

From habit, we can think that the Internet is an option; some consumers and organizations will embrace it, for some it makes sense, for most it is an extra option they can do without. It is probably what we thought about fire when we first started using. Some will use it, some will not. ... Just like fire, the Internet once deployed, is not an option. It is a life imperative. Embracing this discovery means sensing new behaviours, and expanding the strategic innovation opportunities. This is the *sensed* attribute of an innovation object.

Sensed: There is awareness of possibility in the signal; it has multiple strategic opportunity directions, yet undefined. The degree with which any invention becomes an innovation, is the *rate by which a sensed signal becomes precise,* see Figure 2.8. Innovation objects that move synchronically through their own attribute cycles, dynamically influencing and expanding the opportunities map, accelerate this rate.

What was undeniable when the DynaTAC was presented in 1973 (Figure 2.4) was the fact that what is visible is not a part; what is visible is a system that is a *component* of a whole. The whole is what you need to be aware of and plan strategy for. When you see Figure 2.4 you must get ready for Figure 2.9.

If by now you think that it is easy to map out events that have already happened, I must point out that all of these signals were in plain sight, and obvious to anyone engaged in seeing, and in thinking about the meaning of what is in plain sight. I am merely illustrating it here for the record.

The strategic potential of any innovation object is there, waiting to unfold, if we ask the right questions. What is undeniable, as a possibility, is understood by people who are knowledgeable and perceptive. When we look at a new device, we need to understand the entire ecology it will create; an interdependent ecology of behaviours and tools that will keep growing, for as long as the innovation object in question is media for the satisfaction of people's goals.

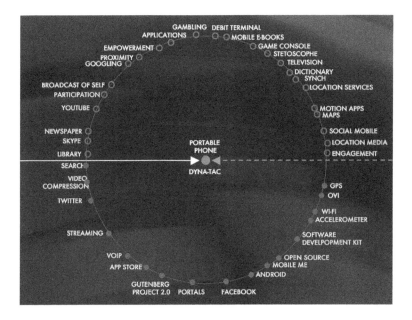

Figure 2.8   Mobile Phone as Innovation Object 4

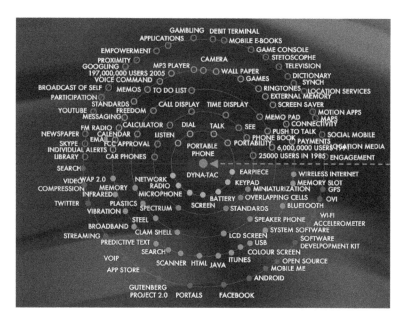

Figure 2.9   Mobile Phone as Innovation Object 5

The predictive statement made by Ken Olsen, and mentioned earlier in the book that *'There is absolutely no reason anyone would want a computer in their home'* has no meaning in the context of unfolding the potential of an innovation object. It is not about 'a computer in the home'; *it is about where would the computer go, once it can reach the maximization of its potential?* Otherwise put, 'if/when this technology happens, what will people want to do with it?'

Unfolding a map of possibilities has little to do with signals we notice in inventions in science and technology. It has everything to do with signals in how these inventions have become innovations, through people's interactions with them. The first instances of behaviour; not YouTube but YouTube *behaviour*, not Facebook but Facebook behaviour, and so on. It is about signals in us, and our desires, wants and needs. *YouTube and Facebook as motivation for behaviour.*

Once we observe a signal, we must be ready to anticipate the path it will take. As we observed before, the future is the changes WE make to our present condition, through our own motivations, our behaviour and our actions. To anticipate the path of change, we must anticipate, or 'feel', what are *we ready to change in our present*, for what *benefits*, and at what *price*. If we observe a new technology platform, we must ask not 'how and when I am going to use this?' but 'how will *they* use it'? How far will they push it? YouTube.

Your readiness to consider yourself and your organization, as a part of 'they', is a measure of your readiness to change with what you already know exists. How does this 'new' enrich what I already know about what I want in life? How will my daily actions be affected? My life and my outcomes? Change is a dynamic ecology in which motivation is manifested in behaviour, and behaviour is the outcome of what is present to the senses. I see a mobile cellular phone; will I ever use one? And if I do, how will my life be marked? How will this modify the way I do business, the way I relate with other people in my family, and my organization? What do I need to unlearn of the old systems that I consider to be my operating constraints?

PART 1

Perspectives for Innovation

3 *The New Context*

The term 'The Internet of Things' was first used in 2005 in a report released by UN's International Telecommunications Union.[1] The ITU defined it as *'a place in which every person, object and space is both a link and a holder of information'*.

You have a mobile phone with you right now; the device is a link, and a holder of information. It is no longer just a radiophone. If it is a smart phone, it contains much more information than you ever thought a telephone could hold. Through it, you are now a part of the Internet of Things.

The Internet of Things can be called by many names – 'the real world web', 'the embedded landscape' – some having to do with the technology deployed, and others with the behaviours it creates or engages. The Internet of Things is a dataspace;[2] a space in which digital data resides, can move, and can be managed. Dataspace is not a 'future possibility' but the reality that surrounds you right now. How is your business being changed by it? How are you changing your business because of it?

To answer both questions we need to understand the behaviour themes of dataspace – what are the new behaviours that dataspace makes possible – and its agents, the groups of people engaging in this behaviours. *The intermixing of themes and agents, creates the culture of the Mobile Society.*

Themes

Three principal themes can be observed: Empowerment, Participation and Engagement.

EMPOWERMENT

The acceptance of new discoveries, and the transformation of invention into innovation, does not necessarily contain elements that increase the social, political or economic strength of large numbers of the population. There was little mass empowerment after Johannes Gutenberg invented movable type in 1440; literacy was not yet widespread, and only the clergy was the immediate beneficiary of the printing press. For a long while, the printing press did not contribute to the empowerment of people, as it did little to allow them to transform *their role* in the distribution of culture. (You have heard the expression, 'Freedom of the press extends only to those who own a printing press'.)

---

1   The Internet of Things: Executive Summary. (November 2005) ITU Internet Reports 2005. Geneva: International Telecommunications Union.

2   Manu, A. 2007. *The Imagination Challenge: Strategic Foresight and Innovation in the Global Economy*. Berkeley: New Riders. 184.

Over time, communities were changed by the availability of books, and new habits were formed; knowledge could be communicated in textbooks, ideas can be shared, and language can be developed and protected around written form. The rest is history. The book as a device is immutable; between its covers, it contains all the words and images that represent the ideas put forth by its author. The reader cannot delete, copy, transfer or contribute to the content in any way, or share favorite passages with friends or colleagues. All of this changed with digital data files; they are re-mixable, they are easy to transform, mush, they can be acted upon. They empower transformation, collaboration and sharing on an unprecedented scale.

The combination of digital data, transmission and reception devices, as well as the existence of a vast support network, hold within the empowerment of individuals to access and generate information and content; to make choices within a wide range of options; to collaborate in collective actions; to gain knowledge and to participate with others.

PARTICIPATION

Hannah Arendt writes, *'No human life is possible without a world which directly or indirectly testifies to the presence of other human beings.'*[3] The presence of others is our requirement for plurality, and because we seek to be with others, we also seek to participate with them, and allow them to participate with us. This has been one of the dominant themes of humanity from the beginning, while not all moments in history have afforded individuals the capability to engage in participation. Participation means the opportunity to make a choice in matters that effect the other. This choice is equally important when participating within large numbers, or when engaging just with our immediate neighbours. The depth and breadth of our ability to participate, is a measure of our belonging as humans. Individuals capable of digital data transmission and reception – now a majority in the industrialized world – are *enabled* participants in the *creation and direction* of the mobile society. Be that political participation in the democratic process, cultural collaboration on social networks, or just trivial broadcasting of 'what are you doing' on Twitter, the architecture for participation is growing proportionally with the level of *engagement* of its users.

ENGAGEMENT

Engagement is a human experience, equally concerned with the meaning of things for the individual, as well as with the capacity of the thing to transform the individual. Engagement is a *voluntary activity* that deepens our connection with what we find meaningful in our context. More meaning means a deeper experience, so the only moderately accurate measure of engagement is depth. How many people have watched the 'Charlie bit my finger' video on YouTube more than once, is a better measure of engagement, than the total number of viewers. (I suspect that in this case, a majority of viewers have watched the video more than once.)

---

3   Arendt, H. 1965. *The Human Condition.* Chicago and London: University of Chicago Press.

Agents

The agents empowered for participatory engagement are members of the Millennial generation, born after 1980, and growing up alongside the developments illustrated in Figure 2.5. They are now of the same age as the desktop computer, this is not a superfluous analogy, but a statement of their capabilities and expectations.

There is whole lot of change between IBM's Personal Computer XT of 1983, and the MacBook Pro introduced by Apple in 2009. From the ten Megabytes hard drive of the XT, to the 320 Gigabytes hard drive capacity of the MacBook Pro, the increase in memory capability *alone,* is what a tall bumblebee is when compared to the height of the Empire State Building. 320GB is 32,768 times bigger than 10MB. This is just on the quantitative side of this example, but not on the qualitative side; there are no adequate metrics, to my knowledge, that can fairly measure the profound changes that took place over the course of the past 25 years, when we look only at this example. The societal, cultural and economic implications, while hard to qualify, have changed the nature of this generation's engagement with technology, and through that, with themselves and their life expectations.

Everything is possible for the millennial. You want to start a web site where classmates at your university can talk to one another? Now you can! So you do it, without asking for permission. And you notice patterns of engagement within this social group that surprise in their eagerness for life's detail; then you and your friends decide that this will be a good idea, and a useful meeting place for students at other universities, and for high school students, and later for the entire world. So you do it, and you don't need anyone's permission, because you can. You have the entrepreneurial spirit, and you also have the tools that empower you to act as an agent of change. Mark Zuckerberg started Facebook in his Harvard dorm room in 2004. Five years later, more than 300 million people use Facebook.[4] Why? Because they can. Because they find value in this engagement. Because they cannot afford not to participate. Because for some, Facebook is not *an option.* According to the site's own statistics, 125 million people log in at least once a day. Imagine having a meeting place that has 125 million visitors every day. Now imagine that these visitors are there because *they are not in your market place*! While they are on Facebook they are not watching your adverts on TV, not seeing your message in print, and not shopping for your products and services. This is significant for the economy on many levels, and, through the interconnected nature of the ecology of commerce, this is significant to your business as well.

And it will remain significant whether you understand why people go to Facebook, or not (incidentally, this is about the same number of people that shop at Wal-Mart in *one week*).[5]

The time spent on Facebook, YouTube, Flickr, MySpace – listed here only as representatives of a whole list of similar engagement opportunities – is measurable *participatory time* for the ones involved in the activity. It is time spent participating in the creation of culture, and in the shaping, one engagement at a time, of their own lives. Some may argue that users creating, managing and distributing their own content online

---

4   Available at: http://www.facebook.com/press/info.php?statistics [accessed: 27 August 2009].

5   Available at: http://wiki.answers.com/Q/How_many_people_shop_at_walmart_kmart_target [accessed: 27 August 2009].

is not exactly 'culture', but when the Pew Internet & American Life Project reports that in 2007, 64 per cent of American teenagers were posting content online, while 39 per cent of teens were sharing art they had created, we are pressed in revisiting what we mean by culture. What we mean by value.

How do we measure value? By the standards of a world in which a 10MB hard drive was the norm? It would have been unthinkable in 1983 to declare that, one day, I will have an 8GB storage device hanging around my neck. It is not only that the technology was not available, but 8GB of memory is not something that anyone could have predicted we would ever need, as individuals. Remember, some smart people already declared in 1982, that *640K ought to be enough for anybody*. But tools create behaviours, and behaviours create new motivations that create new tools. As we explored in a previous chapter, once an *innovation object* captures our imagination, our goals change, our motivation changes, and we revisit our expectations. Once we have invited the innovation object into our life – be that the DynaTAC, IBM's Personal Computer XT, the MacBook Pro or the iPhone – we are in a permanent state of disruption, as our curiosity drives new knowledge and opportunity. The Millennial generation grew up precisely in this context of permanent disruption of habit. Their 'normal' is empowerment and participation in the creation of *their* culture. For them, this is a fundamental and non-negotiable way of life.

You want to share videos of your birthday party online, with some of the friends who could not make it last night? You give it a try, and it is more difficult than you think. But if you want to share videos online, this means that others like you want to do the same thing, so it makes sense to start developing an easy to use website, where people *just like you, will* find value in the empowerment to upload their own videos, and watch videos uploaded by others. So in 2005 you register www.youtube.com (and yes, 2005 is not a printing error, the official launch of the site for the public was in November of that year). Because you can! By 2007, just two years after inception, YouTube was used by people in 22 countries.

The empowerment and participatory behaviour that are the essence of people's engagement with YouTube, are not manifestations of technological innovation. They are manifestations of innovation as a behaviour outcome.

WHERE TO FROM HERE?

What started with little over 25,000 users in 1983, has transformed us – our aspirations, productive outputs and broad engagement with others – becoming an integral part of our everyday life, an extension of who we are. By 2005, there were over 2 billion mobile phones world wide, and the Internet became society itself; every person, object and space is both a link and a holder of information. Connectivity to anything, from anywhere, by anyone, anytime. Where to from here? What innovation outcomes are foreseeable, if we treat digital mobile media as an *innovation object?*

Lets examine first where we are. Figure 2.7 illustrates innovation behaviours that are now (2009) in plain sight. Labels such as Flickr, Wordpress, Hulu, Linkedin, Sellaband, Twitter, PS3, GTA4, etc., are not meant to illustrate technologies, but rather, the engagement of people in the behaviour of Linkedin and all. I am repeating this point on purpose; *Flickr the website, would not exist without Flickr the behaviour.* As we manifest behaviours, new social interactions take place leading to engagement with new forms of cultural output, which in turn, create new behaviours. This means that we are looking at a *dynamic system ecology of behaviour.*[6]

Briefly described, we live in a system of continual change and adaptation, in which each 'new thing' entering a system already in place, and attaching its own needs – for networks, mobile power, bandwidth, shelf space, behaviour engagement, and more, as in the example of the DynaTAC mobile phone – to the demands already present in the system. This dynamic enhances existing motivation through new expectations, which become new behaviours to be satisfied. This may sound like a complicated way to express that what we know, for sure, is that the 'new thing' will change our system; we just don't know the dimensions and shape of that change. What is clear in this dynamic is the fact that 'new things' and 'new behaviours', will constantly appear and constantly modify expectations. For your business this is another illustration that *change* and the search for beneficial behaviour outcomes is a *constant*. Your *business is the variable*.

The digital media behaviour map in Figure 3.1 contains seemingly disconnected labels. The first objective of the map was to place behaviour events in the approximate order in which they have occurred. Now we can connect the dots. Take a look at the second layer; it contains the iPhone, the PS3 (PlayStation 3), DRM (digital rights management), the iTouch, the Xbox as well as a few more labels. One layer higher, starting at 10 o'clock, you will find Hulu (hulu.com) and moving around the layer Joost (joost.com), Vimeo (vimeo.com) and P2PTV (peer to peer TV). Can these dots be connected? And can they spell the end, at one point in the very near future, of television broadcast as we know it?

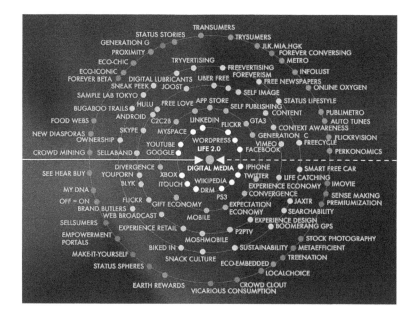

Figure 3.1   Digital Media Context Map

6   Manu, A. 2007. *The Imagination Challenge: Strategic Foresight and Innovation in the Global Economy.* Berkeley: New Riders. 102–4.

I mentioned before that the future is the changes we make to the present through *our motivation, behaviour and action*. In the presence of Hulu as a web based broadcast platform, the PS3 as the receiver station of the web based signal, and any flat screen TV as a display terminal, the end of cable TV broadcast as we know it is just a matter of the scale of the motivation, behaviour and action. Combine the iPhone into the mix – both a receiver and a display terminal – and now you have mobile TV. Can this be also a danger – or new opportunity – signal for the advertising industry? It all depends on what you know about people and their individual – as opposed to organizational – readiness to embrace change.

On 28 August 2009, as I was writing this chapter, the following headline appeared in my email inbox: 'Hulu Has More Viewers Than Time Warner Cable'.[7] A succinct article followed, informing readers that 'Hulu's reach as a video platform keeps growing, now reaching more video viewers than the second biggest US cable company.' What? More video viewers that the second largest cable company?

Digging a bit deeper, I went to the source of the data leading to the headline above. The source was a press release by Comscore:[8] '*TV Viewers Turn to Internet for Fresh Content with Shows on Summer Hiatus; Hulu Reaches All-Time High with 457 Million Video Views*'. I naturally have to ask myself, what is the number now, when you are reading this book? According to Comscore, in July 2009 158 million US Internet users watched online video, the largest audience ever recorded. Online video reached another all-time high in July with a total of 21.4 billion videos viewed during the month. Goggle (YouTube and Goggle Video) continued to rank as the top US video property, with a record 8.9 billion videos viewed, making up 42 per cent of all videos viewed online.

Let's step back for a second, and look at this number: 8.9 billion videos represents 42 per cent of all videos watched in one month. The total videos watched online in July of 2009 (one month) in the United States was over 21 BILLION! Now let's assume, modestly, that each video is just one minute long, giving us 21 billion minutes of content. Did you create any of this content? Did your company create it? Do you know what 21 billion minutes means? It means 356 million hours, which is over 14 million days, which is 40,000 (forty thousand) years. IN ONE MONTH! And this is just the beginning of web based TV.

Comscore reports[9] that '*Canadians Watched Nearly 150 Videos per Viewer in February*', 21 million Canadians – or 88 per cent of the total Canadian Internet population – viewed more than 3.1 billion videos online during the month of February 2009. The average Canadian online video viewer spent 10 hours viewing videos in February, up 53 per cent from their average viewing time last year. Google Sites attracted the most viewers with 18.2 million watching an average of 89 videos per viewer during the month. Microsoft Sites drew 7.1 million viewers, while Facebook ranked third with 5.8 million viewers.

Other findings from February 2009 include:

7   Available at: http://www.businessinsider.com/chart-of-the-day-hulu-has-more-watchers-than-time-warner-cable-2009–8 [accessed: 28 August 2009].

8   Available at: http://www.comscore.com/Press_Events/Press_Releases/2009/8/U.S._Online_Video_Market_Soars_in_July_as_Summer_Vacation_Drives_Pickup_in_Entertainment_and_Leisure_Activities_Online [accessed: 28 August 2009].

9   Available at: http://www.comscore.com/Press_Events/Press_Releases/2009/4/Canada_Leads_World_in_Online_Video_Viewing/(language)/eng-US [accessed: 2 June 2009].

- The average online video was 4.1 minutes in length, up nearly 25 per cent from the previous year's 3.3 minute average;
- 18 million viewers on YouTube.com viewed more than 1.6 billion videos in February, representing nearly 90 videos per viewer;
- Nearly 88 per cent of the total Canadian Web population viewed online video in February, the highest penetration of the five countries currently reported by comScore Video Metrix (France 82 per cent, Germany 82 per cent, UK 81 per cent, US 76 per cent);
- The average online video viewer in Canada watched 605 minutes of video in the month, the largest amount of time of the five countries reported by ComScore (UK 540 minutes, Germany 466 minutes, France 390 minutes, US 312 minutes).

How does this activity affect your business? You may think that if you are not in the TV broadcast business, or in any way connected with its business model, all these numbers mean nothing to you and your organization. You may after all be in a businesses to business (B2B) activity, so you are far removed from anything happening on, or with, YouTube. As your business makes equipment for other companies, you are not affected. Well, look at the map again (Figure 2.7); there must be a label somewhere that is part of your value chain, either as a content creator, an advertiser, an advertising agency, a brand marketer, a distributor of branded goods, a printer, a maker of packaging, a transportation company, a retailer, or the bubble wrap maker for which you are supplying a piece of equipment.

Everything is connected. And your business is connected directly or indirectly with the activity of the humans that form the market place. According to Comscore's findings, the average video viewer spent ten hours in February 2009 watching free content on line. This is ten hours not spent doing what they used to do; watch TV, read the newspaper, shop or play. This is ten hours in which *the user is not debited* for the consumption of entertainment. YouTube is free entertainment and more importantly, it cuts the share of the individual's consumption time by almost 40 per cent on a daily basis. When the eyes of the consumer are on YouTube, it follows that they are not somewhere else, where your message as an advertiser used to be. YouTube is another example of a meeting space soon to become a market place. If your users are there, you should be there too.

Phenomenon and Theory

The map in Figure 3.1 illustrates the nodes of the phenomena. In the opinion of German writer, philosopher and scientist Goethe, *the manifestation of the phenomenon is its own theory.* Lift your hand in the air, about head high, then let it drop around your body. This is the phenomenon of gravity. Now, you can wait for a theory of what you just experienced, or you can proceed in life knowing how gravity *feels*, and what you have to do to master it. I propose that we can apply the same attitude to business and the design of innovation outcomes; engage in the discovery of manifestations of what is happening, understand the values the people are after, then design and deliver new opportunities for new manifestations. This will be the strategic position acting dynamically within the phenomenon[10] taking place. The other position will be to wait for others to define the theory[11] behind the manifest behaviour. By the time they do, you no longer have a competitive advantage. For an example of dynamic strategy in which business is always the variable, think of Apple and iTunes. On 3 April 2008, Apple Corp announced[12] that the iTunes Store surpassed Wal-Mart to become the number one music retailer in the US.

In strategic terms, this means operating a business either in the *new dynamic meeting space* characteristic of phenomena, or operating in a competitive market place characteristic of the theory. In the former, the business is a variable, characterized by the ability to change with the conditions and nature of the phenomena. In the latter, the business is seen as a constant, while change is dealt with only in terms of risk; how to manage risks in order to maintain the marketplace definition we currently operate from.

The diagram in Figure 3.2 illustrates four quadrants of business activity planned around the opposition between Constant–Variable and Phenomenon–Theory. Each quadrant can be a profitable place for business, provided that one recognizes the pressure imposed on the user's behaviour by the existence and attractor power of the phenomenon. Where do you place your business on this diagram?

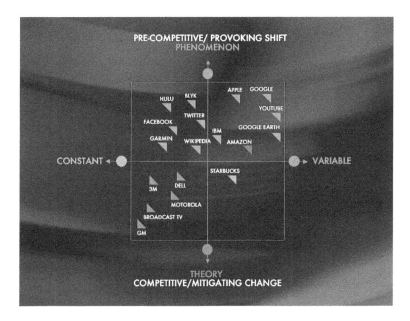

Figure 3.2   Constant and Variable in Business Positioning

---

10   In this context, we define Phenomena as behaviours and disruptive business models that change the rules of the market space.

11   We define Theory as processes, rules and tools that react to the presence of the phenomena in a market place.

12   Available at: http://www.apple.com/pr/library/2008/04/03itunes.html?sr=hotnews [accessed: 25 May 2009].

Challenges of Mobile Digital Culture and the Mobile Society

What are the strategic directions and actionable tactics for organizations in order to successfully navigate the transition between analogue and digital mindsets? What are the challenges?

First, let's deal with the terminology currently in use: Mobile Media, Digital Media, and the Digital Landscape, stand as descriptors of both a technology – digital data and the devices that transmit and receive it – as well as a behaviour, a user engaged in retrieving data while being mobile. As discussed earlier, the innovation object here is the fact that data is now mobile *and* digital. Mobile digital data could be transferred from one user to the other, from multiple entities to one, and from one to multiple. It is fair then to term the environment in which this activity takes place a Mobile Digital Culture – the expectations of the users and the deliverables of organizations, are tied to the understanding of 'mobility of data' as a cultural outcome, and one that results in new sets of relationships, new community structures and new forms of organization, all leading to a new society, the Mobile Society.

The mobile society is the sum of the lifestyles of its participants, and the participants are in a constant state of searching for media to navigate it, for media to engage with from play to work, learning to knowledge, entertainment and leisure. In the mobile society the innovation object is mobile; thus Mobile Media is the only media of relevance in the mobile society. Naturally, for organizations it will become the primary media for engagement – brand engagement – and because of that, a new challenge to be overcome.

The challenge of the mobile digital culture is *not about technology, but about strategy.* Nowhere is this challenge more immediate than in the domain of marketing and communications affecting brand management and brand building.

BRAND BUILDING AND BRAND MANAGEMENT IN THE MOBILE SOCIETY

What is the challenge? The challenge of mobile digital media for brand communicators is simply this: *mobile digital media is not a channel.* Mediums are not channels, they are modes of individual action. In the mobile digital mode of action, Brand Management is Brand Building; the actions of the user, his/her engagement with the brand via multi-platform portals of participation, are the cornerstones of brand building. This statement simply reflects the nature of mobile digital lifestyles and the role reversal now evident between brand building and brand management.

Consumer packaged goods companies – Procter & Gamble, Unilever, Kraft, Nestlé, et al. – have generally treated brand building as a global function (although the US and other large markets are regional). In other words, they have defined the attributes of the brand experience for a targeted but broad group, in a large geographic area. Based on studies of behaviour – what people are doing, how people are reacting to questions or situations, in other words, *manifest behaviour* – brand builders defined the vision and the values of brands, the emotional characteristics that will resonate with consumers, the rational benefits; in short, the personality of the brand.

At the local level (state level in the United States, province level in Canada, country level in Europe), brand managers were charged with delivering the brand values to consumers, in the form of marketing campaigns. This all worked well at a time when interruption was the norm; someone is watching a TV programme, and he or she is the targeted consumer for the brand, what do you know, I will buy some advertising time and interrupt the show with my brand's message. The planning principles of particular campaigns included multiple channels of support for the brand message, a mix of tactics and layered executions in each channel. The marketing budget will be divided between TV, Print Media (newspapers, consumer magazines, directories, trade magazines) out of home billboards and Live Interactions, etc., and once the Internet starts to matter, Digital will be added to this mix.

This is simplified of course, for the purposes of illustrating the changes brought to this behavioural landscape by the mobile digital media. According to Price Waterhouse's forecast[13] on advertising, worldwide expenditures in 2013 will be slightly below half a trillion dollars ($467 billion). Half a trillion is a significant number at both ends of the equation; for the advertisers spending it, and for the parties receiving it – agencies, production houses, TV stations, newspapers. And the forecast number does not include the salaries of brand management and communications personnel; added all up, the number is closer to three trillion dollars. This activity creates part of the economy. A large part. And this activity assumes that the people identified as the target group watch TV, read newspapers and magazines, listen to the radio ... what happens to this activity when this demographic no longer obeys habit?

Against a backdrop of tough economic conditions, we believe there will be nowhere to hide from the implications of digital migration. As economic pressure increases, so does the pace of change; aside from short-term challenges posed by the economic downturn, the real challenge lies in how to take advantage of the digital reality.[14]

The ability to engage and mobilize the community of users around common interests, and the ability to initiate and sustain a meaningful dialogue, are the new measures for the operations of brands. And while these tasks are vastly different than the brand model of the past century, corporations have not yet altered their models. Image based attributes which worked fine in product specific branding on the familiar display of the TV set, or in the pages of a magazine, *do not engage in dialogue*, and do not provide the impetus for a engagement. Ideas do, and ideas are independent of the devices that hold them; ideas are mobile, and they can transform the individual, and inspire transformation in his or her immediate group of friends.

What changes need to be made to respond to these challenges? Here are just a few headlines:

1. Agility in attitude and response.
2. Intelligence based strategy adaptiveness; this means the ability to continually reshape strategy with the dynamics of the context and in a synchronic timeline.
3. Rethinking of Marketing – its role, tools, methods – for the mobile digital culture, its agents and themes.
4. Rethinking of Brand Building in Mobile Media terms – from *location strategy* and tactics, to engagement strategy and tactics.

---

13   Available at http://www.pwc.com/gx/en/global-entertainment-media-outlook/index.jhtml [accessed: 13 September 2009].

14   Available at http://www.pwc.com/gx/en/global-entertainment-media-outlook/index.jhtml [accessed: 13 September 2009].

The major shift is from the stationary and captive audience watching a TV spot, to a *mobile crowd* that has to be transformed into *an audience for the brand*. How do you transform a crowd into an audience? With magic! Magic does this all the time by understanding the nature of the media at hand, the nature of the crowd, and by transforming their reality by design, creating an innovation outcome that is *compelling, engaging, surprising and delightful*.

The nature of the media at hand: In the Mobile Society, the nature of the media used is transformable, portable, mobile, transmittable, customizable, re-mixable, local and global at the same time, and multiplatform. In the very near future it will also become context aware, location based, individually filtered, sensor triggered and independently storable on small read-write transponders.[15] This is the technological reality in which we need to frame both the challenges, and the opportunities for brand management and brand communication.

With the mass acceptance of smart-phones, and their guaranteed penetration in all demographics, mobile digital life has become a reality. This simply means that the instrument of choice – the media by which individuals choose to manifest and actualize themselves – is now a portable computer and communication platform that fits into one's pocket.

PORTABILITY REFERS TO SIZE, MOBILITY REFERS TO LOCATION

Life, in this context, refers to the nature of the media being ON all the time, and its ability to both SEND and RECEIVE. It is in these two functions that we find both the challenge and the opportunity, as it is these functions that are unique from prior forms of media. For brands this means:

- the ability to contact individual users with individual messages;
- the ability to contact multiple users with the same message; the ability to receive feedback at all times from users;
- the ability to engage users 24 hours a day; the ability to trigger users' responses of engagement via defined stimuli;
- the ability to control and define stimuli on a daily basis; the ability to define stimuli on location basis;
- the ability to define stimuli on proximity basis (users close to other users) and much, much more.

Mobile Digital Culture is a way of life in which everything becomes media for the *individual empowerment to create, manage and distribute content*. Again, this is not about technology, it is about strategy.

Clarification of terms: What is the NEW in New Media? From the perspective of strategic focus as well as resource allocation – people, money, time – we need to clarify the term New Media as used in the marketing mix. Using the label New Media in reference to Digital Media or Mobile Media does a great disservice to the phenomenon we are

---

15   ZigBee technology – just one of the examples of read-write small scale transponders. More on ZigBee at http://www.zigbee.org/

observing, as well as diverts resources into domains that no longer have currency with the demographic.

To clarify, there is no such thing as 'New Media'. There is only current media, the instruments and agents we use NOW to actualize ourselves. We can also talk about 'contemporary media', the media still around, but not preferred for our current need to maintain, expand, enhance and actualize the self. This is an important distinction for brand management, as it informs the very core of strategy. Using the term New Media to distinguish from past forms of media – print, TV and radio, more recently the Internet – triggers focus and resource allocation in disproportionate percentages to the value of the engagement possible.

Trends, Sub-trends and Trend Watchers

Who keeps an eye on the manifestations of the phenomena? Its own newly empowered, participatory and engaged agents! Trendwatching.com is an independent and trend firm, scanning the globe for the most promising consumer trends, insights and related hands-on business ideas. With a network of hundreds of spotters in 120 countries, trendwatching.com is sourcing its data gathering to the crowds. Information is collected through Happy Spotting,[16] a network of spotters that submit contributions, when accepted, the contributions are rewarded with points that can be redeemed for gifts. The network participants receive, via email, monthly requests for spotting specific trends. Trendwatching.com produces monthly trend reports – which are emailed to over 160,000 professionals in 180 countries – as well as an annual trend report. This is the dynamic system ecology of behaviour in action. And here are some of trendwatching's findings (some of which appear in Figure 3.1).

THE EXPECTATION ECONOMY[17]

The Expectation Economy is an economy inhabited by experienced, well informed who have a long list of high expectations that they apply to each and every good, service and experience on offer. Their expectations are based on years of self-training in hyper consumption, and on the biblical flood of new-style, readily available information sources, curators and BS filters, which all help them track down and expect not just basic standards of quality, but the 'best of the best'.

Tracking and understanding the Expectation Economy is not a science; in fact it's a nice mix of experience, intuition, and knowing your sources. Some examples of sub trends are:

> *Vicarious Consumption*: Consumers can now vicariously consume everything and anything through the eyes of curators and other consumers, and the written/spoken/taped reports they freely share. Once high(er) expectations have been set, they are bound to go largely unmet, since the majority of brands still choose not to keep up with the best of the best.

---

16   Available at: http://www.happyspotting.com/index.php?page=index [accessed: 2 August 2009].

17   Available at http://trendwatching.com/trends//expectationeconomy.htm [accessed: 8 March 2008].

Fake Loyalty: Consumers will continue to purchase from underperforming brands if the 'real thing' isn't available. To the underperforming brand, all may seem quiet on the western front, until the best of the best suddenly does become available. Good examples of fake loyalty can be found in the airline industry; millions of frequent flyers around the world know that Virgin Atlantic, Singapore Airlines and Emirates offer a superior experience, but since these airlines don't fly on all routes, consumers have no choice but to fly with subpar airlines now or then, or all of the time.

Postponing Purchases: Some 'best of the best' brands like Apple actually manage to indirectly convince consumers to postpone certain purchases. Many consumers would rather wait for the iPhone or MacBook Air to become available, than to buy a new phone or laptop. Again, due to the dissemination of information, even local product launches are instantly global. Digital services have already succumbed to phased distribution, the physical world is next.

STATUS STORIES

The shifts from brands telling a story, to brands helping consumers tell status-yielding stories to other consumers. Some companies no longer inundate consumers with their 'brand stories', but instead help customers tell a story to other consumers. Not to promote that particular brand, but to make those customers more interesting to others. As more brands (have to) go niche and therefore tell stories that aren't known to the masses, and as experiences and non-consumption-related expenditures take over from physical (and more visible) status symbols, consumers will increasingly have to tell each other stories to achieve a status dividend from their purchases. Some examples are:

Everything Niche: Consumers moving away from familiar, trusted mass brands may soon find themselves truly addicted to everything niche. Old, physical status symbols won't disappear overnight, but preferences are shifting.

Experience Demands: Besides the shift from mass to uniqueness, mature/prosperous consumers now predominantly live in experience economies. Experiences not only are inherently more unique, they also do a better job of providing instant gratification, they are often more affordable, and thus more numerous than old-world status symbols.

Virtual Status: The shift in consumer attention toward online, virtual worlds, means yet another challenge for visible, physical, real world status manifestations.

Life Caching: Peoples need to collect and store memories – collecting, storing and displaying one's entire life, for private use, or for friends, family, even the entire world to peruse. In an economy in which many consumers favour the intangible over the tangible, collecting, storing, displaying and sharing experiences is exciting, and even necessary.

ECO-ICONIC[18]

Eco-friendly goods and services sporting bold, iconic markers and design, helping their eco-conscious owners show off their eco-credentials to their peers. At the heart of ECO-ICONIC is a status shift, many consumers are eager to flaunt their green behaviour and possessions because there are now millions of other consumers who are actually impressed by green lifestyles. As the *New York Times* put it: 'Why are Prius sales surging when other hybrids are slumping? Because buyers want everyone to know they are driving a hybrid.'

This is not about all green products, it's about those products that through their distinct appearance or stories actually show that they're green, or at least invoke some curiosity from onlookers, and thus help their owners/users attract recognition from their peers. In an ECO-ICONIC world, visibility counts, for big and small products alike. Which, in the case of cleaning products, means exposure will start the moment others check out your shopping basket or cart. Will that bottle of washing-up liquid scream 'green!'? Some examples:

> *Eco-Embedded*: While the current good intentions of corporations and consumers are helpful, serious eco-results will depend on making products and processes more sustainable without consumers even noticing, and if necessary, not leaving much room for consumers and companies to opt for less sustainable alternatives. Which will often mean forceful, if not painful, government intervention, or some serious corporate cuts, or brilliantly smart design and thinking, if not all of those combined. Think green buildings, or a ban on plastic bags or gasguzzlers – anything that becomes truly embedded into daily life, and by default leaves no choice, no room for complacency.

> *Eco-Boosters*: Expect smart companies to quickly move from 'merely' neutralizing and offsetting their undesirable eco-effects to actually boosting the environment by doing something extra. From planting more trees than is strictly required, to cleaning up not only your own mess, but someone else's too.

FREE LOVE[19]

The ongoing rise of 'free stuff', the brands already making the most it and the millions of consumers who are happily getting into a free-for-all mindset.

The war for consumers' ever-scarcer attention and the resulting new business models and marketing techniques, also benefits from the ever-decreasing costs of producing physical goods, the post-scarcity dynamics of the online world (and the related avalanche of free content created by attention-hungry members of GENERATION C), the many C2C marketplaces enabling consumers to swap instead of spend, and an emerging recycling culture.

Contributing factors:

---

18   Available at http://trendwatching.com/trends//ecoiconic.htm [accessed: 20 July 2008].

19   Available at http://trendwatching.com/trends//freelove.htm [accessed: 8 March 2008].

- The *online world*, with its capacity to create, copy and distribute anything that's digital, with costs that are close to zero, forcing producers to come up with new business models/services, which are often purely advert-driven;
- The ever-*decreasing cost of physical production* makes it easier to offer more (nearly) free goods in the offline world;
- The avalanche of *free content* created by attention-hungry members of GENERATION C;
- C2C marketplaces enabling consumers *to swap instead of spend*, making transactions cash-neutral;
- An emerging recycling culture.

Tryvertising and Trysumers: A new breed of product placement in the real world, integrating your goods and services into daily life in a relevant way, so that consumers can make up their minds, for free, based on their experience, not your messages.

Brand Butlers: Instead of stalking potential and existing customers with unwanted, hollow advertising slogans, why not assist them in smart, relevant ways, making the most of your products and whatever it is your brand stands for, for free?

Premiumization: Entice one's audience to buy a premium/more extensive product only if they truly like the free version.

Cunning Cartridges: Hook users by giving away or heavily subsidizing the machine/ device, then have them pay for the (proprietary) batteries, cartridges, blades, bulbs, pads, minutes, and so on.

Uber Free (Paid Love): Companies paying consumers to use certain goods and services.

Give and be seen: Never before have we witnessed such an explosion of free content, courtesy of individuals who are happy to share their thinking, novels, photos, movies, music, knowledge and expertise, advice, crafts and more in exchange for visibility, respect and status.

Examples: Newspapers and magazines (*Metro*), Free mobile (Blyk, Talkster, Jaxtr), Free airfare (Ryanair), Food and beverage (Apex), Photo prints (MesPhotosOffertes) Wifi (Metrofi, WIGO, Starbucks, Google), Navigation (adNav), Finance (Mint, Weabe), Games (EA), Music (Qtrax, Ee7, SpiralFrog).

4 *Rethinking Innovation*

I proposed earlier that innovation is behaviour – as outcome – changed by technology. YouTube, the App Store, the Kindle and iTunes, are some of the manifestations of this definition. The innovation of YouTube is not in technology, but in people's engagement with it. The innovation of YouTube is behaviour; when behaviour engages technology in an innovation outcome, we have a *disruptive business model*. This is not about a product or a service, but about the creation of culture. It follows that the ultimate capability of a business, is *the knowledge of initiating, managing and monetizing, the creation of culture*. This is why rethinking the role innovation plays in culture, starts with rethinking innovation.

The popular concept of what constitutes an 'innovation' usually encompasses technological breakthroughs and new products. This definition is limiting, and inhibits the imagination, for in truth, the scope of possibility for innovation can extend well beyond our established notions of the term itself. It falls to our capabilities as innovative individuals to define and re-define the term, through our organized explorations of what could be possible in any chosen domain. The latent innovation potential that lies in every individual, can be – and must be – mobilized and leveraged to produce new pre-competitive value for corporations, which in turn can influence the quality of life of humanity. Bringing forth the latent innovator in individuals towards this goal, requires not just effective management, but leadership qualities as well. The empathetic character, courage, and playful qualities of a leader, must accompany the systematic and diligent attention to process and systems inherent in effective management.

'Where From' Innovation?

Successful innovation outcomes are answers to *conscious or subconscious goals residing in human motivation, and motivation starts in desire*. This position is consistent with the history of innovations that have changed, improved and reshaped human life, and are also consistent with their roots and ethos. The ethos that pushes us to discovery is our continual search for media for becoming. This means that the drive to innovate – the actions taken toward innovation outcomes – is not primarily the result of our competitive spirit, but the result of our desire to be beyond competition, and pre-competitive as far as the other animals are concerned. Not a search for a new way of doing things, but a search for a better way. A qualitative life change that echoes with our motivating goals as individuals.

What tools do we employ to both achieve and measure this goal for '*a better way*'? Or a better question still: are the tools we employ in developing and measuring ideas, connected in any way with the conscious or subconscious goals that we seek to satisfy?

Most tools and methods currently used to manage innovation, are holdovers from the industrial-era economy, an economy in which efficiently satisfying an identified consumer need was an accurate predictor of sustainable success.

The industrial economy's primary values of efficiency are well-served by the 'funnel' innovation process model, by which the scope of possibility begins as broad, and is gradually narrowed to an outcome with the highest likelihood of success, in an established market. But in a post-industrial, globally competitive economy, innovation is no longer about *serving the market*, but about making – or transforming – markets. It is no longer about adding value, but about creating value. As the rules of the global economy evolve, so too must our notion of what it means to be an 'innovative company' in this changing context.

Change and Frameworks: This is Not Our Business!

A few years ago, I was involved in a foresight mandate for a global communications company. The task included research of current technologies and future trends, conceptualizing user scenarios of individual or integrated applications, and defining opportunities for new business platforms aimed at integrating the core technologies of the company.

We started with four broad questions:

1. What is the *capability* required for transforming the company's knowledge into Wealth?
2. What unique *cultural role* can the company play in the future, in the life of users and business, and how current developments and trends might affect this role?
3. What unique *business role* can the company play in the future in the life of users, and how current developments and trends might affect this role?
4. How do we leverage the company's technology and core capabilities, to achieve higher profits and market penetration?

We discovered that in the very near future (this project took place in 2004) everyday brands would need capabilities closely connected to the enablement of technologies that were the strength of our client company. Specifically, that *content* will need to be transmitted and received; *situations* will need to be detected, monitored and mitigated, and *customized* levels of service will need to be designed for the above. The opportunity to shape the future was at hand; it was closely tied to the company's agility for change, and its ability to play a leading role in the redefinition of the *meaning of communication in the mobile society*. By recognizing and acting on the potential of this concept, the company could become a critical partner in enhancing and expanding the experience users have with everyday brands and everyday spaces.

We proposed[1] the following strategic directions:

---

[1]   A version of this listing first appeared in Manu, A. 2007. *The Imagination Challenge: Strategic Foresight and Innovation in the Global Economy*. Berkeley: New Riders. 187.

Enabling sense: This is the strategic decision to take on the role of making sense of raw data. In the awakening data-permeated environment of the mobile society the challenge will be first to realize the scope of opportunity made possible by the existence, and transferability, of data.

Knowledge enabled: Developing a new standard of expected intelligence within products.

Knowledge ready: Every person, place and object should be ready to learn, and that each of these elements should have the capacity to communicate this knowledge when called upon to do so.

Making everything make sense: The resolution to meet the challenge of making the world intuitive and meaningful to all, individually. This strategy demands complete clarity of all user experience. It is the refusal to accept environments and objects that do not recognize and communicate their purpose.

Wisdom sets: This is the belief that data, when properly indexed, can itself become meaningful to the user. These sets are the retrievable benefits of the immense collaborative filtering of the Knowledge Enabled landscape.

The embodiment of the strategy was a device we called 'The Enabler'. What was making the Enabler distinctive, was the wealth of user upgradeable applications and features, as well as the unit's basic configuration based on three primary functions: as a *conduit*, as a *catalyst* and as a *provocateur*. The big idea was moving away from 'smart devices' – it was clear in 2004 that this field would become very competitive, and our client may have been too late to enter the field – to 'dumb devices with smart sensors'. This was the positioning of the Enabler:

Today we have brands designed to support and enhance lifestyle. Your Lifestyle. Tomorrow, YOU WILL BE THE BRAND.

YouBrand: your Objects, Services, Environments, will know you.

They will sense anything; they will sense light, weight, emotion, position, location, temperature, patterns of action. We are moving from smart devices with dumb sensors, to dumb devices with smart sensors.

These devices will know your friends, your family, your music, your movies, your time, your business, your banking. They will know your emotions, they will know your activities, they will know your environments, so they could enhance your experiences, by introducing you, to more of you.

The list of capabilities is too long for the purpose of this story, but here are a few highlights:

- The Enabler performs all the traditional functions of the cell phone, mp3 player, day planner, PDA, entertainment device, or remote control, while adding layers of information and communication beyond that;
- It is a data collection point and a virtual translator of meaning, advising on possible actions and choices for specific moments in time, while the user is at specific locations;
- It uses a combination of programmed personal details and behavioural tracking, to ensure that everything you interact with is tailored just for you;
- It monitors the availability of services and features, and only offers the ones that you want;
- It will communicate with everything you own, including your household appliances, media devices, computers, smart clothing, smart spaces, acting as the information hub and interpreter, between you and all the devices in your life.

Well, you get the point. Pretty much what the iPhone, and other smart phones are soon to become. The presentation of these ideas went well, the questions asked by participants were smart, and the general dialogue revealed that everyone in the room was 'getting it'. However, at the end of the meeting, the senior executive in charge summed it all up by saying: 'This is great, *but this is not our business*'.

There was no need to get into details. The research mapped the phenomenon of mobile lifestyles as an occurring, precise, signal. The company was simply lacking the agility for response, and the attitude and tools to deal with it. It took our team a while to fully understand the roots of the decision not to move forward in prototyping the Enabler as a business model; the proposed directions were not addressing an *existing market space*. The mobile society was not yet defined as a key innovation area for the company. People were just not engaged, yet, with devices of the sort we were describing. *Our solutions were not solving any problem!* No user was complaining or demanding more, no vendor was asking for this, and no competitor was offering anything even close.

The lesson for the company, now in retrospect, should be this; innovation as strategy is not about what *people are doing now*, but about *what people are about to do*. The field of business opportunity is in *the future*, always. So the challenge at hand was not how to fit the Enabler into the existing business, but how to fit the business to the Enabler. Treating the search for innovation outcomes as constant, and your business as the variable – but more about this in a subsequent chapter.

AGILITY AND THE CORPORATION

'This is not our business' was probably a rewarded strategic attitude a few years ago. The executives defining 'what is' and 'what is not' *our business* were seen as focused execution specialists, praised for keeping their eyes on the ball, and for keeping results at the forefront of decision-making. The organization that can declare *this is not our business,* is a model of a body that has grown to a state of numbness; it can no longer make use of what its extremities are sensing. In such organizations, process dominates; and while process may be good at managing facts, it is not so good at managing ideas. New ideas have a hard time penetrating existing processes and the grids that manage them. The grid is the closest structure we can use to illustrate the physical spaces, offices and cubicles you are familiar with. This grid creates more than physical barriers, it creates fundamental

fear, which builds barriers to creativity, and people do not transmute ideas between these barriers easily. Have you, in your own organization, ever had a great idea and taken it to a group? What was their reaction? Here is a list of probable reactions; see where your experience fits:

'We are doing something similar'

'We did something like this a few years back'

'We don't have time to do this'

'No one needs this'

'This is too expensive'

'We cannot market this'

'This is not our business'

These are just a few of the remarks that will send your great idea into oblivion.

Why do large corporations seem to loose the agility to react? The shortest answer: *risk aversion*. Agility is a measure of an organization's ability in four domains:

1. The ability to act on intelligence received from the field (from the periphery of the business, from media reports, from unfolding signal maps, from consultants, etc.);
2. The ability to unlearn legacy processes;
3. The ability to reshape legacy supply chains;
4. The ability to reframe and rethink tools and metrics.

From the perspective of processes, supply chain, tools and metrics, the declaration *'this is not our business'* makes a lot of sense. It means: I am not equipped to deal with this; I do not have a process in place, have no way of measuring it, and have no tools to work on it. Not engaging is a safe way to protect the status quo. It is also a measurable mitigation; the certain risk of *not acting* versus *the uncertain risk of acting*. This attitude has defined for long the problem mitigation nature of most product and service innovation efforts. The motivation for developing new products and services has been rooted in competitive pressures, and for the purpose of competitive advantage. This encourages a starting point where a problem to be solved is the most desired outcome. If an innovation outcome does not solve an existing problem, it is not deemed to be helpful in substantially altering the competitive position of the company. The Enabler device and service mentioned earlier did not solve any problem. Therefore; *'This is not our business'*…

This model is no longer sufficient or desirable. In innovation as mitigation you know what you want to discover – you also know what you will discover; the solution to the generating problem. This type of innovation does not create a strategic advantage but mitigates a weak position. When rethinking innovation as *behaviour changed by technology*, I propose a pre-competitive strategic mindset that aims at innovation outcomes that are beyond competition.

Beyond competition as a mindset for innovation starts with *questions* rather than *problems*. How can I live in comfort? How can I feel pleasure? How can I keep warm? How can I cook my food?

Life Beyond Competition

'CHIMPS GOT FIRST CRACK AT STONE AGE'

This was the newspaper headline on 14 February 2007,[2] announcing that a Canadian discovered that primates used rocks as tools 4,300 years ago.

'We used to think that culture, and above anything else, technology was the exclusive domain of humans, but this is not the case,' Dr Julio Mercader, University of Calgary.

We were told that humans evolved from the great apes and that some forms of life are more evolved than others. This was evolution. As long as we were the evolved, it all made sense. But what do we have, of what we want, that a great ape does not? The development of language? The civilization of great cities? Music? Poetry? What if ... devolution is the cause of every innovation? What if we invented what surrounds us today because we were weak?

What if we needed language because we cannot run? We build cities because we can't breathe underwater. And we write poetry because we cannot fly.

We are the only animal that writes poetry. Poetry is not music, as music can be made by other animals; we write poetry because we want to send a meaningful message to other human beings. We want to create meaning in our life, and the lives of the ones we care about, meaning that goes beyond the tangible. Our sense of self, our spirit, is the force that gives humans the ethos to change our condition continually. It is this spirit that creates the ethos of innovation, a prerequisite for creating the conditions we want in life.

Humans have been beyond competition for a long time. Throughout our early history, humanity has developed tools and innovated ways of life out of the necessity to compete with other animals. In order to do that, we needed to define how we had been short-changed by our physical limitations, and where the danger from other animals lay. We invented ways of moving faster, jumping faster, building better shelters, and later on, flying. That all came from a competitive necessity and from a problem/solution framework; I need to run faster; how can I run faster? This is tactical innovation, protecting a competitive position in an existing market. Tactical innovation allowed us to compete with the other animals for the same sources of water, the same sources of construction material, and the same plants and vegetables. We developed tools that allowed us to be prolific at maintaining ourselves, and at protecting our immediate social groups. We developed these tools out of the necessity brought forth by our physical constraints; we are not the fastest of the animals, so we developed tools to compensate for that, and other shortcomings of physical nature.

---

2   *Globe and Mail*, Toronto Edition, 14 February 2007.

But we did not stop at simply compensating for our weakness; our desire, as demonstrated by most of the artifacts we created, was not just to compete with the other animals, but to be faster, more lethal, better than them. Slowly, we improve and start dominating. We are now safe to desire more. Once fully capable of surviving amongst the faster and stronger animals, and being able to compete for the same food sources, we found it necessary to attempt to transcend our animal condition, and started looking at pre-competitive innovations, manifestations of our desire for more, for better, a search for quality in our survival. What the Greek, Roman, and Egyptian civilizations left behind had nothing to do *with running from the tigers*. But everything to do with manifestations of: 'If I happen to be killed by the tiger, this is what I left behind, *this is who I was*'. It is from this ethos that pre-competitive innovation comes.

But what happens when we move to a framework beyond competition? How do we innovate new frameworks for life? On what basis? How did we move from building shelters to building *comfortable shelters?* How did we move from survival to *the quality of survival*, to manufacturing soft pillows and creating an entire industrial and economic structure that produces comfort?

We did it by defining ourselves as different than the other animals and by imagining new destinations. The concept of comfort is one of these destinations. Pillows have nothing to do with need, or competitive drive. A pillow is an innovation beyond competition, or what we call in this book, a strategic innovation. Strategic innovation does not have preceding artifacts to compare it with, its behaviour outcomes create a pre-competitive opportunity and a new market space.

How did we move from eating food for survival to drinking coffee for pleasure? I cite coffee here because it is the second-largest trade commodity on the planet, yet it has little to no nutritional value, thus no practical function. Coffee is not food! *It is an expression of our desire for pleasure*. Coffee is fragrant and flavourful intoxication – it just tastes really good. What is the benchmark for good coffee? 'Mmmm, *good* coffee!'

Life beyond competition is about 'Mmmm', purely human in its intention, and rooted in the ultimate source of action; is desire.[3] As Bertrand Russell puts it in *'The Analysis of Mind'*: *'Desire in behaviour is like force in mechanics'*. Can it be any other way when it comes to pursuing innovation? The case for desire in the next chapter, for now, let's us look closely at benchmarking life beyond competition. What is the benchmark for flowers, and why do people give flowers to one another? Entire industries are built around cut flowers, the cut flowers you give your mother on Mother's Day might have come from Colombia on an aircraft, packed in a plastic box, a few days before you bought them. Cut flowers are Colombia's fourth largest export earner after coffee, oil and bananas. And what do we do with flowers? In a competitive framework, where survival was primordial, we might have eaten them. Now we give them to each other, as a means of communicating meaning.

These are not the same frameworks. We think of events as taking place in relationship with fixed coordinates, and we measure them against those coordinates. Remove the coordinates from analysis, and the event or object is independent of measure, and worthy of its own scales of value. So how do we measure the value of flowers in our life? Against what coordinates? This example speaks about the need to reframe and rethink the metrics of habit, both at the level of the individual and that of the organization. This reframing has to be a dynamic and synchronic capability of every organization involved in the

---

3   Aristotle in De Anima declared that: 'Desire is the ultimate source of action.'

development of products and services. And the only coordinates that matter should be those of the *constant human desire for a better experience of life.*

Change and innovation: In an environment of continuous change, innovation is the constant and business is the variable; does this statement shake the foundation of your organization? It should not. It did not for IBM.

For International Business Machines Corporation, the period from 1995 to 2007 saw the company acting voluntarily to repurpose their traditional technical expertise. Imagining a new destination, IBM repurposed itself as an 'Innovation Company', declaring in the 2005 Annual Report:

> *IBM today, perhaps more than any time in our history, is an Innovation Company. We have a distinctive point of view on how innovation is changing, and a unique set of capabilities to enable our clients to capture its benefits. In a word, we are their innovation partner. We make them innovative – the innovator's innovator.*

The company established early on in the process of transformation, an organizational capability to develop and maintain strategic advantages in the areas of Global Enterprise, E-business, Business Performance Transformation Services and Global Integration. This ability to respond, the readiness to adapt and most importantly, predetermine the course of shifts in the market landscape, made IBM fit to embrace change and let go of habit, let go of mature businesses.

In 1995, IBM made note of the profound transformations that would become manifest as information technology matured, specifically that connecting *the right information, with the right person, right now* is an area of business competence that will refocus IBM's expertise and value for business. Moving away from their computing hardware design and manufacturing business, IBM focused on UIMA (Unstructured Information Management Architecture), collecting and analysing massive amounts of data and defining valuable insights for clients from this data. The company mapped the future scope of its business in relation to signals that were evident in 2001. Some of these signals were described in IBM's annual report of that year as:

- Autonomic Computing: Computers will care for themselves;
- Biomimetics: Advanced computing devices will take a lesson from a mollusc;
- The e-workplace: Enterprises will dismantle industrial workplaces;
- Supercomputing within the reach of individuals;
- You'll be able to manage an army of 'you', one 'virtual identity' – single, encompassing and under total control through all our daily interactions and transactions;
- All computers (and computer users) will join 'the grid', 'millions of computers will be interwoven into a gigantic grid which people will use like a utility'.

By developing their expertise in emerging high-value spaces, they were able to reconfigure their traditional concentration in computing hardware, while anticipating the social transformations that would eventually demand of the computing industry the redesign of its own 'organizational software'. They saw a new computing model, where the combination of infrastructure and ubiquity created a distributed model of economy and industry, with forms of human and technological capital interacting to realize greater collective benefit.

Engaging in this transformation, IBM involved itself in the story of its own future. Internally the company was experiencing a resurgence of the sense of self-assuredness, enabling the scope of the organization to look forwards by creating opportunities, rather than reacting to threats; shaping the future became not only a goal, but a series of manifest actions as well.

For the first time in a very long time – probably since my early days with IBM 30 years ago – I'm seeing a company ready to focus more on opportunities than on threats, more intent on setting the agenda than on reacting to the moves of others. Our deep-seated optimism – a fundamental belief that IBMers have always possessed in progress, science and the improvability of the human condition – is reasserting itself.

(IBM Annual Report 2003)

In 2006, IBM recognized three shifts that will change the IT industry and articulated them as fundamental in their change imperative:

1. We believe that our clients would place a premium on innovation;
2. We believe that both our industry and our clients would seek to reintegrate;
3. We believe that globalization would fundamentally change business.

The result was a four-tier strategy that delivered on the promises made during the course of the previous decade:

1. In their software activities, they had expanded beyond the previous one-on-one and team collaboration suites, opting to introduce tools through which communities of expertise could be built.
2. Their Global Services division came to be ranked first and second worldwide in consulting, systems integration and Web hosting among others, ending 2006 with an estimated backlog of $116 billion.
3. In their Systems and Technology business, they headed up shifts towards the use of multicore processors.
4. Of all the areas in which IBM was most active, the one with the greatest potential for re-drawing the boundary of the computing business as a whole was innovation and global integration.

After decades of new technology invention, we are entering a phase familiar to economic historians who study technological revolutions. This is when new technologies get infused into every aspect of business and society. And this is when lasting value is created and real money gets made. Increasingly today, it's playing out on a global stage – and that, in turn, is driving a new model of the corporation itself. We're shifting away from the 20th century multinational and toward a new way to integrate the components of business activity on a global basis. We call this the 'globally integrated enterprise'.

(IBM Annual Report 2005)

IBM's structural, operational and cultural transformation is a model for fundamental change, in the face of imperatives faced by all business; new technology adopted as behaviour, and the new meaning of globalization made possible by information technology.

Samuel Palmisano,[4] IBM's CEO, writes in 'The Globally Integrated Enterprise':

> Sustainable competitive advantage has never come only from productivity or inventiveness. Today more than ever, the premium comes from the fusion of invention and insight into how to transform how things are done. Real innovation is about more than the simple creation and launching of new products. It is also about how services are delivered, how business processes are integrated, how companies and institutions are managed, how knowledge is transferred, how public policies are formulated – and how enterprises, communities, and societies participate in and benefit from it all.

The 'fusion of invention and insight' that leads to transformation is *the design process* leading to innovation. A process that can be measured, has methods, has inputs and has outputs. Which brings us to the complete picture of the innovation producing ecology: *Innovation is the outcome. Design is the process. Humans are the subject.*

The Power of Design as an Innovation Process

The power of design lies in its capability to make change usable and marketable for corporations. This translates into different things at the different ends of this capability; at the manufacturer's end, design's primary capability is that of making *technology* and raw materials marketable as a 'machine', a 'telephone', a 'coffee maker' or a 'chair'. At the user's end, design's capability is that of making technology and raw materials *usable and recognizable* as a 'machine', a 'telephone', a 'coffee maker' or a 'chair'. Usable as an innovation providing beneficial responses to the question 'how is this coffee maker media for me?'

In performing at its full capability, design is in effect restoring the equilibrium between the corporation and the change affecting its world, and in this context, designers act as the Equilibrium Integrators. They integrate the complex values of the consumer with, and into, the products, services, and environments of the corporation. For the corporation, design gives change its tangible and usable form. Towards an integrative definition of innovation – inclusive of both the design process and the behaviour outcome – I propose the following definition of design process leading to innovation outcomes:

Design is the conscious activity of creatively combining technological invention with social innovation, for the purpose of aiding, satisfying or modifying human behaviour.

Design plays an active role in creating the context of social, economic and cultural development, by establishing the formal and normative conditions within which all human activity in the industrialized world takes place. In doing so, design is the process that leads to innovation outcomes that make possible the relationship between human beings and their world as illustrated in Figure 4.1.

---

4   Palmisano. J.S. *Foreign Affairs*. 85(3), 132.

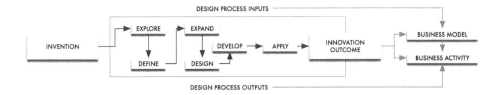

Figure 4.1   Design as the Process of Innovation

5 *Purpose in Innovation*

Creating Culture: The Multiple Dimensions of Creating a Compelling Experience

It was habit for hundreds of years to sharpen pencils with a knife. About 1847, Therry des Estwaux invented the manual pencil sharpener.[1] Hundreds of improvements were made over time to this invention – double blades, a holding chamber for the shavings, mechanical rotation devices, electric rotation devices – and yet the outcome has remained the same: insert the dull pencil in the round opening of the device resting its sides against a sharp blade, rotate the pencil a few times, take it out of the opening and enjoy the inviting sight of a sharp pencil.

Where is the innovation here? If you have a pencil sharpener around, take a look at it. *It* is not the innovation. The sharpener is *the invention.* You, the user, engaging it its use – all the activities described above – is the innovation. Innovation outcomes involve behaviour. They actively involve your actions. Innovation does not exist without an action, and *no action exists without an experience.* From this, we have a simple proposition to make; innovation is an experience. The more compelling the experience, the more delightful and useful the innovation.

Innovation creates culture and experience, not products. With the iPhone, Apple did not invent a technology, but new ways of engagement with technology for desired and beneficial outcomes. In other words, *ways to make us happy.* Ways to make us productive. Each iPhone application makes the experience of using the device more compelling, and changes its nature by reinventing the device into a new possibility, each time we download a new application. Download 'Stanza', and the iPhone transforms into an e-book reader. With a few taps on the screen the iPhone becomes Plato's *'Republic'*, or *'The Notebooks of Leonardo DaVinci'.* Download 'Navigon' and you now have a GPS navigation capability. Download 'Level' and you can now use your device as a surface leveller. 'Voice Memo' and you can now record your thoughts. 'Bug Spray' and you can protect yourself against mosquitoes, by broadcasting high pitched sounds through the tiny speaker of the iPhone, annoying enough to keep the bloodthirsty insect away from you.

The iPhone is an innovation object; it is also a model of innovation as the creation of ways of being. Engagement in the iPhone innovation is defining, *one moment in time*, the best circumstances for the way you experience life. Every time one uses the iPhone the experience is improving slightly one's most recent memory of what the product is, and that is the realm of compelling experiences.

---

1   Bellis, M. *History of Pens and Writing Instruments.* Available at: http://inventors.about.com/library/inventors/blpen. htm [accessed: 13 August 2009].

Usability and Esthetics

The journey of any discovery from the condition of *invention* to that of *innovation*, involving adding to its form – the state in which we find the discovery, or the original practical function state of any invention – the goals of motivation and the actions of behaviour. Transforming a piece of technology into a *behavioural object*, something that invites use, directs the user and responds – providing feedback – to his or her actions.

Toys are a perfect example of a behavioural object; by themselves they mean and do nothing. They are designed for 'relationships' or for the 'experience of use' and not simply for their practical features or form aesthetics. The functionality of a toy resides in its potential for creating a relationship, either between user and toy, or amongst users; I believe that here we can also find the development brief for the iPhone. When we intentionally add elements *for* behaviour to any object or system-behaviour in the form of the manner we address the object and relationship we can create with it – we are transforming that object into an innovation outcome. And the aesthetic of the object is only an invitation into its possibility. In the case of the iPhone, anything is possible. The underlying issue thus becomes one of reassessing the meaning of innovation from the reliance on new function and utility, to the new proposition of what makes a media – object or service – wanted and useful, is the relationship it creates with the user, while providing one, or multiple answers to, the purpose question of 'How is this media for me?' 'How does this help me satisfy my motivating goals?'

The conceptual model of innovation as a relationship experience is: Motivation leads to Behaviour; Behaviour leads to Action; Action leads to Relationship; Relationship leads to satisfying the goal (maintain, enhance, actualize). The satisfaction of these conditions creates Value (media for me) see Figure 5.1.

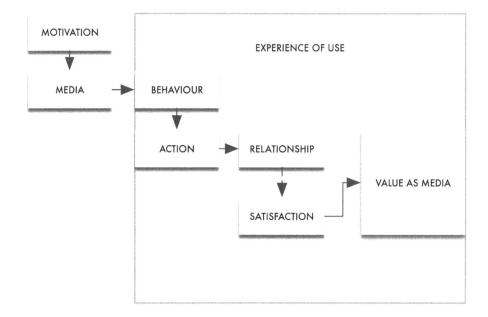

Figure 5.1   Value as Media Map

Innovation is the Experience of a Big Idea

There is a Big Idea at the root of every innovation, and engaging in the process of producing innovations with the Big Idea in mind is key in delivering outcomes of benefit to users. A few years ago I termed this process[2] of creating experiences the *'Big Idea of Design'* and defined its components as Product, Event and Experience. The Big Idea concerns the fundamental purpose of an artifact, or service, and in this respect there are few Big Ideas and many forms to represent them. Technology frequently reshapes the artifacts we use, but rarely does it reshape the Big Idea. Making whipping cream is transforming milk into a new dimension. There is no taste difference when the whipped cream is made by a manual, mechanical or electromechanical mixer-blender. So the Big Idea was not improved upon; what was improved upon is the way we address the task and the convenience of performing it.

Let us say your company is developing a new coffee maker; where do you start and what element do you consider in the development process? Some might start by looking at the competition and shape the new product offering within the gaps that can be observed in competitive products, thus striving for 'differentiation'. Others might step back and ask 'What is a coffee maker?' 'Why do we drink coffee?' 'What role does the coffee drinking experience play in our lives?'

The Experience of coffee consists of many things, such as the taste of the coffee, the shape of the cup, the sugar bowl, the use of fresh water, the roast of the coffee beans, the size of the grind, the grinder and so forth. Each of these contributes to substantially altering the primary stimuli object of this experience, which is taste. But the experience itself takes place in a context; the context is the Event of drinking coffee and its system components; the table, chair, light, time of day, noises surrounding the user, the conversation or other activity one is engaged in while drinking coffee, and all other attributes of the environment hosting the event. The event takes place within its own context, and that is the context of the Big Idea, or the original idea of coffee consumption; roasting the coffee beans, grinding them, and using hot water to extract the flavour in a brew, for the purpose of savouring the experience in the company of others, as a digestive or special offering. The presence of 'others' might be an essential part of this picture. And the seed for the success of Starbucks. Opened in Seattle in 1971 by three coffee enthusiasts, the company migrated from the sale of coffee beans and coffee making equipment, to a retail experience in which coffee is the core of a relationship with life; it is not about the beans, but about the culture that we, as users, create around the experience of the beverage, the surrounding space, and the others enjoying the same experience. For Starbucks, coffee is an innovation object worth $10 billion dollars in sales in 2008.

INNOVATION AS A RELATIONSHIP

Your wristwatch. Is it an innovation or an invention? And where is the innovation? It is your relationship with time that is the innovation, and the wristwatch plays just the role of media for this relationship. The watch is media for your ability to manage the passing of time, your time, and time in relationship with the actions you must engage in, at

---

2   Manu, A. 1998. *The Big Idea of Design*. Copenhagen: Dansk Design Center.

fixed moments of the day, week or month. Outside the Big Idea of *time management* your wristwatch is just a piece of jewellery.

The watch is an excellent example of a product that means nothing when you take it out of its context. Without the Experience, the Event and the Big Idea, a product by itself does not exist. In any innovation, context is meaning, without Context, there is no meaning, and no relationship.

TECHNOLOGY IN INNOVATION: BRIDGES TO A BETTER SELF

My view of technology is that of a bridge, for both corporations and users, it is something useful in helping us negotiate our journey towards becoming the next best representation of ourselves. From a foresight perspective, specific technology artifacts are not good guides of what the future holds; the culture they create and will leave behind, and how technologies have changed people's expectations is what we need to focus on. The residue that is left in us, and how do we become better human beings because we used this device, or this service.

All these technologies are just temporary bridges into the future. We are not after the computer screen; what we are after is the relationship with the other, the people behind the screen. And the faster we can find another way to achieve this relationship with the others, the faster we will move away from devices called 'computers' to a different type of interface we don't yet know what to call. The next interface will not be on a device, but the interface with knowledge. Smart places will give people the ability to engage in meaningful dialogue with locations themselves. That is why we go to Florence in the end, because we want to learn, we want to ask Florence the question, 'Why have you become the centre of the Renaissance?' Who is going to tell you this story? The best storyteller could be the building itself, Il Duomo. Il Duomo knows a lot about Il Duomo. Right now it doesn't have the means to transmit that information, but that is what technology is for.

A Model for Innovativeness in Corporations

From any perspective, two major factors confront innovation practice today; the discourse of innovation as a methodology – a processed based, task solving activity – rather than a behaviour outcome, and the management of innovation as a *process* capability of the organization. The latter effort is akin to trying to *manage*, rather than deliver, the experience of a particular wine. The statement made earlier in this book that innovation is not a process, may seem radical to many people in business, academia and government. These organizations like processes, because processes have inputs and outputs, they can be managed, they can be measured, they can be authorized and theorized about, they can be taught, they can be put in a timeline against which funding can flow. Processes are good. Redefining innovation as a behaviour outcome – a noun – possesses real difficulty for managers; how do you manage a noun?

Treating innovation as a process capability divorces it from the desired value outcome of the product or service; in any method, the tools used to initiate inputs and measure the outputs of the process, have little in common with the metrics of how an innovation outcome is measured, experienced, and felt.

Treating innovation as a process reduces it, its practitioners, and results, to the basic elements of any process. A plentiful supply of innovation methodologies and innovation management processes, guarantees neither demand for the products and services of the organization, nor quality in the innovation outcome. Specialization in a process-based activity further fractures the innovation practitioner's role in the organization, to one of assessing and addressing a given problem. This is the Problem Based innovation method; it works well for management because problems have solutions. If solutions are found, then innovation is happening, right? But solutions to what? The originating problem.

The differences between the old and the new value chain (see Figure 5.2), are not drastic in terms of allocation of time and resources; but they are drastic in terms of the output they generate, as well as in the metrics used at every stage. For any business, innovation within the existing value chain is rather easy to manage because we have already identified needs, expressed by the artifacts and services we are already using.

We have a defined framework, and we know the players, as well as their ability to add value at the identified points of the chain. In this framework, we are concerned with designing, developing, making and marketing the artifact to service a previously defined user need, but in a new, more beneficial form. Essentially, we are satisfying a user need that was determined *prior* to our activity of developing something to satisfy it; the process of innovating in this chain does not create a new output from the point of view of invention plus behaviour, but responds to a competitive condition. It may create more features to an existing device, make it more user friendly, improve its serviceability, improve the brand proposition, all within the competitive landscape that existed prior to commencing the process. As for metrics, we know how to measure at all stages and we know the timing that will satisfy our metrics, measured against the investment in money and human resources. Developing innovations within the existing value chain is a comfortable proposition for management, because it carefully avoids ambiguity; we know what the outcome is, and we have an identified market for it already, so we also know the potential ROI if everything works as planned.

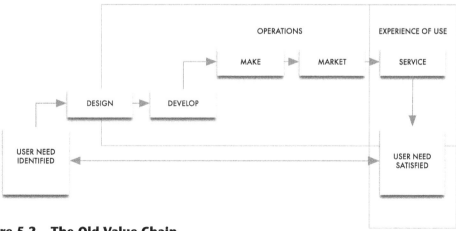

Figure 5.2   The Old Value Chain

The process funnel illustrated in Figure 5.3 is also a manifestation of carefully avoiding the ambiguity of new and potentially disruptive ideas; the disruptive elements – causing either internal or external disruption – are mitigated with the aim of fitting the new idea into the existing business.

The danger embedded in this approach is that all our competitors have an equal opportunity to innovate on the same value chain, and we may end up rolling out a product only marginally different than that which the competition is rolling out the very same month. And we take the risk of having this happen time and time again.

The risks associated with this approach can be avoided by defining a pre-competitive *innovation challenge*, a challenge that starts not with an identified need, but with the discovery of emerging behaviours and emerging technologies – disruptions of the status quo in the market space in which we currently operate – and the mapping of new opportunities at the intersection of the two as seen in Figure 5.4. With a bit of courage, we may map opportunities that fall outside our core competence, but opportunities which are obvious once we start asking questions, and once we understand that new market spaces may open as a result of what we just discovered. These discoveries are not assumptions or forecasts: they are logical extensions of reasoning, extensions of our human ability to understand cause and effect. Fire and cooked meat, changes in diet, and the domestication of animals. Fire and light; light and knowledge.

I mentioned courage briefly in the preceding paragraph, when referring to discovering opportunities that fall outside our core competence. Courage is mostly needed after we made the discovery, in the actions we take to transform the opportunity in a new competence for the organization. Cognizant that we may hear others say, 'This is great, but *this is not our business*,' we need to equip ourselves with the courage to *make it our business*.

Once we have defined what the opportunities are, we need to simultaneously engage in exploring in three dimensions of behaviour, at the same time; experiences, products and services, and define what we can design for each one of them. The innovation outcomes that will make these opportunities manifest in the marketplace, will create new spaces for

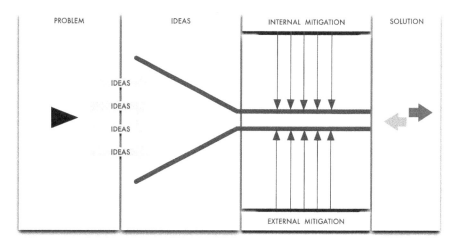

Figure 5.3   Mitigation Funnel

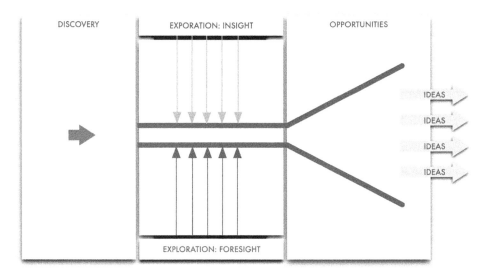

Figure 5.4   Innovation Funnel

commerce and reveal latent behaviour, and the process results in an innovation outcome; a new behaviour, a new form of engagement with the user, and a new market space. An opportunity for which we have defined the space, and created the rules of engagement. The three process steps mentioned above – discovering emerging behaviour, emerging technology and mapping opportunity – are not expert competencies for most companies, as they were not part of the old value chain. It is natural then, to fear these steps and to ask: How do we innovate? What do we need? Do we need creativity, or do we need imagination?

This third query begs the further question: What is the difference between creativity and imagination? According to Webster's dictionary, creativity is: *'The ability to use the imagination, to develop new and original ideas or things.'*

Creativity is, in effect, an application of your imagination. Without imagination there is no creativity. Which leads to an interesting idea: creativity allows us to manage the process, but it is the imagination that starts it. The required capability for the new value chain, is imagining possibility (see Figure 5.5). Possibility requires foresight, and foresight is how we invent the future.

THE BUSINESS MODEL

Traditional business models consist of two primary elements; *what your business does, and how your business monetizes what it does*. The concept of the value proposition is widely used in all business model design (as seen in Figure 5.6), with models having the 'value proposition' in the very centre of the scheme. And yet, this is not seen as one of the distinctive elements[3] but rather as a starting point for a neat diagram. The value proposition in this context, is simply a description of what is being sold, but with the

---

3   Weill, P., Malone, T.W., D'Urso, V.T., Herman, G., and Woerner, S. 2004. Do some business models perform better than others? A study of the 1000 Largest US Firms. *MIT.* 5.

twist of defining it as an outcome. Not mobile phones, but 'Seamless Mobility' (Motorola, 2003), or 'Connecting People' (Nokia, 2002). It is the position on which the business wants to build its distinctiveness in the market place.

The emphasis of these models is on 'How' the business makes money. What they rarely contain is an emphasis on *creating* value, the 'why'? Why would people want seamless mobility? Why would people want to be connected? In other words, what is the value for the individual? *How is this 'Seamless Mobility' media for me?* In my view this is where business model design should start: *defining how the value proposition is media for its users.*

Let's look at a rudimentary business model design (Figure 5.7) for the Apple App Store.

How is the value proposition of 'Opportunity' media for the satisfaction of users' needs? The App Store SDK (Software Development Kit) is the answer; it gives a crowd of potential developers the technical capability of engaging in the activities that will lead to the creation, testing, debugging and distribution of as many applications as the user is willing to create. The user is in complete control of all modules of the value chain. What

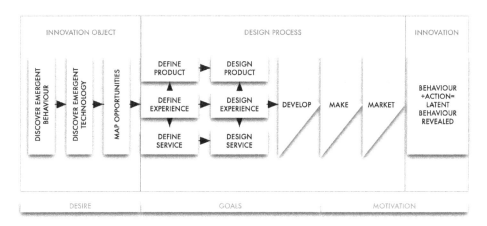

Figure 5.5   The New Value Chain

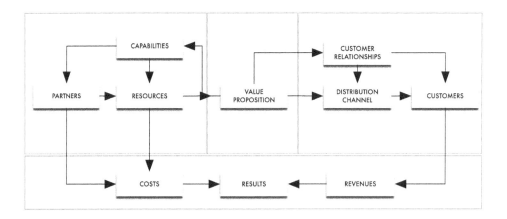

Figure 5.6   Classic Business Model

is interesting about this model is that it contains sources of revenue for Apple at both ends of the model; one is connected to the number of applications sold, the other with the number of SDKs sold. Apple acts as both distributor and broker of an asset created by the crowd, *without having ownership of the asset*. The App Store model is an example of an organization attuned to the world of its users. It flawlessly answers the question: 'How do you attract your customers forward in their life?' By creating the App Store, Apple has invited its audience to become fire, by providing the tools and the ecology that attracts one to the future, and makes one responsible for it, Apple has engaged in the shared project of shaping the future alongside. The Business Model now redesigned, is that of an Innovation Producing Enterprise (see Figures 2.2 and 5.8).

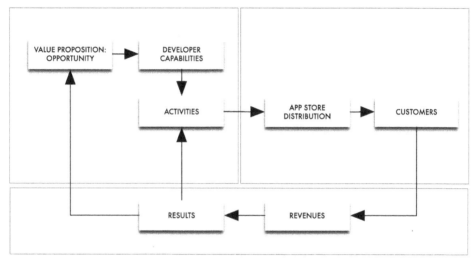

Figure 5.7   Rudimentary App Store Business Model

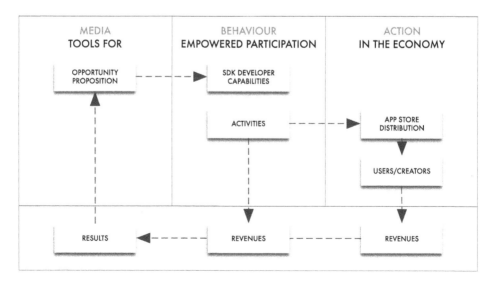

Figure 5.8   App Store Business Model

6 *Ethos and the Role of Desire in Innovation*

I Want Something You Have and You Want Something I Have

Indulge the idea that the economy may be as simple as this: '*I want something you have, and I am willing to exchange for it.*' My want comes from *seeing* what you have to offer; I am motivated to buy the product or service you are selling. Mine – *buying* – is a motivation. Yours – *selling* – is a behaviour. Both are rooted in the goals we have set for our lives. The more I am motivated to buy – by different factors including your persuasive advertising – the more your behaviour will engage in this exchange by producing more goods. And we have commerce. On your end, we have the production and distribution of certain goods I want. On my end, we have the exchanges I am willing to engage in, in order to obtain your goods, as well as their consumption. You are the producer, and I am the consumer. Or is it: 'I am the consumer, and this is why you are the producer?'

How important is this reordering? Who is the engine of the system we have just created? It is: '*I want something you have,*' that starts the process evolving into this economic system, which will eventually grow, as soon as my friends, my family and my colleagues, define themselves as peers that want to have the same things I have. By necessity, other elements of the system develop to support my desire for your goods, including engineering, management, administration, money, and finance. Gold, silver, copper, and zinc. Oil. Trade. Customs and trade routes. Markets. The management of all these systems is what we call today the economy. The variables are my wants, as '*I want something you have*'. Demand and supply. This is the *motivational basis* of the economy. The constants – in as much as they are constant for as long *as I want* the something you have – are the elements of the system, which you have put in place to supply this want. As soon as '*I want something else*' you need to have the agility to reshape the elements of the constant. Not easy. But necessary for moving forward in our *relationship,* me the consumer, and you the producer.

Adam Smith in: 'An inquiry into the nature and causes of the wealth of nations,' writes about the exchanges between consumers and producers:

> *Whoever offers to another a bargain of any kind, proposes to do this. Give me that which I want and you shall have this which you want, is the meaning of every such offer; and it is in this manner that we obtain from one another the far greater part of those good offices which we stand in need of. It is not from the benevolence of the butcher, the brewer, or the baker, that we expect our dinner, but from their regard to their own interest.* He continues: *we address ourselves not to their humanity but to their self love.*

It is this interest that both parties have, that is both the core of our exchanges, and also the ethos for innovation.

The ethos of innovation is a sequence of pre-competitive goals that initially start in self-preservation; not based on mere fear and survival, but on the desire to exist and achieve. To know, and to understand. These fundamental desires have created the *desire economy*, where goods and services are driven by the human desire to become, to achieve, to exist at a different level, in the sense of transcending one's current condition towards betterment in all forms.

And what is it that we desire? The media that both define where we are, and where we want to go in life. How do you know that you exist? You know because you desire. Because you want. Because you strive for more. We humans, exist not because we are here, now, but because we want to become. Readiness to exist starts when you understand that you have a choice to transform your world and transform yourself, and you start existing in the moment you engage in its pursuit. In the moment you define yourself as separate from the trees, the flowers, and the butterflies, all of which do not have a choice. So, you exist in the moment you *define yourself* as more than a tree. This is where the human animal is different than nature and all its creations; you exist not because *you are*, but because *you will become*. Desire, striving for more, wanting to become, are foundations for the architecture of existence. The keystones: make your choice; have the will; engage. Think IBM. To exist means to take a stance. I want something that will help take this stance, help me engage, help me become.

THE ETHOS OF INNOVATION HAS LITTLE TO DO WITH TECHNOLOGY. IT HAS ONLY TO DO WITH WHAT WE WANT OF OURSELVES

The goal of becoming – rather than just simply being – may be unique to the human animal, and it is at the root of our behaviour of engaging in new experiences of learning, of exploration, of permanent search for more. More understanding, more worth. Our goals are closely tied to our purpose; that of creating artifacts that will transcend our mortality, and will attest to our presence on Earth.

Our worth is measured in what we are worth for others, in their eyes. It is our condition of plurality. Human survival is more than just being alive; it is the quality of being alive that matters to most of us. This is why we go to school, this is why we participate in society, and this is why we build careers. We are leaving a mark for others. We are telling them what our destination was. We are asking them to continue our journey. For all of us, in the community. These are the choices we make as humans, choices that define not only the journey, but also likely, the destination.

In a first reaction to these ideas, you may feel they have nothing to do with business, with markets, with the financial and economic system. Think inside yourself. You will discover you want something, and you will discover that you are ready to make the choice of engaging in an exchange to get it. This is business. The choices we make on the journey to transform ourselves *are the economic system*.

Change, Transformation and Sustainability

There is a lot of noise being generated by supporters of sustainable consumption theories, and a lot of business opportunities as well. It is not the place here to debate the pros and cons of sustainability as an ideology, or as a tool for convenient legislation; it is however imperative that we look at sustainable proposals as disruption signals, and thus, sustainability as an innovation object and potential generator of innovation behaviour. In this context, my view is that the place to start change and transformation is in retooling the individual – our desires and expectations – as a first step, rather than retooling the products and services we create by design.

Sustaining 'human life' on Earth is too complex a task to embark on, before understanding what is 'being human' in the first place. I have the view that art is not sustainable for the planet in the ecological perspective, but humans without art are not sustainable as a species. We humans are either the proof that nature is not perfect – our ways not being in tune with the ways of most other species – or we are an example of transcending our nature as species.

Is it possible that at one point human beings decided that nature is not enough? The abalone does not seem to have reached that point, so it will be pointless to go and ask the abalone – as some bio-mimicry enthusiasts advise us to do. Nature, after all, may not have all the answers. We are not just a species any more. We need art to survive, and grow, and art is by practice and definition not sustainable. Art demands and consumes red pigment for the sake of red as a colour, and not for the sake of red as a signal for danger. Red as a colour speaks about our human conditioning to communicate through symbols and archetypes: red is symbolic of love, passion, life.

Human life is not only about efficiency – which is the chief lesson we can learn from nature. Human life is about storytelling, literature, music, all of which are not sustainable. Human life is about meaning, and meaning that is well beyond the efficiency of survival – which incidentally, is about the only lesson the abalone can teach us. So let us recap the essentials so we don't fool ourselves:

- *We read books,* and that is not sustainable. Literature is not sustainable – it consumes in production, manufacture, marketing, transportation, purchase of books, and the act of reading.
- *We like watching movies,* and that is not sustainable. The totality of the entertainment industry – second largest on the planet – is not sustainable, as it consumes voraciously everything from film, tape, equipment, etc.
- *We like listening to music,* and that is totally unsustainable. Music consumes energy without returning anything back to the ecosystem. It consumes at every single level – creation, duplication, production, marketing, purchasing, and listening.
- *We like looking at paintings and sculptures,* as we feel that art is a means for transcending our nature. Art is TOTALLY unsustainable. We not only enjoy looking at art, and producing art, but we TEACH art, an activity, which is COMPLETELY unsustainable, as it compounds the original unsustainable nature of art itself.
- *We like sports,* both as an activity to perform, and an activity to look at as spectators. Is anything more unsustainable than sports? Probably only art, music, painting, sculpture, movies and literature combined.

- *We pursue knowledge,* can anyone imagine any activity that consumes as much energy in the act itself, and results in the consumption of more energy in all the discoveries we make by this pursuit? Totally, completely, utterly UNSUSTAINABLE. So what if we are searching to cure a disease? In the course of that research we are consuming and destroying NATURE – admittedly, not as much as we will do if we actually find a cure.

Are these generalizations? Read again, human. This is your life, and the reason you live it. We think and act from the gut, through the heart, and into the brain. This is where we live *from*. This is where we have created masterpieces from, the monuments that we leave behind for our children, and for their children after that, as proof that we have existed.

It is in the gut of our humanity that change needs to start taking place. The current discourse around sustainable models of living seems to ignore the main actor in the transformation, and that is the human actor. The discourse is constructed on academic coordinates, around a thesis based on selected sets of data. We are being given life prescriptions – see Al Gore's '*An Inconvenient Truth*' – with little or no interest in allowing us to think, to discover the why and the what. The danger lies in the fact that these are prescriptions for thinking; they create belief systems that will render many individuals intellectually atrophied. And so the discourse is not about ideas, but about facts, numbers, and tools.

It is not about WHO WE ARE, but a means by which we can run away from talking about who we are as humans, what we feel, the limits of one's own possibility, one's own responsibility, what we desire and how did we get here in the current chaos. I want to know where, and what I need to change IN ME, instead of being given prescriptions to attenuate the withdrawal from a life of consumption.

The Role of Desire: What Do I Really Want?

It becomes necessary to discuss the role desire plays in creating the ethos for designing products, services and the ways of life these create in return. We need to face the reality that in 'product design', we humans, are the 'product'. We design ourselves every time we create new tools for our survival and betterment. We are re-designed by these tools in profound ways.

The desire to survive, the desire to procreate, the desire to achieve a different level of existence; these are the ultimate sources of action. The question for you right now is: *What do you desire?* How open are you to understanding what you desire and to believing that this desire can transform the way you look at everything else? Understanding the nature of your desire can actually create a path for a new journey of life.

Wants are choices. Once you articulate your wants, they become choices for your existence, and as a result, wants become destinations. The question, 'What do I really want?', determines a variety of destinations that are getting closer, and closer, to what you really want to become.

When looking at changing from the gut of our humanity, we need to understand how we are different from other animals. We have constructed entire industries based on the offer of pleasure, or hope, in the form of various products and services: sugar, coffee, tea and the many other things that form and inform our immediate existence, and the existence of the ones we love.

Hope is the highest human artifact of the mind; the artifact for possibility. There are many artifacts that are manifestations of our hope, made and distributed commercially, products that we use every day and form the core of our economies, and industries. From skin creams, to the tooth brush, tooth paste, perfume, soap, books, shirts, pants, neckties, pillows, socks, blankets, beds, carpets, mobile phones, forks, knives, vacuum cleaners, lamps. ... They are all in the name of hope. All in the name of what the human animal is all about; the transcendence of our nature as animals into some form of immortality.

Of all animals, we are the animal that knows about our limited time on Earth, we all learn very early in life, that we will die. So our life becomes a series of plans for achieving, in any way possible, continuity on Earth. It is in these plans we make to insure our life has meaning, that we can find the seeds of change and transformation. Until we look at the *actions of being alive*, we will just continue to be intellectually dishonest about change and sustainability.

What do we ultimately want? It may not be easy to change the destination, but it may be worth pursuing, because it seems there is a lot of talk these days about changing destinations. What we need to analyse more deeply is where the idea of that destination originates. The destination is in us.

So, where do you want to go from here? This is the question, and every question we ask is a desire; so what is it that you desire? Are you, the reader of these words, ready to recognize the nature of your desire as an individual, as an organization? If you are ready, the answers you give will provide your map.

The Map of Choices

What you see here is the map of the automobile (Figure 6.1). Once accepted by our behaviour, by choice, the automobile creates its own ecology of dependencies, which forms the big picture, and the background for any discussion about sustainability as a business opportunity.

What does the automobile create? What tools are created, and what further behaviours are created in turn? On analysis, we will find a number of positive and negative attributes (negative now in retrospect, such as exhaust fumes). We created a number of ways to improve our lives through the transportation of goods; we have reshaped the food chain, and increased our standards and our quality of life. Do the costs balance the benefits? The answer is on the map, as are many other answers to yet unasked questions. As you start seeing the connections between the map's components, you begin to see how we are transformed by the choices we make, and conditioned by the tools we have created.

Look carefully at the map: Which of the items listed on it are not part of your everyday life? *In what way is this map not you?* Which items could you remove from your life and still be able to live the same way? Or, how would your life change if certain items were not there?

The value of mapping is that it helps us to understand the complexity of the system that artifacts create. Would the urban ecology be any less complex, if we had the Smart Car from the beginning? Posing these questions shows that issues are not as simple as they look. We cannot solve problems by mitigating two or three of the unpleasant consequences of using the automobile; *the automobile is us*, a whole and not just a component. Technical solutions are not the answer to the complexity of the ecology created by the invention of the automobile. Can the electric cars fix this? Fixing is a mitigation of the problem, *not a solution to the problem*. The solution is re-imagining. Having the empowerment to re-imagine your own life, not to fix it.

If the tool is broken, we fix it. If the tool is emitting dangerous levels of CO_2, we fix that, we put a filter on it, and we legislate others to do the same. But in order to change behaviour, we need to *change motivation*, and for that we need to re-imagine. We need to re-imagine our way of life, we need to re-imagine our values, and we need to move them to a new level. So what is that you want to do? Imagine or fix?

Change starts with ideas, and ideas depend on imagination. This is why it is hard for us to move forward, because we are trying to fix and mitigate our way out of problems that require re-imagining. (*The future is the changes we make to the present through our motivations, our behaviour and our actions.*) Change also starts with understanding who, and what, we are; products of desire.

From the moment you can point, you desire. Desire shapes values, and values shape our tools. This has been so for thousands of years and people sometimes divert themselves from this reality, because we learn very little history in schools, and we don't deal with business in cultural terms. The desire to survive, the desire to procreate, the desire to achieve a different level of existence; these are the ultimate sources of action. The question for you right now is: What do you desire? How open are you to understanding the nature of what you desire, and believing that this desire can transform the way you

Figure 6.1   The Map of the Automobile

look at everything else? Understanding your desire can actually create a path for a new journey of life.

The question, 'Who are we?', is in good measure a statement about *who we have become through our desire.* Consider the question, 'What do you want?' If you ask this question of yourself, the first couple of answers are predictable: Money, love, happiness, health, comfort, etc. – any number of things that are obvious. But ask yourself this question five or six times. A couple of years ago, a few students of mine (Rayelle and Cayla Hache) asked the question: 'What do you want?' multiple times, to the same group of people. Here are the results:

In the first layer of questioning, the answers were the obvious: We want money; the purse that will always be filled with gold. We want the table that will cover itself with food, and will clean itself afterwards. But what do you *really* want? We want invisible servants. The seven-league boots so we can get places very quickly. We want the Hat of Darkness (Harry Potter anyone?) so we can snoop on other people. Snooping on other people may not necessarily be the first thing you think of when asked, 'What do you want?', but it turns out using the Internet is one form of snooping on other people. The Internet allows you to snoop on other people's tastes, on their behaviours, on their likes and dislikes, and so on. Snooping is a form of power and control. But what do you *really want?* Immortality. Excitement and adventure. Safety and security. And the list starts getting long when you understand how deeply this question hits you.

What do you really want? We want those we love to love us in return, and be loyal to us. Gold, obviously. The ability to fly, which might explain why we dream of flying, and why Superman and Spiderman are such successful franchises. And the list keeps growing as we keep asking, 'What do you *really* want?' Delicious food, for sure. Smart children, attractive visual objects. We want to speak with the animals. We want to have sex with a large number of attractive people. We want wisdom. Hope. To be good. To be envied.

Reflect on this: *Wisdom. Hope. To be good. To be envied.* Suspend your cynicism for a moment. Think about yourself right now. Do you want to have wisdom? Do you want hope? Do you want to be good? Do you want to be envied? Wanting to be envied is not something we regularly admit to, but perhaps somewhere deep inside, don't you want certain people to wish they were you, or to wish they were like you? The point of the exercise is to show that *wants are choices.* Once you articulate your wants, they become choices for your existence. And these choices become your goals. As a result, wants become destinations. The questioning, 'What do you really want? What do you really want? What do you really want?' determines a variety of destinations that are getting closer and closer, and closer, to what you really want to become.

What Do People Love?

Themselves, chocolate, coffee, touch, smooch, hugs, kissing, compliments, etc. It is important to make these lists. Face what you love and hate; make a list. 'What we want' is connected to what we love.

'What do you desire?' is a question answered very simply by the physical and virtual manifestations that surround you, now, in the *desire economy* (see Figure 6.2). You may think that the economy – the list of the industrial sectors on the stock market – may

have nothing to do with desire. But consider this: What do we use oil for? To make plastic. To transport ourselves from Point A to Point B. If we analyse the economy of the industrialized world on the map of desire, you will find something very striking. Basic materials, utilities and energy, are used to maintain us. Health care and other sectors expand and enhance us. Some sectors, such as consumer staples – which are perfumes, soaps, and detergents – actualize us. We may not see it this way at times, but the brand managers in these companies do. They see *actualizing* as an opportunity and a scope for their efforts to sell products and services. Nickel, iron, zinc. Ore, coal, oil. What do they have to do with desire? You don't eat them, do you? Nor do you have friends that do. But you cook with them. You make your home and your life comfortable with them. This is why I do not believe in need as being at the root of innovation; need would not exist without desire. Toothpaste would not exist if you didn't want to brush your teeth; and you want to brush your teeth because you want to be a healthy participant in society. Why? Because you desire knowledge, so you can be part of the social plurality of people.

I propose that you ask this question everyday: What *they* – your target demographic – might desire next? How will that desire shape the next behavioural and business disruption and initiate the design process illustrated below, in Figure 6.3?

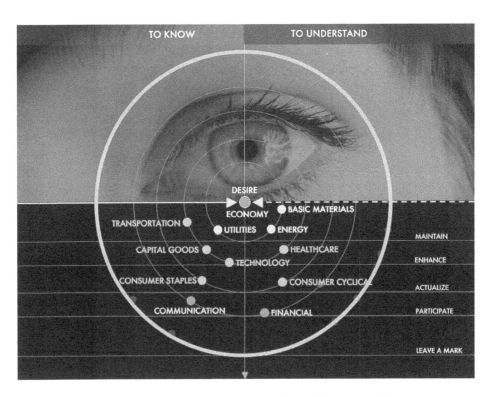

Figure 6.2   The Desire Economy and the DJ Industrial Categories

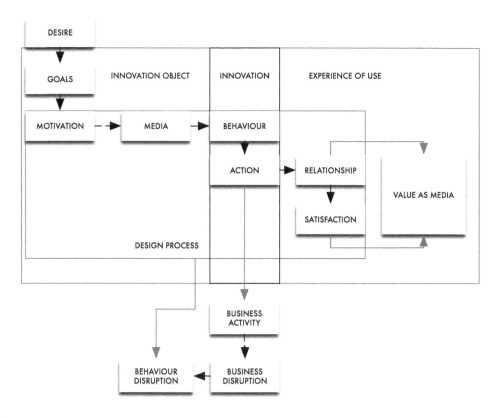

Figure 6.3   The Complete Map of Innovation Processes and Outcomes

Desire and Innovation

How does 'what we want' become a plan of action for the organization? How do we transform this ethos into a strategic ethos?

Here is a simple, and rather familiar example; how we went to the Moon and back. Think about the Moon. It is an object we all see from Earth. It is the closest extraterrestrial body, but do we really have to go to the Moon? Is there anything on the Moon, that will contribute to maintaining, enhancing or actualizing ourselves? What was the Moon '*a media for*' for the United States in 1960s?

The memorandum reproduced below may have never existed, if NASA would have been successful in sending an astronaut in orbit before the Soviet Union did, in March 1961. But they did not, and only days after cosmonaut Yuri Gagarin established the Soviet Union as the first nation in space, President Kennedy authored this memorandum, a model of declaring his nation's desire in all things connected to the space programme, as well as a model of becoming competitive through a pre-competitive strategic desire; to the Soviet Union's success of sending a man to orbit the Earth, America will respond by sending a man to the Moon, and returning him back safely to Earth. Strategically, President Kennedy had no other choice.

The White House, 20 April 1961

MEMORANDUM FOR VICE PRESIDENT

In accordance with our conversation I would like for you as Chairman of the Space Council to be in charge of making an overall survey of where we stand in space:

1.   *Do we have a chance of beating the Soviets by putting a laboratory in space, or by a trip around the moon, or by a rocket to go to the moon and back with a man. Is there any other space program which promises dramatic results in which we could win?*
2.   *How much additional would it cost?*
3.   *Are we working 24 hours a day on existing programs? If not, why not? If not, will you make recommendations to me as to how work can be speeded up.*
4.   *In building large boosters should we put the emphasis on nuclear, chemical, or liquid fuel, or a combination of these three?*
5.   *Are we making maximum effort? Are we achieving the necessary results?*

'*Do we have a chance of beating the Soviets?*' – in the first paragraph is Kennedy's *expression* of desire. Once we recognize this desire, and understand its nature, we are able to express it and then able to *articulate* the want: to put a man on the Moon. And the manifestation of that became the space programme that created amongst other tools, the Lunar module.

The *desire to* 'beat' the Soviets led to *wanting* to put a man on the Moon, which led to *needing* a lunar module, and the other capabilities required to get it there and back as illustrated in Figure 6.4. This is the connection between desire and strategic innovation.

Desire is the expression. Want is the articulation. And need is the manifestation. Products, services, the things that we can touch and use, are all manifestations of desire.

'How much would that cost?,' 'Are we working 24 hours a day on existing programs?' – Imagine this memo in an existing company and replace 'Soviets' with 'Apple' or 'Siemens' or 'Nokia'. Are we making maximum effort? Imagine the CEO who actually sends out this memo. The race to the Moon is a perfect example of Bertrand Russell's definition of Desire: '*A mental occurrence of any kind – sensation, image, belief or emotion – may be a cause of a series of actions, continuing, unless interrupted, until some more or less definite state of affairs is realized. Such a series of actions we call a behaviour cycle.*'

Anatomy of Action: Desire, Want and Need

Our actions are instigated by the desire for, and in pursuit of, something. Our behaviour is goal directed. And here are the goals directed by desire:

- *Basic desires for the nourishment of the body*: Smooth, Soft, Shiny, Sweet, Fragrant, Intoxicating, Beauty and Pleasure.
- *Motivating desires for the growth of the individual*: To participate, to leave a mark, to maintain, to enhance, to actualize, to propagate.
- *Ultimate desires for the nourishment of the mind*: Knowledge, Understanding, Hope.

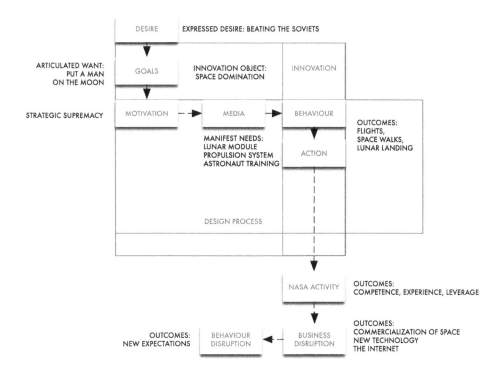

Figure 6.4   How We Went to the Moon and Back

These are the compelling motivators for human action, as illustrated in Figure 6.5. We frame our life around strategies designed – consciously or subconsciously – to experience manifestations of some, or all, of these desires, through the products we consume, the services we use, and the actions we undertake towards our contribution to society. We permanently seek higher and higher media for the manifest satisfaction of these goals.

Each moment of experience leads to another goal: there is no benchmark for how smooth 'smooth' can be, or for how sweet 'sweet' can be, or for what is knowledge. If we accept the premise that desire is the driver of the economic system, we also have to accept that desire is also the driver of the innovation outcomes that engage behaviour, and create business opportunities. Where would the Coca-Cola Company be (2008 revenue $32 billion) without our desire for sweet? Where would Procter & Gamble be (2009 revenue $79 billion) without our desire for smooth and soft skin and our constant search for beauty? Where would Google be (2008 revenue $21 billion) without our desire for knowing and understanding?

And finally, where would all the companies of the Dow Jones industrial index be (see Figure 6.6) without our *desire for, and in pursuit of, something?*

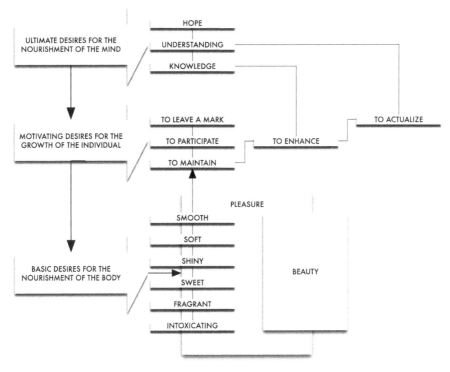

Figure 6.5   Anatomy of Action

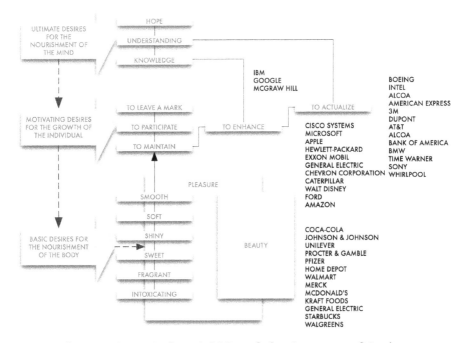

Figure 6.6   The Dow Jones Industrial 30 and the Anatomy of Action

The Ambiguity of Compelling Motivators

The compelling motivators for human action, illustrated above, have one common characteristic; they are not measurable, they are all ambiguous. Ambiguity is a fertile ground for interpretation, and interpretation is a fertile ground for diversity in products and services. What is important when defining a design process leading to innovation outcomes, is establishing at which point of the diagram illustrated in Figure 6.3 do we want to start. Do we start with the 'VALUE AS MEDIA' we want users to experience through the relationship with what we are creating? Or do we start with the 'ACTION' we want the user to engage in? The starting point will define *both the process and the nature of the outcome*. But no matter where we start, we must be clear about the meaning of the compelling motivators, and the reasons we seek them.

SMOOTH

Why do we desire smoothness? A baby's skin is smooth; smooth means youth. For smooth, we create an industry that creates the tools that make material smooth. Is there any logic to make things smooth? It is all about pleasure. It is pleasurable to run your hand on a smooth countertop, or a smooth piece of sculpted marble. It might be safer to walk on a smooth wooden floor, than on a rough surface. What is the inspiration for smooth? Nature. Many things in nature are smooth – the surfaces of leaves, fruits and stones. We want to achieve smooth and manufacture it. It is a choice we made as humans.

Smoothness is not a rational choice, as it cannot be benchmarked; smoothness is *an emotional choice*. Something can always be smoother. So you realize that the real 'benchmarks' of our life, of what we really desire, are open-ended. They can always become better. So why do we like smooth? Because we want to be young, we want to live forever; we want the pleasure of touching smooth skin and smooth surfaces. And if I was Unilever, or Proctor & Gamble, I would not ignore human desire, and they do not. The revenue line of both companies proves that they understand that you want to be, feel, look, young.

SOFT

Soft is pleasure and comfort (see Figure 6.7), and it comes in plenty of forms; the petals of a flower and the material properties of cotton and silk, or the manufactured properties of foam rubber. And why do we like soft? Because it is pleasurable, because we like coffee, because we give flowers to the ones we love, and because we like 'smooth'. Because we are human. To make things soft, we need to use oil, electricity, fire. Soft is the manifestation of the transcended condition in which we, humans, were just a few thousand years ago. Soft is the measure by which we define ourselves as different from other animals; we can manufacture it. A soft pillow is the distinction between pleasure and hardship, *between the before, and the after we discovered ourselves in, and through pleasure.*

SHINY

What does shiny express? Shiny means new. Shiny also means healthy – would you buy a tomato with a skin less than shiny? Shiny reflects. Shiny is light. Mirrors are shiny. So

Figure 6.7   Soft

are windows, and we live surrounded by windows; we seek to have the environment we live in, reflected in our homes. We also want to see ourselves in the shine of water. And we create tools to make things shiny, because shiny is the pleasure of something intrinsically good. By choice, we have made 'shiny' one of the conditioning factors in our lives. Happiness is *light that shines on you, and all you care about.*

SWEET

We desire sweet; we are the only animals that consciously manufacture sweet for the purpose of consumption. How much of the industry of the civilized world is involved in the manufacture of 'sweet'? How many pieces of equipment, how many transportation devices, how much effort? What is your guess?

What is the benchmark for sweet? The benchmark is, 'Mmmm!' Sweet is one of the basic taste sensations alongside bitter, sour and salty. These are the cornerstones of our gastronomic preferences. In contrast with the others, sweet is pleasurable. But how much pleasure we get out of it we don't know, as detecting sweetness varies between people. If you are so inclined, I'd recommend that you search 'theories of sweetness' on your favourite search engine. A world will reveal itself to you, a world that you have always been a part of. And you will learn a lot about the value – or silliness, as the case may be – of metrics, when it comes to human sensations; you will learn about high potency sweeteners, and especially about *lugduname*, which is about 225,000 times sweeter than sucrose. WHAT? How do you graph *'225,000 sweeter than'* on a neat chart?

FRAGRANT

Perfume-making is the pursuit of pleasure in the form of scent. It is also the pursuit of memory; we recall scents faster than we recall flavours or images. Scent can unlock memories of long forgotten moments or people. Your mother's smell. Your first day of school. Smells are embedded in us, identifiable and yet hardly describable. Smells that make us happy, or make us sad; smells that bring about emotions and feelings. We manifest ourselves both through the scent that we emit, and the scents that we remember. The world's largest[1] cosmetics producer, L'Oreal, had revenues of $24 billion in 2008, from a market share of only 15 per cent. Add to this the number of retail outlets involved in the distribution of perfume and cosmetics and you complete the picture of an industry that is bound to grow every year, as more individuals attain both the age – older groups demand more cosmetics according to L'Oreal – and the income levels allowing them more sophisticated cosmetics.

Or think of Pepper. The small berry changed the course of world history. Christopher Columbus went toward India in search of pepper and other spices. Pepper gives fragrance and flavour to food, and because of that peppercorns are the most widely traded spice in the world.

BEAUTIFUL

What is beautiful in this picture? (Figure 6.8). What is beautiful for you will be different than that I consider beautiful. The observable attributes are of a smooth and shiny surface. The balance between the attributes gives the emotion of tranquillity. All of these combined create the feeling of 'Beautiful!'

- The feeling of being delighted by something, receiving satisfaction from something;
- A state of mind;
- A state of pleasure, one moment at a time.

Figure 6.8   Beautiful. Nature at Rest

---

1   Available at http://www.wikinvest.com/wiki/L%27oreal_(LRLCY) [21 September 2009].

PLEASURE

Animals like pleasure, we like pleasure. How much time do we dedicate in our lives to the acquisition of things that give us pleasure – physical things, intellectual things, knowledge. Why are you reading this book? You are reading in the hope of becoming better. That is connected somehow to pleasure. The cushion on the chair you are sitting on is connected to pleasure; the picture on your wall and the flower you gave to a loved one recently are connected to pleasure. We search for media that will bring about the state, or feeling, of being pleased. And in turn, we create media for the satisfaction of this temporary, and subjective state of mind that is pleasure.

HOPE

Hope is the biggest product and service sold on Earth. It is also the biggest – most successful – business model. Hope is a longing for a new possibility, a belief that personal actions will positively affect outcomes in our life. Hope unlocks our latencies, and makes our subconscious goals manifest. In some measure, hope is what we buy in all products and services, it is what we are all about; hope is how we are different from other animals. Hope is about the possibility of life. Don't fool yourself thinking that large industries, oil and electricity are not about hope; oil, electricity and large industry are about creating the things that give us hope.

7 The Ecology of Innovativeness

Where can we find the competence and ability to satisfy the goals and new behaviours of the Mobile Society? In the corporate ecosystem most likely to encourage the free flow of ideas capable to generate new revenue models. The challenge is that of creating a culture in which platforms for the exploration of possibility are encouraged, funded and free of the day to day metrics of the organization, balancing risk, ambiguity, courage and imagination with a pragmatic business ambition in a timely manner. '*Move fast and break things*',[1] is Mark Zuckerberg's (founder of Facebook) directive to his developers and team. 'Unless you are breaking stuff,' he says, 'you are not moving fast enough.'

A New Mindset

In creating an innovation culture, you are armed with the new understanding that innovation is a noun; innovation is an outcome. To achieve this outcome, you need a new mindset. You also need a new spirit. In the context of an organization, spirit means the will to transform, the will to become, a renewed sense of self which brings about the enthusiasm and optimism of new possibilities. Spirit gives us the meaning; why are you doing what you are doing. Spirit provides the ideas, and the mindset provides and manages the tools. The mindset creates the means.

To innovate is the verb, and it works as illustrated in Figure 7.1. From people's desires to innovation outcomes, we need a good measure of ideas that are matched by the tools of implementation. But the tools are not ends in themselves; the tools are just used to enable the technologies needed to satisfy our desires, in the form of innovation outcomes. The innovation ecology needs a few more things:

> *Strategic Focus* – Why are we doing this in the first place? Where does it fit? What needs to change? Where will it lead in our future?

> *Tactical incentives* – Why and how would my internal and external resources engage themselves in this process?

We also need rules of engagement, rules of defining and measuring value, rules of defining when we start and when we stop the process. Once in place, this leads to a working diagram in which the innovation is generated from the incentives outwards, reaching desire at one end, and the outcome at the other end. The ecology also includes

---

1   Available at http://www.businessinsider.com/mark-zuckerberg-innovation-2009-10 [accessed: 3 October 2009].

the new values, the language we use to communicate our ideas, as well as the networks we will use to diffuse these ideas to the mass market. What we are constructing in effect, is a bridge between our organization and society, culture and current technology.

FRAMING THE INNOVATION CHALLENGE

The challenge of any large organization when it comes to imagination, creativity and innovation outcomes, is that of creating a culture built around platforms for the exploration of possibility, platforms which are free of the day to day metrics of the organization. The exercise of freedom is different from freedom as a concept, and I see this as a major challenge in the next three to five years. The challenge is expressed both in terms of infrastructure (the very design of work spaces) as well as in terms of human resources.

The possible solution: companies need to create a completely new entity – a Place of Possibility, an entity that is lean and nimble, can take risks, can partner with spectacularly different competencies than the obvious, and can prototype fast, fail fast, and fail cheap. A place where everyone feels empowered to explore and to share ideas, and there is no fear of consequences. A liberating ecology for the mind. Does this remind you of your kindergarten days? It should, as you need to be able to say and do silly things. You need an ecology in which you allow yourself, from time to time, to believe that anything is possible. Innovativeness is a way of approaching decision-making. By inspiring and engaging the imagination and creativity of the people within the organization, a company can focus the talents of many toward common growth – creating a culture of courage, passion and perseverance.

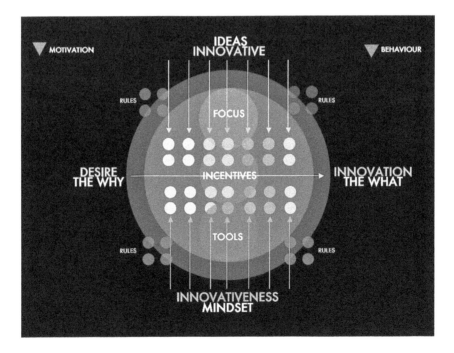

Figure 7.1   The Ecology of Innovativeness

Unleashing an innovative mindset is not about adding new tools, it is about creating this culture that empowers inquisitive minds to imagine the future, and think beyond the legacy of the past.

The process aims to:

1. Introduce new strategic visions/possibilities;
2. Deliver compelling experiences that target the imagination and thus the creative potential;
3. Transform a strategic goal into a shared story.

There are two immediate advantages to the place of possibility model: the first is the agility advantage, the second is the asymmetric advantage.

Agility is manifest not just in giving time and space to be imaginative and creative, but in accepting the ideas generated with an open mind. Accepting they are in a play-space, in an 'unlearning' frame of mind, a place where nothing is judged from the perspective of the past.

Asymmetric advantage means the freedom of not being measured against a competitive landscape – either in features, materials, expectations, price points, distribution and all other sets of data already in the market place, data that usually forces the development of symmetric offerings. IBM understood this in the early 1980s, when it undertook the development of the IBM PC.[2]

'Rather than going through the usual IBM design process, a special team was assembled *with authorization to bypass normal company restrictions and get something to market rapidly*. This project was given the code name Project Chess at the IBM Entry Systems Division in Boca Raton, Florida. The team consisted of twelve people directed by Don Estridge with Chief Scientist Larry Potter and Chief Systems Architect Lewis Eggebrecht. They developed the PC in about a year. To achieve this they first decided to build the machine with "off-the-shelf" parts from a variety of different original equipment manufacturers and countries. Previously IBM had always developed their own components. Second, for scheduling and cost reasons, rather than developing unique IBM PC monitor and printer designs, project management decided to utilize an existing "off-the-shelf" IBM monitor developed earlier in IBM Japan as well as an existing Epson printer model.'

Massive Innovativeness: Play at Work

In the first year of operation (since the release on 9 July 2008) the Apple's App Store released over 70,000 applications and reported that two billion applications have been downloaded. This is massive crowd sourced innovation in action. What makes this model compelling? How can it be applied in other lines of business? What are the immediate challenges?

---

2   Available at: http://www.computernostalgia.net/articles/IBMPC.htm [22 September 2009].

ANALOGUE VERSUS DIGITAL IN THE WORKPLACE

Large organizations have a significant Human Resources challenge at both ends of the generation spectrum; for the baby boomers in management, the question is, 'How do we retain the trained work force the millennials[3] represent', and, 'How do we empower them to make significant contributors in the new competitive spaces of the mobile society?' Both these conditions need to be addressed by present-day organizations, before embarking in creating innovation ecologies, and defining new innovation outcomes.

Job satisfaction is the primary factor in retaining talent, and the number one contributor to a creative and productive performance while in the workplace. Why are millennials leaving the workplace in search of better challenges for their life experience? To answer this question we need an understanding of the typology of this social and cultural group, their experiences and expectations. A few more questions need to be explored in search of a defining typology:

- What do millennials want?
- What do they expect from the workplace?
- What is the shape of the experience the millennials expect from work?

A MILLENNIAL PROFILE

According to empirical data, the millennials face disappointment when they reach the organization; raised to believe that everything is possible and the sky is the limit, these are people of ambition, purpose and experimentation. They have grown up in an environment in which technology allowed them early participation in culture, as well as hands on experience in the creation of a new network society in which they feel they are in control. At least this is what they believe. Schooled and ready to contribute in a work environment, they join the ranks of the employed in organizations that have recruited them aggressively and with best intentions.

They were promised all the freedom of thought and action worthy of their generation's aspiration, just to discover once they join the organization, that the old structures of the workplace are not as permeable to change as they claim to be.

Once in the workplace, millennials are now part of a system that does not necessarily recognize merit, imagination, play and the cultural and economic participation that characterized the millennials' behaviour up to joining the workforce. The old structure of the organization does not see the empowerment and participation of the millennial, as necessary attributes for the prosperity of the corporation. In such an environment, they become stifled in their work and slowly disempowered. This undesirable consequence of the inability of the system to change around new behaviour, is made worst by the inability of their superiors to *even identify that a problem exists*. Their superiors are the baby boomers.

The analogue culture group represented by the baby boomer, is part of a generation that in turn, felt everything was possible, a generation that achieved a certain degree of transformation in society but one that did not challenge the very structure of 'work', and thus the structure of the system itself. They made the status quo work for them rather

---

3   Anyone born after 1980. Also known as the digital generation.

than changing it around them. My friend David Edgar – who has worked at the executive levels in a number of large and small enterprises – made the observation that organizations are spending millions on new employee orientation programmes and presentations – and almost all of the time, these present a theoretical picture of the organization, whereas the reality is in fact totally the opposite (no procedures, no control, no manuals, no process, etc.). The millennial sees immediate disappointment on leaving the orientation presentation as he/she looks around for all the 'stuff' he was just told, existed. In the 'old' days we didn't do orientation presentations, so there was never a disappointment. So perhaps one of the solutions is a major overhaul of *orientation thinking*.

The baby boomer (Analogue) and the millennial (Digital) are not generations separated by age; they are separated by *experience and expectations*. For the Millennial, empowerment is a condition *sine qua non*, and as such, it is also an expectation. With empowerment, the Millennial has learned about participation in the shaping of culture and society and with that, they have learned that one can – in a satisfying way – operate from a condition of freedom. For the Millennial, freedom is not a concept – as it is for the baby boomer – but an experienced percept.

FREEDOM MANIFESTED

The Millennial grew up in a time in which the conceptual mythology and its characters became quickly part of everyday play life. *Star Wars* characters, locations and situations, became quickly perceptual objects that further released their imagination while engaged in play. The same can be said about Ninja Turtles, Voltron and in the 1990s, the world of *Toy Story*. The immediacy of this availability allowed a rapid transfer of the imagination from thought to action, so these are action orientated people who concern themselves little with the analysis of situations in terms of metrics – 'Is it needed, does it bring significant revenue?' – believing instead, that what they like, others like them will like as well. Google, Facebook, MySpace, Wikipedia, are manifestations of this belief system. They are also manifestations of the return of play, and the freedom associated with it, to the latter life of the adult. There is no room for 'work' in this behaviour.

There is only room for life as it is worth living, with pleasure and immediacy of action. Facebook as a 'need' will make no sense to a baby boomer, and less so as a revenue platform for business. But this is not what Facebook is all about; it is more than that, it is culture. And millennials KNOW about the creation of culture because they grew up being a part of it at every step.

For in as much as the Millennial is an empowered individual who acts on this empowerment by participating actively in the shaping of his/her own world, the baby boomer was empowered in thought but not in action. They never lived up to the promise of their generation and worst still, succumbing in a majority to the rules of the status quo. The majority of the baby boom generation did not change the world, but witnessed it being done by rebels from their own midst, in the garages of Silicon Valley. And this is the key in understanding the gap between the two generations: the millennial wants to have fun *as a life attribute*, while the baby boomer has fun *as entertainment*. Programmed fun, within its time limits and specific formats and places. This is why YouTube makes no sense to a baby boomer, and less so blogging or texting. There is little cultural connection between the two groups. Eminem or 50 Cent are seen as annoyances by the baby boomer, while being essential ingredients of daily life for the millennial. This gives rise to a number of new questions:

- How can these two behavioural groups achieve a productive collaboration within the structure of an organization?
- What is the shape of the strategic vision that will mean the same thing to these two different cultures, and enlist their enthusiasm towards tactical implementation?

The most significant differentiator between the two groups, is the dimension given to 'freedom' and its understanding. For the baby boomer, freedom was a political concept at best, and it was generally associated with freedom of thought. These are people who wanted to be free 'in principle', but not in detail. The late 1960s and early 1970s were times of political struggle for this generation, but not times of significant political change. In other words, the struggle did not result in tangibles. Many went to join the very 'system' they were criticizing, with no challenges being offered.

By contrast, for the millennial, freedom is a percept: the freedom to engage, to participate, to contribute, and to have not only their voice heard, but their actions seen. Some with consequence and some without, but by the sheer number of evens, we can claim that millennial freedom is being used to change and challenge. The cultural and social significance of YouTube and Facebook cannot yet be predicted, but they will certainly change the way we look at both content creation and social groupings. While the millennial sees value in such networks of apparently disconnected entities, the baby boomer can only raise an eyebrow in wonder. *Why would anyone use Facebook?* This is just a small measure of the disconnect between these two culturally estranged groupings. While this cultural disconnect is just a minor nuisance in a household where these two generations cohabit, or in society, where they occasionally share space, in an organization, this nuisance affects everyday actionable strategies, and the bottom line. One generation calls for caution and restraint, while the other calls for experimentation and courage.

What is lost if these two groups do not communicate, and what is gained if we build a bridge? Imagine a workplace where these two generations collide. They meet every day, they talk every day, and they plan action every day, but they never truly communicate, transferring knowledge and wisdom to one another. For sure, some tactics get implemented, but what will be the result if true communication would have taken place in advance? What would be the benefit for the organization? On one hand you have the wisdom, knowledge and experience of life of the boomers, and on the other hand you have the urgency, the imagination and the free spirit of the millennial. What are the possibilities for the organization if these two capabilities were combined? One imparting method while the other imparting experimentation and courage? And more than anything, an unabashed desire to succeed.

FREEDOM TO SIMPLY BE

What the boomer sees as a minor technological achievement – the MP3 player as an example – the millennial sees as a new form of culture, a new mode of expression, a new tool for empowerment. Herein lies the most profound difference between the generations: *one looks at tools as means* while the other sees them as ways *to transform and give meaning*, and believes deeply in the right and freedom to do so. Freedom is critical in this context as it underlines the power of technology when used by the millennial. We are not looking here at the freedom to think, but at the freedoms to both think and act. Action is where the two generations draw the line. The distinction between the theory of freedom, and the phenomenon of freedom. It is true that with this freedom we may encounter triviality, but the quest of the millennial is not for triviality, but for consequence, for making a difference, for participation in the stream of change. For the millennial, words are not actions. They need to transform feelings into reality, and they have the means, the desire, and the will to do it.

This difference in expectations manifests itself in behaviour, and further increases the gap between the two groups. What is a *dream* for the baby boomer is seen as *a right* for the millennial. At times, due to these vastly different attitudes, the two groups cannot hear each other, let alone understand each other. And what is more, the makeup of the two is vastly different in the experience leading to expectations: the analogue baby boomer grew up in an atmosphere of respect for elders, in the household, and later in the workplace, both places in which his/her own voice was not 'seriously considered'. *Respect vs Rights* sums up the difference between these groups, as the digital millennial grew up with a sense of entitlement of rights. On one hand we have respect and responsibility while on the other rights and no implied sense – or fear – of responsibility. At one end we have judgement, and the benchmarking of everything ('what is the purpose of this, what is the market, who will use this,' etc.), while at the other end we have the immediate understanding of purpose and acceptance based on 'wow'. What I feel for this NOW. What experience it allows for. How am I transformed after the experience has ended. Life.

One – the digital generation – instinctively 'gets it' when it comes to technology, taking purpose for granted. The millennial will never ask, *'Who will use this?'* or *'What is the purpose of this?'* as they do not concern themselves with such questions. For them the purpose is a continuum of life. It is as obvious as breathing. At the other end of the cultural and expectation spectrum, for the analogue, every object, service or new technology must have a purpose rooted in 'need'.

'Who needs this?' is a question frequently asked by this group in an effort to measure change by their own ability to comprehend where new devices and services might fit, in the prescribed framework of what life 'should' be about. With the analogue in control of the organization and the digital performing the daily work, clashes are imminent and inevitable. Even when they face each other, the dialogue is between the deaf and the mute, as there is no common experience that unifies these two groups allowing for a comprehensive dialogue. And this is where I see the URGENT need for a new platform for communication, collaboration and dialogue, leading to a productive working relationship.

A BRIDGE BETWEEN PLEASURE AND PURPOSE

One will be hard pressed to describe as 'work' the daily activities of Michael Faraday, the inventor of the electric motor; none will fall under the definition, behaviour or processes that work represents. However, all will fit within the characteristics of play and play behaviour. Faraday spent his days building a device that was impossible to use for any practical application, but enough of a signal to others to define the opportunities that it held. Faraday's contraption was the classic inventor's nightmare; good enough to supply proof, but inconvenient enough in size, architecture, and complexity of parts assembly, to discourage any possible contemplation of practical use. Its success could not be measured, the contraption could not be benchmarked. Most innovations are the result of play behaviour and the mindset of possibility it creates. As a result, a play ecology in the process of innovativeness is also a requisite, as the mindset of innovativeness needs a suspension of reality – another characteristic of play – in the process of evaluation.

Two directions emerge from this understanding of innovativeness as play: the first is the need for companies to create an ecology of play innovation. The second is related to the mastery of play being a crucial capability for innovativeness; the millennial generation has engaged in play patterns of a complexity and diversity that far exceed that of any other generation. They are play wise and play ready, and they will bring this expectation and capability to the workplaces they enter. The future of work will be determined by their facility with play, as it outpaces all previous generations. This presents organizations with the unique opportunity of using this expertise toward strategies that will lead to massive innovation, and permanently redraw the value chain.

How do we build a bridge between these two groups? By constructing a temporary play space – a place of possibility – where the generations can meet, work, and collaborate. And by giving both groups the same tools of the mind: a Play/Full/Mind.

Schematic for a Place of Possibility

Imagine an organization where everyone works as if at play for leisure. Call it a Place of Possibility, and empower a group of your most talented resources to form a Futures Group as an experiential activity. The rules are simple: each member of the group expands on the potential of their imagination, supports their colleagues to do the same, enhancing the competitiveness, innovativeness and business potential of the organization. A participatory play organization is the culmination of an enabled and empowered people; it is the prototype of a society that has cultivated the psychological tools to manifest their presence and express it, both individually and collectively. The Futures Group is a new platform for communication, collaboration and dialogue leading to a productive working relationship. The Futures Group programme activities attempt to anticipate. You will ask: *What has already happened that has yet to make its full impact felt?* What can we do with the events? This place of possibility does not concern itself too much with all the things we cannot do. It always asks: 'What CAN WE DO – what shall de do – what do we want to do?'

To ensure continued growth and relevance, your organization must understand and interpret the world from the position of the people who are trying to change the field today. The most effective way for you to identify the high-potential opportunities, is to create a series of knowledge forums for the high potential leadership of your organization, in order to gain insights into:

- The themes and motivations of people;
- How to identify significant strategic shifts at their early stages;
- Describing the potential of these strategic shifts in as potential markets before they can be measured.

The primary objective of the programme is to ensure that your organization recognizes, understands and benefits from the next strategic shift, no matter what its origin, technology or user behaviour. This requires communication and collaboration between the digital and the analogue demographics toward common objectives. A five-point purpose statement for this activity might look like this:

- To unify the experience and aspirations of all groups in the organization, by providing for a common platform of experience and competence;
- To guide participants into a renewed way of looking at the business, and the world it works in;
- To experience how to manage the design process toward innovative breakthrough ideas into products, services and experiences;
- To change the participants' outlook from reacting to technological or behavioural disruptions, to the proactive exploration of the beneficial innovation possibilities for branded goods and services;
- To discover/unveil existing, but still invisible, potential market areas and means of operations;
- To integrate, unleash and accelerate the sensitivity, imagination and capability of innovativeness into the core business functions of the organization.

A Place of Possibility: Structure and Outcomes

Play is serious business. And so are the activities that you will undertake in the newly constructed place of possibility, as illustrated in Figure 7.2. These activities could be grouped under the following outcomes:

STRATEGIC PLANNING AND STRATEGIC FORESIGHT

In the face of accelerating technology pressures and complex consumer behaviour, organizations must be prepared to recognize, manage and generate sound strategy in order to provide relevant product or service offerings, while maintaining shareholder confidence. Focus is on enhancing the perspective required to distinguish, evaluate and improve the benefit of strategic foresight in informing free spirited innovation. This insight informs strategic decision-making and creates wiser policy options.

PROJECT MANAGEMENT

Focuses on how to identify new opportunities in people's behaviour, how to validate ideas and create new project management tools outside the context of traditional management frameworks. Provides new tools that nourish and trigger the imagination of individuals in teams, and transforms the result into innovation outcomes.

TEAM INTEGRATION

Participants will work in teams to evaluate global behaviour shifts in the context of the economy, and define opportunities for new business models. They will develop the ability to unlearn in order to see from new perspectives, and recognize and assign meaning to local and global patterns of emergence in behaviour. The aim is to translate these behaviour signals into future opportunities, explore the experiential value of these opportunities, and describe the support structures required to support these experiences. Finally, to design and propose business models that translate these experiences into corporate wealth.

INNOVATION

Understanding of the role, value and limits of play and freedom in pre-competitive innovation, team members will create methodologies to discover and assign meaning to macro behaviour trends. The methods discovered will deliver an imaginative and practical mindset that can inspire discovery and learning within teams, identify and validate ideas, and then transform these results into beneficial products, services and systems.

PRODUCT DEVELOPMENT

Through experiential exploration, participants will transform shifts in behaviour and technology into feasible, useful and desirable concepts, systems, communications, products and services that fit or expand the competitive space of your organization.

BRAND STRATEGY

This module might be designed around generative questions such as:

- How will new technology help your organization reach their current users, define new market segments, and create new revenue opportunities?
- What are the characteristics of these new markets?
- What, therefore, are the characteristics of the organization that will best respond to these markets?
- What are the key business model issues that will determine your ability to develop a ubiquitous business model?
- What are the market issues, that when addressed, will create frictionless growth and superior margins?

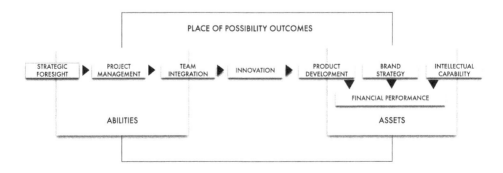

Figure 7.2   A Structure for a Place of Possibility

The Futures Group: Methods

In Chapter 3, 'The New Context', we outlined a few of the challenges of the Mobile Society, and also asserted earlier in the book that specific moments in time have specific innovation objects and further, that Mobile Digital Data is such an object. It will be natural then to use this object as the focus of the Futures Group methods and activities towards innovation.

How do we do this? Two steps:

1. Define a vision of the future.
2. Work to make it a reality.

VISION: THE MOBILE SOCIETY

A place in which every person, object and space is both a link and a holder of information. The Mobile Society is the emerging system of intangible environments created by the proliferation of smart phones, smart tags and other context-aware technologies. In a Mobile Society, people are the carriers of 'place' and meaning into the spaces they enter. Upon entering a space, a person transforms it through the chain of links they provide. This transformation is not unidirectional; the space will in turn leave its mark on the person, thus touching all subsequent spaces that person will enter. The Mobile Society topologies are generated by the very flow of the people who travel through them. They will shape, and be shaped, by human experience. Once enabled to do so, people will reveal their needs and wants through their very interactions and behaviours. When places and objects are data enabled, they take meaning from people. When meaning is enabled, it becomes benefit. In the Mobile Society every different combination of people, devices and places will create a wealth of unique social and information possibilities. Presence is proximity, and data is potential for an unlimited number of opportunities beneficial to users.

The Mobile Society expands the scope of transferable data to an unprecedented magnitude. Due to the scale of this data, the obvious question is how and when does this data become information – how do we make sense of it? Every time that data is collected it must be organized for expression and transmission. The transfer conditions should not simply measure access to data; they must also reflect purpose, context and method.

The context described above is an ever-expanding market of opportunity for device builders, application software and operating systems protocols, all presently under development or already deployed. The inevitability of an interconnected digital and physical network of spaces and objects, where devices communicate using location sensors and other networked devices, is also related to new user behaviours and the ever growing dependence on social networks. Business success in the next decade will require understanding the impact and nature of this transformation, and taking advantage of it, by providing new services that exploit the new environment, understanding the resulting new needs, and opening new channels of communication.

So the first questions facing your organization when dealing with strategies for the Mobile Society might be: 'What is the value proposition of my existing business in a networked Mobile Society ?' 'What is my brand vision for this new context?'

BRAND VISION AND THE MOBILE SOCIETY

We operate from visions of what could be possible. But before we can engage in the pursuit of new innovation outcomes, we need the courage to spell out this vision (see Figure 7.3). *This is the destination.*

The mobile society is fast changing consumer behaviour in an irretrievable way, while placing new demands on companies. These demands are:

- We will respond to this challenge by understanding it and by transforming it into the opportunity it represents.
- We understand that our consumers are expecting new forms of engagement with our brand.
- We recognize that we need to become experts in understanding value, and also in understanding where *value resides*.
- We recognize that digital media in all its emergent forms represents a new form of engagement with life, and we are committed to deliver vitality to this new space.
- We recognize the need to engage in new ways, building better and more expansive relationship with the user, on multiple platforms of experience and on the user's terms.
- We are determined to develop the ability to move swiftly from one platform to the next, and from one compelling experience to another.
- We understand that brands are not about lifestyle, but about life choices. The choice to live healthy, the choice to look good, the choice to feel good. The choice to eat well. These choices transcend lifestyle. These choices are the voice of expectations. And expectations now include people's participation in the shaping of their daily life, and access to new tools of empowerment and new media for expressions of this participation.
- To add value to this new life, the Futures Group will provide the tools and inspirations for engagement and participation; we will construct new platforms of experience and engage our users as participatory individuals.
- *Our vision is to be part of the user's multidimensional expectations of themselves and their life.*

The Futures Group: Strategic Innovation Planogram

The Mindset: Expand the implementation, scope and monetization potential of any innovation goal as illustrated in Figure 7.4. The following methods maintain an open perspective throughout a project:

- *Impact Intensification* focuses attention on new user behaviours and the impact of their intensification on what people will expect.
- *Disruption Amplification* focuses attention on emerging behaviours and technologies and amplifies them to map what will become normal.
- *Market Maximization* focuses attention on other 'peripheral' markets to broaden the scope of threat and opportunity analysis.

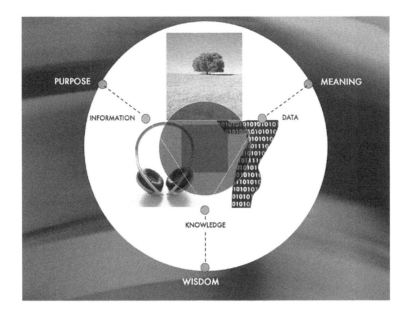

Figure 7.3   Wisdom, Meaning, Purpose for Data

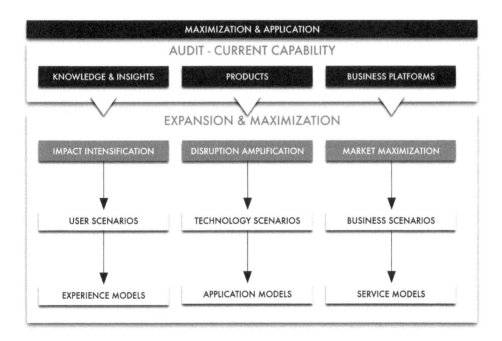

Figure 7.4   Strategic Innovation Planogram

THE PROCESS

- *Opportunity Discovery* – 'The Why' of change: The incentives to innovate and the opportunities that they represent.
- *Opportunity Expansion* – 'The Focus' of change: Innovative ideas that expand the scope and potential of the innovation goal.
- *Opportunity Application* – 'The What' of change: Define the outcome that will best meet the innovation goal.

OPPORTUNITY DISCOVERY

Understanding external disruptions, by connecting changes in consumer behaviour with new technologies and associated business responses, as seen in Figure 7.5.

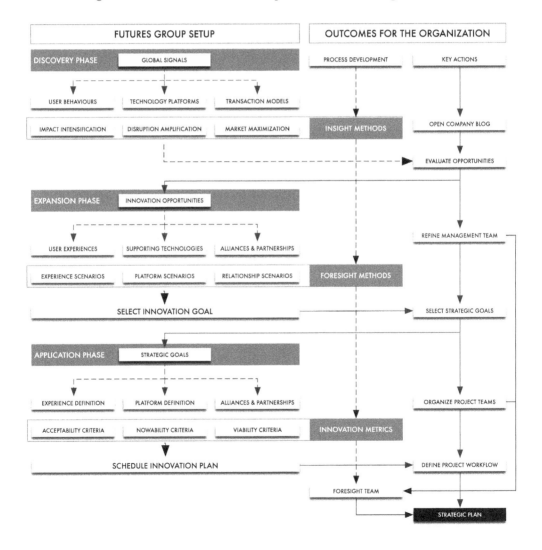

Figure 7.5   Futures Group Setup Diagram

- *Consumer Behaviour Mapping* – How are consumers changing the way they relate to companies and how you might leverage these changes?
- *Technology Possibility Mapping* – Which new technologies are transforming the rules of engagement and what this could mean for your company?
- *Pre-competitive Market Mapping* – Which other services are now positioned to change your market space and what can be learned from them?

OPPORTUNITY EXPANSION

The objective is to broaden the scope and potential of your business ambition by exploring and presenting compelling visions of what could be possible:

- *Ideal Experience Proposals* – Explore how the ideal experience might feel without current constraints to identify the essential qualities of the innovation goal.
- *Technology Platform Proposals* – Describe the technology and infrastructure that would best deliver the desired experience today and in the future.
- *Strategic Partnership Proposals* – Explore models that leverage the experience, assets and business ambitions of others toward your innovation goal.

OPPORTUNITY APPLICATION

Identify the essential qualities of the innovation model and develop metrics to manage its successful implementation:

- *Acceptability Evaluation* – What are the qualities that must be included and promoted to ensure that the outcome meets the innovation goal?
- *Nowability Evaluation* – What aspects of the plan are adequately achievable today and what should be reserved for tomorrow?
- *Viability Evaluation* – How sustainable is the new model and how do we make best use of its collateral benefits?

PART 2 *Collaborative Innovation*

8 *Massive Innovativeness*

SAMI VIITAMÄKI

Sami Viitamäki is one part marketing practitioner and one part management academic. Having always been drawn to design, he created his first visual identity for corporate use at age 12. After completing a minor degree in advertising and graphic design, Sami enrolled at Helsinki's School of Economics to pursue a Master's degree in Marketing. During this time, he also completed a design management programme studying in the Helsinki University of Technology and the Helsinki University of Arts and Design. He completed his studies with a Master's Thesis on Crowdsourcing, which eventually led to the conception of the FLIRT model presented in this book. For the past ten years, Sami has been working with marketing, design and the Internet for both client and agency sides in various organizations as well as an independent entrepreneur. He is currently a partner at TBWA/Helsinki, where he is also a co-founder of TBWA/DIEGO, an agency focused on enhancing the innovation, management and marketing processes of their clients through utilizing digital and social tools to their full potential. He is an active blogger and speaker on the topic of crowd sourcing and social media.

Flirting with the Crowds: Contemplating a New Framework for Collective Collaboration

Leading businesses have already for decades built and utilized networks and collectives external to their organization for increasing innovativeness, fuelling growth and maximizing efficiency. At present, this opportunity is in the hands of virtually any business, as companies worldwide are engaging online communities and integrating external, voluntary and autonomous workforces, into their operations and decision-making processes.

Traditional frameworks for marketing, management and operations, fail to address the unique nature of these systems, for they are built for another era – an era of top-down processes and communications, of institutions used to possessing control of their environments, and of annual marketing plans that didn't need monthly, weekly or even daily adjustment. Effective business development and marketing at present requires constant collaboration with external entities. What's more, collaboration with communities and individuals empowered with the collective knowledge of the web, requires a new framework for planning and managing collaboration – one that reflects the fundamental changes in the environment and in people's behaviour.

The FLIRT model presented in this chapter is a framework that identifies the key issues and the drivers of collective collaboration for commercial purposes. The model enables the utilization of the power of the globally connected community, by fully exploiting the opportunities of modern digital networks and tools. The model has proven its applicability as a comprehensive handbook for planning and managing this kind of collaboration in a business setting, and is also a recognized academic contribution to the field.

SUCCEEDING IN COLLECTIVE COLLABORATION

A major US biotech company was in a hard place. Its internal science team had been struggling to develop a method for a cost-effective detection of DNA sequences that would be robust enough for extreme field conditions. In the end, none of the efforts were producing results. However, solving the problem was seen as crucial for the company, and management decided to explore radical alternatives for traditional R&D. Ultimately, they opened the challenge to an open community of outside scientists through Innocentive's web community, an open innovation marketplace where scientists use their spare time to solve problems for companies large and small around the globe. A significant reward was also offered for a viable solution.

In the course of just one month, over 500 community members investigated the problem, and 42 scientists submitted their potential solutions to be evaluated by the company. Finally, it was a Finnish scientist – who didn't even work in the biotech industry – who took an off-the-shelf methodology, applied it in a novel way, and submitted the winning solution. In addition to solving the initial problem, the solution also opened up further research in a new domain and resulted in a valuable patent for the company.[1]

FAILING IN COLLECTIVE COLLABORATION

The retail giant Wal-Mart found itself venturing into the social networking arena in the late summer of 2006, as they launched their social networking site 'The Hub'. The purpose was to harness young students as spokespersons for Wal-Mart and their back-to-school campaign, by letting kids set up personalized web profiles (think MySpace) and having them promote Wal-Mart products in exchange for product gifts and other rewards. The company was tapping into the power of the people, offered relevant payoff in exchange, and naturally expected to follow the path of the likes of MySpace to huge success. After all, what could go wrong? 'The Hub' fell flat on its face. The young people didn't really find their way to the site – and those who did, didn't find it to be particularly interesting nor engaging. Participation never took off, as very few visitors created profiles of any kind. Even fewer engaged in actually promoting Wal-Mart's products. What's more, both expert and citizen journalists flocked to the site, to publicly mock the failed effort in social network marketing. Ultimately, the site was discontinued after a few weeks.[2]

---

1   http://hbswk.hbs.edu/item/5544.html

2   http://adage.com/abstract.php?article_id=110520

AND THE SECRET IS ...?

What is it then that makes a fairly young start-up like Innocentive a convincing success, while a giant such as Wal-Mart flounders in this field? Surely the question is not in the amount of resources available, as Wal-Mart dwarfs most companies with its financial might. Nor can it be the amount of data gathered on the target group, as understanding consumer behaviour is one of Wal-Mart's recognized strengths.[3]

As can already be seen from the Innocentive example, open collaboration and co-creation using the power of web communities, is not any more an arena only for non-profit, cause-driven open-source successes, like the Linux operating system or Wikipedia. Open and wide-scale collaboration can and does also work in a commercial setting, provided it is done right. The secret lies in how resources are utilized in a disruptive process where people are invited to voluntarily collaborate, co-create value and form relationships. It is about nurturing the culture of *joining, sharing and participating*, as well as creating things together with other people – customers, staff members and partners – that share one or more common interests. This kind of activity can't be driven by formal or material rewards alone, but instead, things of immaterial and social nature are what matters. It is about investing time instead of money, pursuing earnest devotion instead of reach and repetition, and expressing genuine and visible interest in the people that are your customers. And it is here where frameworks for traditional marketing and marketing management fail.[4, 5]

THE NEED FOR A NEW FRAMEWORK

Is it not the very essence of the '2.0 mindset' to experiment and try out as many things as possible, in different contexts, in order to see what works and what doesn't, rejecting the initiatives that won't fly and pushing forward the ones that promise to take off? It has been argued many times over that a certain amount of waste needs to be embraced in order to succeed in the digital realm.[6] An open and experimental mindset is surely essential when venturing into new areas, finding new platforms for growth, and creating truly disruptive models for future businesses. Could it be that any kind of *formal framework* would simply block us from realizing these opportunities?

I believe that in order to make the most of our efforts, and particularly when venturing into the fuzzy and open human interaction and co-creation areas of doing business, we need proper tools for planning, designing and managing activities. Also, in addition to being potentially wasteful as regards to resources, intruding in people's social spaces without understanding their rules and the implications of your actions can be harmful for your brand. Voices coming from the loudest 1 per cent of your target group can command substantial power in moulding opinions within social networks – online or offline. And once the opinion is on the wall, it will stay there virtually forever – and can be found every time someone does a search on your brand.

3   http://hbr.harvardbusiness.org/2006/04/localization/ar/1

4   http://hbr.harvardbusiness.org/2008/12/which-kind-of-collaboration-is-right-for-you/ar/1

5   Vargo, S.L. and Lusch, R.F. 2004. Evolving to a new dominant logic for marketing. *Journal of Marketing*. 68, 1–17.

6   http://www.wired.com/techbiz/it/magazine/17-07/mf_freer

THE FLIRT MODEL OF COLLECTIVE COLLABORATION

FLIRT is a framework for planning, designing and managing an open goal-oriented collaboration with broad audiences. In order to achieve the best results in harnessing a voluntary external (e.g. customers in open crowd sourcing activities) or internal (e.g. voluntary 'communities of practice'[7] within a company) workforce, the activities can, and should be planned and managed with tools designed specifically for the purpose. These tools differ from those presently used to plan and execute conventional marketing activities – traditionally focused on one-way, top-down communication in a controlled context – and they also differ from the tools used to manage and lead internal staff, as they aim to employ voluntary action by individuals outside the control of a corporation.

Fully embracing crowd sourcing[8] and open collaboration on the social web means going one step further from the concepts of Lead Users (e.g. Hippel) and Mass Customization (e.g. Piller). It means going beyond customers simply personalizing offerings or improving them on their own, or in small groups. FLIRT is about harnessing the brainpower, judgement, collaboration capabilities and communicational clout of the vast, globally connected community, and utilizing this power to drive actions that benefit the marketer, as well as the market.

The FLIRT model is intended as a pragmatic framework for understanding and utilizing the key elements in reaching out (see Figure 8.1), engaging and empowering individual volunteers and communities, for business purposes. It identifies five major components that need to be addressed in order to enable effective participation: *Focus*, *Language*, *Incentives*, *Rules* and *Tools*. These components are further divided into smaller elements as shown below.

Focus

Of the various things you as a marketing director can do in order to fire up your brand's presence on the social web, the worst one is marching up to your advertising agency and telling them that: 'As we have very little resources available but tough objectives to achieve, we need a viral video – and by the way, it needs to adhere to the brand guidelines.' Viral phenomena do not get born this way. An equally lacking alternative is to sit down with your digital agency, or IT vendor, and ask them to deliver a platform to be used to *create a community*. They will most likely deliver to you a feature-wise nifty platform that either they get a sales commission on, or runs on a technology they have coders available for, or both apply.

In both cases you are most likely to receive something that might have a high production value, but that is not designed or built to answer your most fundamental needs. These needs can include: how to make your offering more relevant and interesting for the market; how to affect the buying behaviour of your prospects and lower the cost of sales; how to increase the value of your customer relationships; and how to nurture customer relations and strengthen loyalty.

---

7   Wenger, E., McDermott, R., and Snyder, W.M. 2002. *Cultivating Communities of Practice*, Harvard Business School Press.

8   http://www.wired.com/wired/archive/14.06/crowds.html

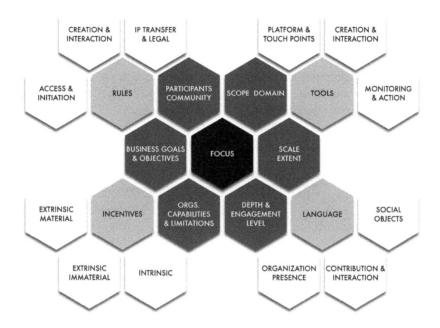

Figure 8.1   FLIRT Elements

The bottom line here is: don't start with technical platforms or trendy buzzwords. Instead, your first priority should be shaping the strategic focus of the collaboration you intend to have with your users. Doing this according to the FLIRT model makes you answer some of the more fundamental questions when starting a collaboration-based activity, and enables you to aim your follow-up tactics in the right direction. This is why the first major component in the FLIRT model is *Focus*.

FOUNDATIONS OF COLLABORATION

I divide the Focus component further into six elements: three have *founding* and three have *defining* roles. The founding elements are so labelled because they are derived from your competitive, market and organizational situation, and require careful mapping. However, this does not mean they are always self-evident or unchangeable; when defining the focus of your collective collaboration strategy, you may take the opportunity to revisit and re-emphasize certain issues over others.

The founding elements are your company's *business goals and objectives*, the external and internal *participants and communities* to be targeted, and finally the *organizational capabilities and limitations*, including your staff and organization culture, as well company policies and practices.

BUSINESS GOALS AND OBJECTIVES

Shaping Focus should start with formalizing business goals and objectives for the collaboration. The goals and objectives can be dictated by a reaction to a market situation or competitive environment, proactive setting of new strategic direction, or a mixture of all three. The objectives for modern customer collaboration can be many, including spotting weak signals[9] as well as trends[10] faster, generating more ideas for new products,[11] speeding up innovation,[12] reducing the risk of product design and development by utilizing collective judgement,[13] strengthening consumer trust through transparency and peer interaction,[14] enhancing loyalty and advocacy through engaging customers,[15] as well as co-creating and spreading marketing messages faster.[16] Goals and objectives for collaboration can be roughly divided into four groups (expanding on Orava and Perttula, 2005[17]):

- *Direct revenue from consumers*, entrepreneurs or companies as occasional, one-off buyers of community output (the Threadless.com/iStockphoto model);
- *Direct revenue from partnerships*, with the partners as enablers and customers to community output (the Innocentive/Sermo model);
- *Direct revenue from companies* as advertisers in the community (the YouTube/Facebook model); and
- *Indirect revenue,* including reduced costs, more efficient product development, better product decisions, more effective marketing efforts, strengthened customer relations and other such benefits (the Dell Ideastorm/P&G vocal point model).

One good example of a high-level goal setting is A.G. Lafley's decision after taking the helm of P&G in the year 2000. When faced with two alternatives that some saw as mutually exclusive – lowering R&D costs and developing better, premium priced products – he concluded that they could both be attained simultaneously. To achieve the two goals, 50 per cent of the innovation would have to come from outside the company, compared to 10 per cent at the time. At present, P&G is bringing in 35 per cent of product development resulting in innovation from outside the company. As a result, the company has gained 60 per cent in R&D productivity, among many other measures of success.[18]

Your objectives should always reflect your organization's current situation, key challenges and your desired strategic direction. Also, proper short- and long-term goals as well as responsibilities, need to be defined and established in this phase, to enable committing staff to reaching those goals and guiding action along the way. However, be

---

9   http://sloanreview.mit.edu/the-magazine/articles/2009/spring/50317/how-to-make-sense-of-weak-signals/

10   Whitla, P. 2009. Crowdsourcing and its application in marketing activities. *Contemporary Management Research.* 5(1), 15–28.

11   Ogawa, S. and Piller, F.T. 2006. Reducing the risks of new product development. *MIT Sloan Management Review.* 47(2).

12   http://hbswk.hbs.edu/item/5544.html

13   Ogawa, S. and Piller, F.T. 2006. Reducing the risks of new product development. *MIT Sloan Management Review.* 47(2).

14   Charron, C., Favier, J. and Li, C. 2006. *Social Computing: How Networks Erode Institutional Power, And What To Do About It.* Forrester Big Idea.

15   Marsden, P. 2006. Consumer advisory panels – The next big thing in word-of-mouth marketing? *Market Leader,* Summer. 33, 45–7.

16   Füller, J., Bartl, M., Ernst, H. and Mühlbacher, H. 2006. Community based innovation: How to integrate members of virtual communities into new product development. *Electronic Commerce Research,* 6, 57–73.

17   Orava, J. and Perttula, M. 2005. Digitaaliset yhteisöt B2C -markkinointiviestinnässä. DiViA

18   http://hbr.harvardbusiness.org/2006/03/connect-and-develop/ar/1

ready and willing to revise your goals and objectives regularly and change them if need be.[19]

POTENTIAL PARTICIPANTS AND TARGET COMMUNITIES

The potential participants and contributors in your collaborative effort can be either your *potential or existing customers* (technical enthusiasts at Dell's Ideastorm), or *other interest groups* (scientists at innocentive.com), but they can also be *individual or institutional partners* (application developers at Apple's App Store for the iPhone) or your *internal staff* (staff members at Best Buy's Blue Shirt Nation). These participants, their characteristics, and the size of the potential participant group have an effect on how you are to design the rest of your collaborative effort.

Even if each and every consumer contribution in an open setting will not be of immense value,[20] it usually pays to target a diverse participant base for the collaboration, and not only the elite or lead users of your product. The wisdom of a crowd functions best with the involvement of experienced and inexperienced, skilled and unskilled participants alike.[21] In addition, one of the key ingredients for successful problem solving with online communities is that the innovation challenges are spread out to people in various disciplines.[22] This is because innovation often happens at the intersection of disciplines, not only within them. Also, keep in mind that the people most interesting to you might not always be your customers, or even buyers of the category that you deal in.

Your primary target group is naturally of utmost importance. How much time these people have at hand, what is their general level of education, what position do they hold at work, how knowledgeable are they on your products or indeed your industry, their general reasons for being online, and the types of digital media, equipment, communities, networks and forums they are using, let alone their motivations for contributing to voluntary projects – all have implications to the structuring of the collaborative effort. And remember that everybody in the target group will surely not be participating with the same intensity level, no matter what you do (more on this in the *Language* section).

ORGANIZATIONAL CAPABILITIES AND LIMITATIONS

Many, especially large, companies are traditionally geared towards closed, secretive, rigid and hierarchical top-down management, culture and processes. There is of course nothing inherently wrong with secretive and closed corporate culture. However, openness towards and collaboration with customers, and other interest groups, are true opportunities for many companies and industries. The challenge lies in the natural organizational resistance to the idea of relinquishing significant control to people outside the company.[23] These challenges in traditional structures, policies and practices need to be well acknowledged when planning collaborative initiatives.

---

19   http://hbr.harvardbusiness.org/2008/10/shaping-strategy-in-a-world-of-constant-disruption/ar/1

20   Füller, J., Bartl, M., Ernst, H., and Mühlbacher, H. 2006. Community based innovation: How to integrate members of virtual communities into new product development. *Electronic Commerce Research.* 6, 57–73.

21   Surowiecki, J. 2004. *The Wisdom of Crowds – Why the Many are Smarter than the Few.* Abacus.

22   Lakhani, K.R. and Jeppesen, L.B. 2007. Getting unusual suspects to solve R&D puzzles. *Harvard Business Review.* 30–32.

23   http://hbr.harvardbusiness.org/2008/10/the-contribution-revolution/ar/2

If two key functions, units or divisions within your company (let's say marketing and R&D, or two parallel divisions) can't find the time or the will for genuine cooperation, it will be hard to coordinate their actions towards your customers as well. And coordination is indeed important, as your customers don't care if they are in dialogue with a sales person, or the head of R&D; in the customer's mind, each agent (e.g. sales person) is a representative of the principal (e.g. your brand) and the two are inseparable when it comes to the customer's feelings towards one or the other.[24]

Where internal cooperation proves an issue, you can either do your best to facilitate and encourage cooperation across the whole organization from the start – or start out small, with only one unit experimenting and leading the way. If you succeed in something that you can manage on your own, and show concrete and visible results, those initially negative or neutral towards your initiative are usually a lot happier to jump in and provide resources. Some other departments you need to sell your idea to when planning collaboration, are brand management (arguing for the need to control brand experience), the legal department (arguing the need to stay off the grey area and on the safe side), HR (whose help you need in educating staff members in collective collaboration) and top management (who might view your efforts as fun stuff, but not entirely critical). Management practices and policies are a very powerful tool for driving desired action, as the following quote by Cisco CEO, John Chambers, shows:

For the first two years after we started using the collaborative model, everyone would have opted out if given the option. [...] We based compensation on their collaborative abilities, as opposed to their individual performance. The first year we did that, two of my top leaders got zero bonus. You can bet they learned very quickly how to collaborate.[25]

DEFINING COLLABORATION

The defining elements are so named because they need to be crafted through active planning, based on the founding elements – goals, participants and organizational capabilities. These defining elements are the *Scope*, *Scale* and *Depth* of the collaboration. These definitions outline the collaborative initiative at the outset, and give direction to many of the planning aspects that follow. Therefore you should make these definitions tight enough to drive relevant action, and provide guidelines for the participants, but still broad enough to provide room for experimentation and the opportunity for disruptive ideas.

Scope

Scope is the functional area or organizational unit to build your collaborative offering around. Naturally, your scope can involve several areas and units, and you need to define other areas or units that are needed in a supporting role. Defining scope in this way is important, because it defines which parts and people in your organization should hold key responsibility in the initiative, which parts and people should be involved in a supporting role, and how the performance of these entities should be measured.

---

24   http://hbr.harvardbusiness.org/2009/07/the-end-of-rational-economics/ar/3

25   http://hbr.harvardbusiness.org/2008/11/cisco-sees-the-future/ar/8

With the proliferation of countless 'Send us your photo/video/song/etc'. competitions, advertising is the most visible area where crowd collaboration is at presently utilized. There are, however, other areas in which smart collaboration might offer extraordinary value. These include, but are not limited to, customer service, marketing, employee support, capital resources, design and development, and production.[26]

Marketing (e.g. word-of-mouth and viral marketing) and design (e.g. t-shirt design communities, such as Threadless) surely are understandable areas for collaboration, but what was that about using collaboration for capital resources? Just think of Sellaband. com which could be best described as a record company, by the people for the people. It is the creation of a former Sony BMG executive, who was tired of deciding what people should listen to during the next holiday season, and decided to give music fans the power to choose. The result is the online community Sellaband, where unsigned bands can exhibit their demos, photos and videos, and the members can enjoy these for free and become fans of the bands they like.

The real genius, however, lies in how Sellaband finances the first professional productions for these upcoming artists (as illustrated in Figure 8.2). All community members, that is, the fans, can invest cash directly into the bands' accounts. They do this based on their assessment of the probability that a band they like might make it big in the near future. The cost required to produce a professional-grade recording – $50,000 per band per album – is in effect invested in the bands by the fans (note that the fans can draw back their investment in full at any time before the band hits the 50k).

Once the records start selling, in digital or physical form, the record company, the band and the fans start sharing revenues accordingly. Taking into account people's enthusiasm for their favourite bands, think how effective a sales and distribution machine they become for bands in which they own a financial interest!

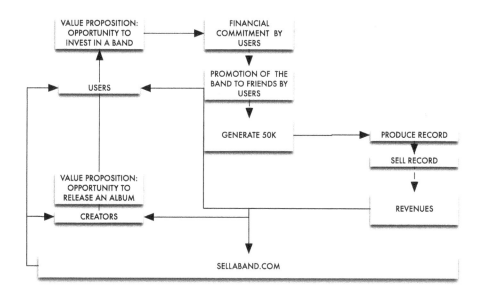

Figure 8.2   Sellaband Business Model

26   http://hbr.harvardbusiness.org/2008/10/the-contribution-revolution/ar/6

While people possess surprising capabilities to contribute to even the toughest challenges, you should be wary to expand the scope too much, and give people too much to do, and too much to decide on within one project. Cambrian House was a company set up on the idea that the members of its community would make up the whole organization, participate in all of its processes, deciding what products would be developed, helping develop them, vetoing non-viable products, helping market them, and so forth.

In May of 2008, the company was shut down, at which point their CEO stated that 'our model failed'.[27] While there might have been many reasons for the failure of the company, I argue that some of the key issues had to do with lack of focus. People simply had too much choice on how to participate, and in the end, this diluted the benefits of the network.

Paraphrasing Dan Ariely, people need runway lights to steer towards, not wholly open spaces where they can do as they please.[28] While user happiness increases some way with the growing selection of things to engage in, it quickly drops after a certain threshold is passed.[29]

Scale

Defining Scale is the next step in the focusing phase. It means defining how much interactivity you're aiming for to realize your goals, how many participants do you need for this level of activity, and what is the time horizon for the activity (i.e. how fast you need to scale to reach the desired level of activity).

What's the right size? Let's say you want to round up 100 product design concepts from amateur industrial designers. Using the widely held 1-9-90 maxim,[30] according to which 1 per cent of visitors contribute (e.g. create product designs), 9 per cent contribute just a little (e.g. rate, comment or make suggestions on the designs) and the remaining 90 per cent simply consume and never contribute, you would need to attract an audience of 10,000 people with an interest in the field and who possess practical capabilities to contribute. Many factors, such as perceived exclusivity, group homogeneity as well as selected levels and forms of participation, influence the contribution rate.

Open or closed? When looking at the size of the community you want to attract, one fundamental question is whether you want to involve users in a fully open or completely closed community (or something in between). Pisano and Verganti (2008) offer a useful framework for assessing this particular issue, as briefly explained below.

In a totally open setting, everyone (suppliers, customers, designers, research institutions, inventors, students, hobbyists, and even competitors) can participate, and you receive a broad range of interesting contributions, sprouting from different disciplines and worldviews. However, screening this potentially vast amount of ideas from fields that you may not have knowledge about, can become an issue.[31]

---

27 http://en.wikipedia.org/wiki/Cambrian_house

28 Ariely, D. 2008. *Predictably Irrational – The Hidden Forces that Shape Our Decisions*. HarperCollins.

29 http://headrush.typepad.com/creating_passionate_users/2007/02/how_much_contro.html

30 http://www.useit.com/alertbox/participation_inequality.html

31 http://hbr.harvardbusiness.org/2008/12/which-kind-of-collaboration-is-right-for-you/ar/1

With closed networks on the other hand, you approach your challenges with one or more parties pre-selected for their capabilities. With a closed mode you are likely to receive, on average, better quality solutions from elite participants, which makes screening easier. Here you are, however, relying on the assumptions that first, you have identified the right knowledge domain for your challenge, and second, that you know who the most valuable actors in that field are (and also that you can motivate them to collaborate).[32]

Campaign or community? One last question related to scale is connected to time. The question here is whether you are setting up a short-term campaign, or building a long-term community. The campaign approach is surely familiar to everybody working in marketing, and the de facto mode of traditional marketing thinking. Here you will most likely build a collaborative campaign site, drive traffic to it through both intensive advertising as well as word-of-mouth activation, inspire desired action in visitors, select the winning contributions, reward the winners, and close the campaign – or at least stop actively maintaining the content. These kinds of media-driven campaigns can naturally be used for advertising, but they can also be employed in product design competitions. Media-driven campaigns can generate fast results, and are easy to maintain and measure. However, generating trust and dialogue, forging strong, loyal relationships with customers, and affecting their long-term behaviour can be hard, as the time available is scarce.

With the community approach, you can start building a whole new kind of relationship with the participants, especially with your most enthusiastic supporters. You can also call your most aggressive dissenters inside your tent, and, by showing that you are ready to listen, ease their dissent or even turn them from enemies into friends. The Community approach, however, is a relatively laborious undertaking, and you need committed resources, both time, money and above all, people who are interested and ready to invest their time in the endeavour. The fruits of long-term commitment are harvested over a long period of time, and if the key people exit your company, you are in danger of loosing the benefits built carefully over time. Another downside of the community approach is that the benefits resulting from building a community are harder to measure, and harder to make visible and thus justify the use of resources for this effort.

Joel Greenberg writes in his blog: 'In a media driven site, the interest increases quickly, but also tends to decay over time. This is the opposite of a community site, which builds over time. My hypothesis is that in a non-community site, a media company will only be successful as they pour money into advertising campaigns to keep the interest up. However, with a community site, the interest is inherent, so people remain engaged.'[33]

Problems can arise when the border between campaign and community blur. Disney noticed this when they shut down their Virtual Magic Kingdom, or VMK after an 18-month campaign. The campaign allowed members to create profiles and avatars in a visually engaging virtual world where they could buy virtual goods to decorate themselves, or their living environments. Having invested both time and money into the virtual world, users were understandably not happy with the decision to shut down the site. As a result, petitions were signed and protests written.[34] You need to remember that although the number of active users might be small, these users are usually the loudest and potentially most harmful to your brand when irritated.

---

32   http://hbr.harvardbusiness.org/2008/12/which-kind-of-collaboration-is-right-for-you/ar/2

33   http://blog.ideacity.com/2007/01/04/contrasting-community-sites-with-marketing-sites/

34   http://www.churchofthecustomer.com/blog/2008/05/closing-a-disne.html

Depth

Depth of the activity is closely linked to your organizational capabilities. It essentially answers the question of whether to invite participants to your lobby, your offices, or your vault. It represents the extent to which the participants in the collaboration are able to view into, and have control over the collaboration inputs, processes and results.

Pisano and Verganti (2008) draw a broad distinction between hierarchical and flat collaboration communities. The fundamental question here is, who has the ultimate control to decide which challenges the community will pursue, and which solutions win? In the hierarchical model, the company has this authority, so it can direct the community toward the most valuable activity, but it then needs the capability to decide on the right direction.

In the flat model, decisions are decentralized or made collectively through cooperation by some or all community members. The advantage in the flat form is the ability to share risks and the burden of decision. However, getting the community to solve challenges and provide solutions that will be profitable for your business can prove a challenge.[35]

At the time of writing this part of the book, we can see on the smart phone market certain movements that well illustrate the lobby, offices and vault metaphors I had in the beginning of this sub-section. In the first generation of the iPhone, users were in the 'lobby' of the experience. Apple invited the users to celebrate the product and embraced the praise. Tech-enthusiasts using Nokia and the Symbian operating system were however already in the 'offices', churning out applications for the operating system. Being able to enhance the functionality of the phones by developing different applications, was obviously a plus for the advanced users, although the applications weren't spreading out to the masses. Then in 2008 a couple of things happened. Google's long awaited Android mobile platform started materializing with product announcements and appearances in trade shows. Although it wasn't as open as previously promised, it was in part open-source, and thus invited people to the 'vault' – to play with the very core of the device's capability, its operating system.

At around the same time Apple launched a new version of its coveted phone and even more notably, the App Store, through which anybody could distribute iPhone application, thus offering a one-stop shop for buyers and sellers alike, with an easy-to-use interface that also inspired tryouts and buying, with free or low priced applications – a channel that Nokia and Symbian lacked.

With the iPhone users also in the 'offices' churning out applications and enhancing the value of their devices, and with masses of enthusiasts just waiting to get their hands on the Android, Nokia made their move: they bought the remaining shares of Symbian (which had been developing the operating system for Nokia) and opened up the code base, thus also inviting their users to the 'vault'.

FOCUS – SUMMARY

In this first, Focus phase of the FLIRT model, six attributes set the boundaries for your sandbox. First you need to map out and crystallize your *business objectives*, or what you are truly after with the initiative. After this, you can start defining the *scope* of the endeavour, which department and people should hold key responsibility and which units in your

---

35 http://hbr.harvardbusiness.org/2008/12/which-kind-of-collaboration-is-right-for-you/ar/3

organization should be included as support. After this, you need map the *participants* you want to engage; who are the potential participants, what can they do and what are they like? After this phase, you need to think about the *scale* of the project, how massive do you need it to be, and over which period of time do you need to achieve short- and long-term goals. An important aspect is also looking at the *organizational capabilities* to support your initiative, and the limitations and challenges your organization possesses. Finally, you need to think about *depth*; how far you're willing to go, and in turn, how deep into the vault are you ready to let your customers go?

Naturally, the order of the process outlined above is meant as a guideline and you need to go back and forth, as well as reflect the elements against each other, as you define and refine a viable focus for your collaboration project. For example, things you discover while mapping out your organizational capabilities might well affect the scale and extent of your collaboration (e.g. are internal key people still going to be involved and with the company in one year's time?). The focusing process can thus be summarized as follows:

Language

'Think like a wise man but communicate in the language of the people' – William Butler Yeats Having gone through the focusing phase in planning collaboration (see Figure 8.3), you have only set your internal orientation for the collaboration initiative. Now is the time to *orientate outwards*, to the people you need to reach and inspire. Your customers, partners, suppliers, whoever you are aiming to engage, are most likely not interested in *your* well-being, but rather what you can offer to make *them* better off. You will need to offer the participants something concrete, in exchange for their participation, and we will review different kinds of motivators in the *Incentives* section of the FLIRT model. But before thinking about informal and formal incentives, you need to establish a connection with your participants on a more basic level – talking about topics that interest them, using a tone that they accept and feel natural with, and offering ways to join the interaction on levels, and in ways, that are possible, relevant and attractive for the target group. Thus the second phase of designing your collaborative initiative is establishing a common *Language* with the participants.

The Language phase of the FLIRT model consists of defining the following:

1. Social objects;
2. Company representation; and
3. Ways and levels of contribution and interaction.

SOCIAL OBJECTS

The social object is a concept that helps in understanding the birth, formation and development of human social networks, online or offline. Initially investigated by academics such as Karin Knorr-Cetina, the social object has recently been embraced and advocated by numerous leading thinkers in the fields of social media, social networks and online collaboration. Social objects are at present considered one of the most fundamental issues in understanding how communities are formed and inspired, for both commercial and non-commercial aims.

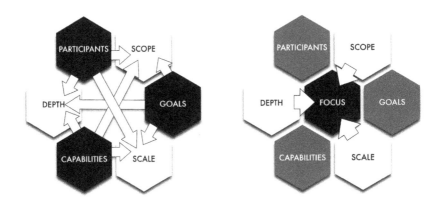

Figure 8.3 FLIRT Focus Phase

OBJECTS MATTER

The underlying insight behind the theory of object-centred sociality[36] and social objects,[37] is that communities are not formed – and social activity is not initiated – simply because people have the possibility to connect and cooperate. While social network theory is good at representing the links between people, it does not explain what connects those particular people and not others.[38] According to the social object theory, the crucial building blocks in social networks are not the links between people, but instead, the social objects that these people gather around. For a given group of people, these are the common shared objects of interest, objects we tell stories about, discuss, celebrate and create interpretations of, or in other ways manifest one's relationship with. Relationships between people then emerge as secondary, as links between people interested in the same social objects.

The social objects, then, are a key element in collective collaboration, and the most important element in the Language phase of planning collective collaboration of the FLIRT model. Social objects can be *tangible* (SLR cameras for user groups at Flickr), *living* (such as dogs, for dog lovers in the Dogster.com community), *intangible* (such as the art of digital photography for the members of Flickr.com), *clearly defined* (such as shared web addresses – or URLs – for the members of the social bookmarking service Delicious.com), or 'messy' and *not easily defined* (such as a terminal disease and related disorders, feelings and worries for people discussing these in online support groups for patients).[39]

---

36   Knorr-Cetina 1997.

37   http://www.zengestrom.com/blog/objectcentered_sociality/

38   http://www.slideshare.net/jyri/bookmarks-babies-barack-and-other-social-objects-presentation?src=embed#

39   Viitamäki, S. 2008. *The FLIRT Model of Crowdsourcing – Planning and Executing Collective Customer Collaboration.* HSE Print, Helsinki School of Economics Master's Thesis.

CHOOSING THE RIGHT OBJECTS

Knowing your target group, their values, priorities, everyday challenges, things they spend their free time on, etc., is important in finding common themes and topics that you can use to connect with them. This data should be readily available for marketers having done their homework on segmentation. But this is only one aspect in choosing topics for collaboration. Another aspect is selecting topics relevant and timely, topics which are part of the ongoing public discourse, and especially part of the average people's current interests. This emphasis on the general public's interests, is in contrast to the traditional two-step model, according to which trends spread first from media to the influential elite, and only then from the elite to the general public.[40] This was emphasized more recently by Gladwell (2000), who states that the spreading of phenomena is dependent on the Law of the Few, or on the involvement of a relatively small circle of people 'with a particular and rare set of social gifts'.[41] However, as Duncan Watts, one of the principal architects of modern network theory, argues: 'If the society is ready to embrace a trend, almost anyone can start one – and if it isn't, then almost no one can,' and continues that 'to succeed with a new product, it's less a matter of finding the perfect hipster to infect, and more a matter of gauging the public's mood.'[42]

Finally, the social objects need to also have a natural link to the collaboration you wish to initiate, to your organization and the brand that is hosting the activity. For example, if you are a communications service provider and wish to sell mobile broadband price plans to young people, a collaborative marketing campaign focused on street fashion and residing on the operator's web domain, might not be the right answer, as a mobile operator might not have the credibility to host such a discourse. However, you could pull this off by teaming with the leading fashion bloggers in your country, giving them a mobile broadband for use for a given period, and let them blog about their experiences on their *own blogs.*

HOW TO STAY ON TOP OF THINGS?

All this goes beyond basic segmentation, and it is worth exploring alternative ways to keep track of the pulse of your potential and existing clientele in real-time. In the current climate you have many tools at your disposal for tracking people's everyday discussions, including Facebook, Twitter, and other such social networks and search tools. However, analysis and production of meaningful knowledge out of the mass of input produced by the public still remains a major challenge for companies worldwide. One example, of utilizing social objects can be observed with the T-shirt design community Threadless. When engaging people in designing t-shirts, it is fairly easy to find a common object of interest; contemporary street fashion. But in addition to the continuous design competition where the themes are free, Threadless also hosts '*Threadless Loves*' competitions that have a set theme around which to design. On many occasions, they challenge people around cultural and social themes, in effect driving discussion around important societal topics,

---

40   Katz, E. and Lazarsfeld, P.F. 1955. *Personal Influence – The Part Played by People in the Flow of Mass Communications.* Free Press.

41   Gladwell, M. 2000. *The Tipping Point: How Little Things Can Make a Big Difference.* Little Brown. 33.

42   http://www.fastcompany.com/magazine/122/is-the-tipping-point-toast.html?page=0%2C2

and therefore strengthening the image of Threadless and its community, as socially responsible and ethical actors.

COMPANY REPRESENTATION

Company representation is an important factor in planning and managing collective collaboration and the second element within the Language component of the FLIRT model. It addresses the proper forms of representing your organization towards the participants within social networks and media. When you start asking people to join your efforts towards a common goal, whether it is for creating a discussion, helping with developing your offering, or evaluating your products and services, it is important to represent your company correctly to gain trust and commitment.

FOUL PLAY DOESN'T PAY IN SOCIAL MEDIA

There are many examples in the short history of social media, where companies have caused damage to their image when entering this new frontier. Many of these examples involve false representation, usually by paying or hiring people to pose as ordinary people, and write about the company and its brands in an overly positive tone. The smart and resourceful community that is the social web, is quickly able to find out things hidden from them, exposing fraudulent representations to the world in the blink of an eye.

The cosmetics brand Vichy launched an apparent consumer blog, 'Journal de ma peau' to connect to the discussions in the blogosphere. After bloggers found out that the blog was a paid effort to promote Peel Microabrasion to the consumers, they cried foul, for the blog was designed to look like an ordinary citizen's diary and didn't disclose any relations to the Vichy brand. Sony also felt the same pain, as they released a video in 2006, in which a young male rapped that: 'All he wanted for Christmas was a PSP', and published the video in a blog that was supposedly his own, with no disclosure about the relation to Sony or its marketing agency. While people instantly denounced the video on Youtube, and their own blogs and social networks, Sony denied any relationship to the campaign, which only inflamed the situation more.

THE CASE FOR COMMUNITY MANAGEMENT

In addition to revealing the company and the brand behind the collaboration, it is important to address the question of who specifically is representing the company. People on the social web discuss with people, and on Facebook, the majority of users are using their own names, not pseudonyms or nicknames. In the blogosphere, real names are the norm; even blogs that are written collectively always identify the writer by name. In this light, speaking to your target groups through an anonymous 'Team MyCompany' is probably not the best way for letting your customers get to know you. Instead, the people want names, faces and positions, so they know exactly to whom they are talking to. The ongoing maintenance of collaboration and presence on the social web is a full-time job, especially in larger enterprises. This is why, more and more companies are recruiting and appointing community managers, an emerging profession that is responsible for multi-faceted tasks, such as representing the company towards the external (or indeed internal) community, being in charge of what social tools are employed and why, measuring return on efforts, and converting the marketing messages for continuous dialogue.[43]

Note that the community manager should also be able to work in the other direction; managing the feedback and contributions coming from the community, representing the needs of the community towards the rest of the company, acting as a binding force across internal functions that are required in the collaboration.

IT DOESN'T ALWAYS HAVE TO BE YOUR FACE

Of course, there are exceptions to the rule of full transparency. The corporate clients of Innocentive might not want to reveal their identity because of security reasons, and the role and nature of the briefs solicited. In short-term advertising campaigns that utilize consumer-generated content, transparent company representation might not be necessary, and the company can be represented by fictional characters. In the end, you need to take into account the context and the assumed media literacy of your target groups, in order to decide which degree of transparency and disclosure is needed for a given situation.

THE NATURE OF CONTRIBUTION AND INTERACTION

While members of the innovation community Innocentive compete for the best possible solution for Innocentive's clients, the editors of Wikipedia clearly collaborate in creating the most comprehensive and accessible dictionary in the world. The members of Threadless, on the other hand, seem to be doing something in between; they are posting their designs online to be judged against other people's entries on which one will be produced. But they also participate in blogs and forums, and leave comments on other people's submissions, to help each other learn and become better. Different modes of interaction fit different settings, yield different results, and need therefore be part of the design process. The nature of social interaction is therefore the last element in the Language component of the FLIRT model.

COMPETITION OR COLLABORATION

What needs to be considered with regards to the nature of contributions and interaction is whether your initiative should be *collaborative* (e.g. Wikipedia, where people build on each others' contributions) or *competitive* (e.g. Threadless, where people submit individual contributions).

In a competitive setting, you will have people fighting for the top spot. While there can be cooperation in a competitive setting too, competition can stifle user's enthusiasm in revealing their solutions, at least before they have made their own contributions and/or the deadline is up. However, in a competitive setting you maximize the amount of time, and the amount of dedication users will put into their individual contributions.

---

43   Viitamäki, S. 2008. *The FLIRT Model of Crowdsourcing – Planning and Executing Collective Customer Collaboration*. HSE Print, Helsinki School of Economics Master's Thesis.

Collaboration implies open sharing and revealing of information, as well as building on others' contributions. This is a viable alternative if the costs of revealing are low – for example, when the participants don't stand to gain significant material benefit from keeping the information to themselves, and using it alternatively. Collaboration develops the knowledge and skill level of the whole community, as people reveal openly and share solutions, experiences and best practices. On the other hand, it can be harder to focus and steer towards a goal that is also useful to your organization.

ACTIVE OR PASSIVE CONTRIBUTION

This means defining the *nature of the contributions* and the *nature of the interaction* around those contributions. According to Cook (2008) the contributions of users can be active (work, expertise or information) or passive and even unknowing (behavioural data that is gathered automatically during a transaction or an activity).[44] Within these rough categories, different levels and modes of interaction are possible:

PASSIVE CONTRIBUTIONS

With passive contributions, you need to inspire people to register with your service, creating a user profile, and using your service as often as possible. This will generate usage data that can be utilized to improve your service, make recommendations to the user or other users, ultimately driving more usage of your service, or related services by new or existing users. An example is Amazon using knowledge on the items people purchase to recommend more purchases.

One key issue in driving this kind of usage is balancing the 'relevance' and 'discovery' aspects of the service, or, as Davenport and Harris (2009) put it you 'must come up with recommendations that stretch horizons with suggestions that are new and a bit surprising, yet not off-putting,'[45] continuing that in *subscription models* (where the user pays a periodical fee for unlimited usage) users tolerate more surprises than in *transaction models* (where users pay per transaction), where they want more conservative and relevant recommendations.

ACTIVE CONTRIBUTIONS

Modern online tools and platforms offer a vast array of different modes and methods of collaboration and interaction. Some of these include sharing social objects, having conversations around them, building relationships with the people with similar interests, grouping and identifying around specific issues, building one's identity, or enhancing one's reputation.[46] The most successful systems relying on users contributions usually focus on certain of these aspects at the expense of others.[47] In planning your effort, you should pick the modes of social interaction that best suit your purpose. This helps you

---

44   http://hbr.harvardbusiness.org/2008/10/the-contribution-revolution/ar/2

45   http://sloanreview.mit.edu/the-magazine/articles/2009/winter/50207/what-people-want-and-how-to-predict-it/2/

46   http://interconnected.org/home/2004/04/28/on_social_software

47   http://nform.ca/publications/social-software-building-block

focus on designing your *Tools* so that they direct participants to the most relevant action and interaction.

KEY MODES OF INTERACTION

Sharing. As already observed in the section discussing social objects, in order to get people sharing things effectively, you need to gauge and tap into the general public's mood and interests, and tailor your message accordingly. In addition, to fully exploit the 'naturally emerging social influence',[48] you need to ensure a wide-enough touch base for the things you want your audience to share, instead of the traditional word-of-mouth approach of going to great pains to find the so-called 'influential few'. Be sure to provide people with effective, easy-to-use tools for sharing,[49] so that anyone has the means to become an influencer when given the impulse (this is a topic to be discussed further in the *Tools* section).

Rating and evaluating. Asking people for their opinion offers an opportunity to make them become advocates for a cause, brand or other social object through the Hawthorne effect.[50] It needs to be noted, that when evaluating and reviewing online, people are not necessarily expressing their unbiased views on the topic, but are indeed influenced by others' opinions, especially the experts.[51] As the wisdom of crowds works best when individuals contribute without the bias of others' opinions,[52] it might be worthwhile to ensure that other people's opinions are shown only after the user has submitted his/her own input first.

Conversation. One of the key issues in driving conversation among people is group homogeneity. While in homogeneous groups members may contribute more to help peers they identify with, in a certain collective setting people might actually contribute less in a homogeneous group, because they feel their efforts are made redundant by others possessing similar knowledge and skills.[53] A certain level of group diversity needs to be ensured in order to best facilitate quality decisions. It depends on your context and aims whether you need a homogeneous or a diverse set of participants.

When driving conversation, another key issue is moderating content. This topic will be expanded in the last, *Tools* section of the FLIRT model, but the most common moderation practices include (1) community-level moderation, (2) personalized moderation, (3) collaborative moderation, and (4) partitioning of the big, heterogeneous community into smaller, homogeneous sub-communities.[54] The latter form of moderation may also partially answer the question of how to attain homogeneity within specific topics, while ensuring diversity within the larger community.

---

48 http://hbr.harvardbusiness.org/2006/09/marketing-in-an-unpredictable-world/ar/2

49 http://hbr.harvardbusiness.org/2007/05/viral-marketing-for-the-real-world/ar/1

50 Marsden, P. 2006. Consumer advisory panels – The next big thing in word-of-mouth marketing? *Market Leader*.

51 Gao, G., Gu, B., and Lin, M. 2006. The Dynamics of Online Consumer Reviews. *Workshop on Information Systems and Economics* (WISE).

52 Surowiecki, J. 2004. *The Wisdom of Crowds – Why the Many are Smarter than the Few*. Abacus.

53 Ren, Y. and Kraut, R.E. (Under review). *A Simulation for Designing Online Community: Member Motivation, Contribution, and Discussion Moderation*.

54 Ren, Y. and Kraut, R.E. (Under review). *A Simulation for Designing Online Community: Member Motivation, Contribution, and Discussion Moderation*.

Creation. Creation of original content is the most demanding task you can ask for from your audience. Asking your audience to produce a video of themselves doing a snowboard stunt, is asking a lot – especially if other factors, such as the issues of *Social Objects*, *Incentives* or *Tools* are not properly addressed. One thing you can do to fire up creativity is to set a concrete example, which people can then easily interpret from their own standpoint. Cadbury's did exactly this as they crafted their 'Eyebrow Dance' video in 2009. They:

- Exhibited an activity that was surprising and delightful to watch (doing a dance with one's eyebrows), and in addition, posed a challenge for everybody to try out (according to Cadbury's, 35 per cent of Britons can move their eyebrows independently, while 18 per cent are fully eyebrow ambidextrous[55]);
- Placed two kids in lead roles (trying out 'stupid tricks' with your friend is always double the fun – and people love to shoot their kids on video);
- Provided people with a catchy song that is in tune with the popularity of retro-styled electronic dance music;
- Finally, to maximize the touch points for things meant for sharing, Cadbury's ran the video on prime time TV.

As a result, the video was extensively shared on YouTube, amassing millions of views, and inspiring the production of numerous video responses from ordinary people, and even a parody on national TV, featuring pop superstar Lily Allen. To provide even more widespread access to join in on the phenomenon, Cadbury's launched the *Jivebrow 09* competition, during which people could use the campaign site to directly record and upload their performance to the gallery.

Incentives

'Joy is not in things; it is in us.'

Richard Wagner

As stated in the previous section, people usually need something in exchange for contributing. However, solving this question solely by coming up with a list of product rewards, gift cards and cash prizes to throw at people, is most likely solving the challenge from the wrong end, resulting in weak incentives – or at least ones driving the wrong kind of participation, and from the wrong participants.

Although material incentives usually play a key role in getting your employees and business partners to cooperate, the majority of the volunteer workforce does not depend for their livelihood on the profits generated from online collaborating with organizations and brands. These people – amateurs, enthusiasts, hobbyists, fans, garage scientists and accidental artists, usually have their daily job elsewhere and contribute for various reasons, some of them self-serving, but all of them sufficient to make formal payment

---

55   http://www.tvadmusic.co.uk/2009/01/cadburys-dairy-milk-eye-brow-dance/

partly or wholly unnecessary.[56] In the following pages, we will go through the different kinds of incentives, categorizing them to *intrinsic*, *extrinsic* and *explicit* incentives.[57]

INTRINSIC INCENTIVES

Intrinsic motivation is derived from rewards inherent in the task or activity itself – the enjoyment of a challenging crossword, or the love of engaging in physical activity, such as team sports. A person is intrinsically motivated when engaging in an activity 'with no apparent reward, except for the activity itself'.[58] Researchers have shown that people contributing to free online user-to-user support forums answer questions in order to learn, rather than to answer, and indeed have 98 per cent of their efforts rewarded via the learning they gain through thinking about a problem before answering it.[59] Contributors also do it for fun and enjoyment, through engagement in the task, and they don't perceive participation as a cost, but instead an enjoyable benefit.[60] [61]

Even such things as efficacy, the feeling of being able to cause an effect in one's environment, can sometimes be enough to get people participating[62] – especially if it is done in a way that surprises and delights people. Subservient 'Chicken', an advertising campaign for the Burger King chain, was successful in gaining traction just because of this: a chicken-suited man shot on video seemed to be performing just about anything people asked it to. There was no exceptional creativity required, no reward promised, no social dimension (other than sharing the link) involved – simply the sensation of being able to affect the content of an online video clip, with an exceptional level of freedom. But it worked; people created their own experiences of the campaign, shared the fun with their friends, and together created a phenomenon.

In planning collaboration, think how you can bring forth these intrinsic incentives first and foremost, in order to truly engage people. Naturally, knowing your target group is key in successfully identifying, selecting and emphasizing the right incentives. A good example of this can be seen on Innocentive's website. When you visit the site's section targeted to the individual contributors (solvers, as they are called), there is no strong visibility for the fact that Innocentive and its partners gives out generous prizes for the winning solutions (from $10,000 to $1,000,000). Instead, the main message you will find is the one that most attracts people with high aspirations: *'The toughest challenges, the most interesting ideas – A chance to touch every human life.'*

56   http://hbr.harvardbusiness.org/2008/10/the-contribution-revolution/ar/2

57   http://buzzcanuck.typepad.com/agentwildfire/2009/04/the-building-blocks-of-word-of-mouth-the-36-reasons-why-we-buzz.html

58   Deci, E. 1972. Intrinsic motivation, extrinsic reinforcement, and inequity. *Journal of Personality and Social Psychology.* 22(1), 113–20.

59   Lakhani, K.R. and von Hippel, E. 2003. How open source software works: 'Free' user-to-user assistance. *Research Policy. 32,* 923–43.

60   Harhoff, D., Henkel, J., and von Hippel, E. 2003. Profiting from voluntary information spillovers: How users benefit by freely revealing their innovations. *Research Policy 32,* 1753–69.

61   von Hippel, E. and von Krogh, G. 2003. Open source software and the 'private-collective' innovation model: Issues for organization science. *Organization Science.* 14(2), 209–23.

62   Wang, Y. and Fesenmaier, D.R. 2003. Towards understanding members' general participation in and active contribution to an online travel community. *Tourism Management.* 25(6), 709–22.

The intrinsic incentives you can employ to motivate participation in this way include, but are not limited to: efficacy, challenge, learning by doing, satisfying curiosity, satisfying creativity, increasing use value, enjoyment and plain fun in participation.

EXTRINSIC INCENTIVES

Both collaboration and competition are forms of social activity in which motivation external to one's self has a natural role. While intrinsic benefits are strong drivers of a person's actions, they are immediate in nature and might not be sufficient to keep up a contributor's interest for longer periods.[63, 64] In addition, effectively employing extrinsic incentives, such as peer encouragement, can lead to feelings, such as competence, that can further strengthen the intrinsic motivations.[65] To successfully do this, you must carefully define and make visible to your participants the value that they can derive from being part of your collaboration and the community around it.

In a collaborative setting, these motivations can be derived from a sense of belonging to, or creating a community,[66] or reciprocity with other people in the community in the form of ideas, assistance and links to others.[67] A relevant form of extrinsic motivation is also *visibly ranking contributors* according to the quality of their contributions,[68] and therefore providing the contributors with potential visibility and reputation gains. Integrating top contributors socially to the community and identifying them, through a 'Top Contributors' list, is also an important form of extrinsic, social incentives.[69] The applicability of different extrinsic immaterial incentives varies according to the context. As an example, if the challenges are of a technical nature, participants are more likely to feel rewarded by company, or 'industry' (expert) recognition, than by peer (amateur) recognition.[70] The Italian manufacturer Alessi, uses both company and industry recognition as a powerful incentive, as they not only share royalties from sales with the designers in their elite circle, but also include their names in product marketing.[71]

Another important extrinsic immaterial incentive for participation can be access to exclusive resources and channels that the company has readily available, and which are unreachable for the individual hobbyist. Doritos used these incentives in their 'Crash

63   von Hippel, E. and von Krogh, G. 2003. Open source software and the 'private-collective' innovation model: Issues for organization science. *Organization Science.* 14(2), 209–23.

64   Sansone, C. and Smith, J.L. 2000. Interest and self-regulation: The relation between having to and wanting to. Intrinsic and extrinsic motivation: The search for optimal motivation and performance. San Diego, CA, Academic Press: 341–72.

65   Jeppesen, L.B. and Fredriksen, L. 2006. Why do users contribute to firm-hosted user communities? The case of computer-controlled music instruments. *Organization Science.* 17(1), 45–63.

66   von Hippel, E. 2001. Innovation by user communities: learning from open-source software. *MIT Sloan Management Review.* Summer.

67   Lakhani, K.R. and von Hippel, E. 2003. How open source software works: 'free' user-to-user assistance. *Research Policy. 32,* 923–43.

68   Sansone, C. and Smith, J.L. 2000. Interest and self-regulation: The relation between having to and wanting to. Intrinsic and extrinsic motivation: The search for optimal motivation and performance. San Diego, CA, Academic Press: 341–72.

69   von Hippel, E. and von Krogh, G. 2003. Open source software and the 'private-collective' innovation model: Issues for organization science. *Organization Science.* 14(2), 209–23.

70   Jeppesen, L.B. and Fredriksen, L. 2006. Why do users contribute to firm-hosted user communities? The case of computer-controlled music instruments. *Organization Science.* 17(1), 45–63.

71   http://hbr.harvardbusiness.org/2008/12/which-kind-of-collaboration-is-right-for-you/ar/3

the Superbowl' contest, as they solicited video advertisements from the crowds for their Cheesy Doritos chips. The prospect of getting the spot aired during Superbowl, the most prestigious ad. placement slot in the world, gave aspiring amateur video artists the reason to put their heart and soul into the project, and the resulting finalist works were truly impressive in terms of both quality and creativity. The winning entry took $12.74 to produce, compared to hundreds of thousands of dollars that the same length spot could cost when produced using professional advertising and production agencies.

EXPLICIT INCENTIVES

Although people could happily participate just for the intrinsic and extrinsic immaterial incentives, it usually pays to also think about *explicit incentives*; cash rewards, gift cards, products and services provided by the company or third party partners, or indeed revenue share plans. These are usually needed for making the transaction fair to all parties, and to stave off accusations of utilizing the crowds as 'cheap labour'. Nobody likes to be used, and even if people would happily contribute without financial incentives, offering them might be necessary in order to avoid the ill will that could result by appearing to take advantage of customers, consumers or partners, without giving anything back.[72]

In some cases, significant monetary or other material incentives can be used in a major role to increase visibility and thus potential participation, so ensuring strong visibility for the campaign. One example of this kind of activity is the challenge posed by Netflix to increase their search and recommendation features by a certain percentage. The publicly announced reward for the winner, was no less than one million dollars.

The longer and deeper the collaboration project, the more considerate one should be with introducing money in the system. Direct monetary incentives can sometimes affect the social nature of the interaction and idea exchange, as people have a very different relation to money itself than to other incentives. The introduction of money can disrupt the social nature of the effort, and wrong kinds of incentives can then dominate, bringing in the wrong kinds of people. Overt focus on extrinsic motivators, such as money, may stifle free-choice activities, such as unpaid innovation[73] and otherwise downplay such intrinsic motivations as challenge, mental stimulation, curiosity and sense of fantasy, negatively affecting interpersonal interactions and creativity.[74]

Rules

Many online services depend on people ultimately wanting to do good things to each other, and to the institutions with whom they collaborate. Wikipedia is the largest encyclopedia ever created, and it is built on the power of volunteers and their donations; social lending platforms such as Kiva.org depend on benevolent people who don't expect a return on investment from the people that they lend money to; the social news service

72   Franke, N. and Shah, S. 2003. How communities support innovative activities: an exploration of assistance and sharing among end-users. *Research Policy*. 32, 157–78 Selection. PasteAndFormat (wdFormatPlainText).

73   Jeppesen, L.B. and Fredriksen, L. 2006. Why do users contribute to firm-hosted user communities? The case of computer-controlled music instruments. *Organization Science*. 17(1), 45–63.

74   Franke, N. and Shah, S. 2003. How communities support innovative activities: an exploration of assistance and sharing among end-users. *Research Policy*. 32, 157–78. Selection. PasteAndFormat (wdFormatPlainText).

Digg.com depends on their users screening and promoting news items that are worthy, and burying ones that they don't deem interesting. It will seem that it is safe to build a collaboration system on the assumption that the majority of users will be supportive, or at worst, neutral towards it. However, it is usually not the majority of the members in a given community or network that is the problem at all, but instead, the minority; vocal, resourceful and motivated to drive their own agenda. Youtube, Wikipedia, Digg, Second Life, all have their misfits, and from time to time, rebellions and misbehaviour. For a measure of control, especially in open collaboration or competition settings, we need rules that are not only established, but also enforced effectively.

The *Rules* of collaboration can be thought of as embodying many of the principles and choices you have already made in the previous phases in the FLIRT model. They make your aims clear, frame the sandbox for the participants, explicitly prohibit the forms of interaction that are not desired, and thus help you gather the kind of people, contributions and interaction that advance your – and the community's – cause.

RULES OF ACCESS

Rules of access dictate who gets in, and who is left out of your collaborative offering. This is relatively easy in a closed setting, where you are able to keep the collaboration within a desired set of people, and invite in only those you deem valuable to the endeavour. Lego chose this approach, as they screened Lego user forums in order to locate the alpha Lego-hobbyists to help them develop the next iteration of their Mindstorms offering.[75]

In a setting where you need to involve a limited group of people and the characteristics of the people are not of major importance (or you want to have a random and diverse set of participants), one approach is to use *shareable invites* – invite in a small set of users, who in turn have a possibility to invite a number of their friends to become test users, and so on. Google chose this method in 2004 when launching their Gmail service for beta testing. For an online email service with 1GB of storage (at the time) and powerful search functionality, the invites were a coveted product in the online world, fetching as much as 200 dollars per invitation on eBay.[76]

Even in a relatively open setting, you might want to let in only people with desired characteristics. Screening questions aimed to identify the people with the right profiles can be one answer here. P&G employed this approach with their word-of-mouth marketing programme Tremor, where users needed to answer questions related to their behaviour and perceived influence and status within their social circles. In 2006 Tremor had a community of over 200,000 teens, working for brands mostly outside P&G.[77]

Rules of access also dictate the levels of access for users at different levels of integration within the community. It needs to be determined which areas are accessible and which functionalities are available for registered and unregistered users alike. It might be beneficial to offer different privileges for registered users at different levels of activity and contribution, in order to *use these rules as motivators* to contribute, as we have already seen that ranking and identification of contributors can act as incentives.

---

75   http://www.wired.com/wired/archive/14.02/lego.html

76   http://www.wired.com/techbiz/it/news/2004/06/63786

77   http://www.sourcewatch.org/index.php?title=Procter_%26_Gamble#.22Tremor.22_for_teens

RULES OF INITIATION

Even if you open up your collaboration to everybody, and access is free for all, you still need to establish the rules of *initiation into the collaboration*. These rules make explicit what information or resources (even money) the participants must give up, in order to become initiated to the community. This is important, as for deriving the most value from your community, you might want to gather a bit more information on your participants than just their emails, desired usernames and passwords.

Gathering the right information on your participants – how intensively do they want to participate, are they already your customers or not, which of your services or products do they already buy, what are they interested in – makes it easier to address them with targeted messages during their participation period. However, increasing the amount of information required when registering comes at a cost. The more you ask, the less people (on average) find the will, or the time, to commit to the registration process.

In general, if you're seeking to engage a lot of people, it is better to ask as little information as possible upfront, and then ask people to fill in the blanks later, bit by bit, as they use your service. Services like Facebook and LinkedIn do this very well. LinkedIn even shows an indicator on your profile that tells you how complete (as a percentage number) your profile is, and also tells you what you need to do in order to notch up this completeness to the next level, e.g: 'adding a recommendation will increase your profile completeness from 70 per cent to 80 per cent'. In this way, information gathering and interaction encouragement is unobtrusive, and the user is not baffled by burdensome request lists, but can instead build his/her profile one small step at a time. In the process, the users cumulatively provide LinkedIn with useful information and contributions.

RULES OF CREATION

Rules of creation make explicit the qualifications of contributions that are eligible inputs to the collaboration or competition process. These rules are important in encouraging contributions that are usable and valuable for your particular challenges, so that the share of completely wasteful contributions is minimized. These rules also ensure a fair treatment to all participants, making it clear to everybody why some contributions might not be accepted while others are. They also help receive inputs that are easy for the other users to interact with, e.g. when users need to evaluate each others' designs using a pre-set criteria.

Rules of creation dictate how many contributions are allowed per participant, what are the desired formats for contributions, what kinds of attributes need to be met for the contribution to be accepted, what are the deadlines for submitting contributions, what are the criteria for selecting the winners, etc. One example of rules of creation is the Threadless Submission Kit,[78] downloadable from the website, which includes t-shirt templates, design placement photos, specialty printing guidelines, and even a separate 'decline reasons' document,[79] that explains in a straightforward fashion, what the reasons might be for a submission to be declined after posting.

---

78   http://www.threadless.com/templates/sub_kit_v1.zip

79   http://www.threadless.com/templates/declinereasons.pdf

In addition to explicit rules of access and initiation, rules of creation can also be used to attract only people with certain profiles. One of Nokia's recent design competitions was the Design Awards Competition in 2005, won by the Turkish industrial designer Tamer Nakisçi of Istanbul, who came up with a phone more like a shape shifting bracelet – a solution Nokia's people instantly fell in love with. The design competition was open for all, but only accepted works in full 3D, effectively ruling out people without the required skills or equipment.

RULES OF INTERACTION

Rules of interaction explain what people are able to do with their own or others' contributions, once they have been submitted online. The rules of interaction relate to the flatness of the collaboration and dictate, which kinds of information and idea exchanges are allowed, and encouraged, between the participants around each contribution.

If you organize your collaboration as a flat, collaborative community, it is usually good to let members comment, rate, vote and even decide on the best contributions. It is still well advised to reserve the ultimate decision power for the institution organizing the collaboration; for this, the organization has to have dedicated resources to make things happen. Free building on others' ideas can be allowed, if the setting is such that people don't stand to gain too much from keeping the information to themselves[80] (e.g. they wouldn't have the means to turn their input into profitable business without the community and the company behind it).

If, however, there are substantial, formal prizes on offer in a hierarchical system, open interaction can become problematic. Imagine one of Innocentive's clients posting an innovation challenge online and offering $100,000 for a winning solution. If one solver submits a solution, to which another one adds a bit of a different emphasis, and yet a third one introduces to it a crucial addition, which finally turns the submission into a winning solution. As there have been many people commenting and shaping a solution, how do you decide who gets the $100,000 – or if they share the prize, what would be the shares of each solver, as their time usage to solve the problem surely has differed from each other? For this reason, Innocentive utilizes a closed submission system, where people submit their solutions without revealing them to others; the client and Innocentive decide on the winner, and announce the solver's name to all participants (without necessarily revealing the winning solution).

INTELLECTUAL PROPERTY AND OTHER LEGAL ISSUES

In the collaboration and co-creation framework, you are going to be working with people who have no formal work relationship with your organization. Legal claims for the exploitation of consumer ideas and inventions can therefore be problematic.[81] A co-creation community nearly always creates intellectual property, and thus you need to think about the process for exchanging the rights in this property from the participants

80   von Hippel, E. 2001. Innovation by user communities: learning from open-source software. *MIT Sloan Management Review*. Summer.

81   Füller, J., Bartl, M., Ernst, H., and Mühlbacher, H. 2006. Community based innovation: How to integrate members of virtual communities into new product development. *Electronic Commerce Research*. 6, 57–73.

to your company. Clear and explicit terms and conditions of use highlighting property transfer issues, are necessary for making the participants feel that they are treated fairly, and also for minimizing the potential liability of litigating IP issues in court.

On many occasions, especially with consumer-oriented collaboration services, the method is to clearly state the terms and points of transfer, with which preconditions this will occur, who will be the affected parties, and what will be awarded in exchange – but still ultimately to reserve rights to use any and all contributions made using the online service, without the consent of the contributor or any payment in exchange. Whether or not this is completely fair is debatable, but it is an effective way to avoid litigation. Clinging too tightly to existing ways of handling intellectual property as well as copyright issues can be counterproductive in the collaboration economy. In an environment where the norm for consumers is to create their own interpretations of the things they love, suing everybody expressing this love can close the door to rising opportunities. Consider Scrabulous, an online version of Hasbro's popular Scrabble game that was developed by two brothers and became a hit on Facebook. Hasbro's marketing and legal department didn't want to consider the opportunities in teaming up with Scrabulous and spreading Scrabble to new audiences, although this was seen as a viable alternative by many.[82] Instead, Hasbro initiated a lawsuit and demanded that Facebook shut the application down.

However, Scrabulous was one of the most popular Facebook applications at the time, amassing millions of users, and people stood up to defend their interests. Many urged their friends to save Scrabulous using their screen names and status updates as means of communication, and the various groups gathered tens of thousands of members. As Jason Madhosingh, the creator of one of the biggest 'Save Scrabulous' Facebook groups stated: 'We have 14,000 people who are very passionate about this brand ... it's a good opportunity for the makers of this brand to engage with us instead of turning us away.'[83] But Hasbro went on with the lawsuit, angering many of potential new customers along the way. The official US and global versions of Scrabble are since up on Facebook, and have gathered in total over a million users within one year, but still short of the 2.3 million active users the original Scrabulous reportedly had.[84]

Tools

Having read this far about the FLIRT method and its different components, you already know that going platform first into customer engagement is probably not the right option. Working your way from constructing your internal *Focus* for the effort, through establishing a common *Language* with your target group, through choosing the relevant *Incentives* for the contributors, and setting up the *Rules* of the collaboration, are all considerations that need to be addressed before screening and selecting the technical platforms available.

Tools are critically important in realizing the potential of collaboration. Especially as digital technologies are developing rapidly, continuous improvements in computing

---

82   http://abcnews.go.com/Technology/AheadoftheCurve/Story?id=5443469&page=2

83   http://abcnews.go.com/Technology/AheadoftheCurve/Story?id=5443469&page=2

84   http://www.huffingtonpost.com/2008/01/11/hasbro-tries-to-shut-down_n_81176.html

power, bandwidth and storage, offer almost constant disruption opportunities for those organizations that best take advantage of them.[85] In this last section in the FLIRT model, we will go through the key issues when considering the Tools of collaboration, starting from the *platform and touch points*, addressing the tools of *creation and interaction*, and lastly investigating the tools for *monitoring and decision-making*.

COLLABORATION PLATFORM AND TOUCH POINTS

Cook (2008) defines *user contribution systems* as systems for 'aggregating and leveraging people's contributions or behaviours in ways that are useful to other people'.[86] He continues, that: 'The system converts inputs into useful outputs in real time with little or no intervention by the company,' creating 'value for a business as a consequence of the value it delivers to users – personalized purchase recommendations, connections between buyers and sellers of hard-to-find items, new personal or business relationships, lower prices, membership in a community, entertainment, information of all kinds.'[87] This is a good definition of what the platform needs to achieve.

Organizations aiming to engage people through digital tools, have numerous alternatives as far as the platform is concerned. Selecting the right platform should be one of the last things to consider in the design process, as the platform should include functionalities and features necessary to fulfil the company's needs and requirements, starting from the objectives of the collaboration and not the other way around.

If the collaboration is meant to be global and high volume, with multiple dimensions and aspects to be taken into account, a dedicated workforce is usually needed for running the aggregation, analysis and leveraging of contributions. In these cases it might be worthwhile to develop the platform using your internal workforce, or an outsourcing partner, and build it to run on-site (on the company's servers). This way, the highest possible level of personalization in design and functionality is achieved, and the competitive advantage gained by using the platform is harder for competitors to replicate. Building a solution like this from scratch is costly and time consuming, and should be pursued only when seeking substantial strategic advantage from the solution. Popular solutions of this kind include Skype (using computing power on its customers' computers to run its systems), Google (utilizing people's web behaviour to introduce meaning and structure to the vast sea of web content), Facebook (harvesting data and interaction between people to find target audiences where and when it matters), Apple's App Store (connecting the sellers and buyers of mobile applications fast and easy) and others.

Moving one step towards lighter and more affordable solutions, there are many types of modular platforms – open-source and commercial – that utilize a base platform and additional plug-ins to achieve multiple functionalities (Joomla and WordPress being among the best known open-source alternatives). These kinds of platforms can be used to set up a collaborative environment with far fewer resources than the ones needed when building your own solution from scratch. Although these platforms are of lower cost – and some are free – the workload for customizing them still needs to be estimated realistically. After receiving pricy proposals from vendors, BestBuy set up its own internal collaboration

---

85   http://hbr.harvardbusiness.org/2009/07/the-big-shift/ar/1

86   http://hbr.harvardbusiness.org/2008/10/the-contribution-revolution/ar/1

87   http://hbr.harvardbusiness.org/2008/10/the-contribution-revolution/ar/2

environment at a fraction of the cost, using open source tools and internal voluntary workforce, complemented with external work sourced using personal connections. The result, Blue Shirt Nation, is a widely referred example of internal collaboration.

If a high level of personalization is not of critical importance, software hosted in 'the cloud', or Software as a Service (SaaS) can be a viable solution. Salesforce.com as well as other vendors, offer ready-to-run solutions that include many tools for managing and analysing collaboration (such as clustering contributions and top-listing most active users). Recently, Dell's Ideastorm – an open innovation and product development service – runs on a hosted solution, and, together with other initiatives under the Dell Community umbrella, has become a benchmark for open collaboration initiatives.

If aiming to simply experiment with collaboration, you can use existing communal media, social networks and online communities for collaborative purposes. For example, if you wish your customers to send you videos or photographs, they can simply upload them to YouTube and Flickr, respectively, tag them with identifiable keywords and you are up and running with your collaboration, without too much time or money invested. Existing professional but communal media can also be used. Doritos did this, as they teamed up with Yahoo to provide the platform for their 'Crash the Superbowl' campaign, soliciting user-generated videos to compete for placement during Superbowl.

TOOLS OF CREATION

The Tools of creation are needed to manifest the contributions. Sometimes these might be built into the platform itself (as it is with Skype providing the VoIP software), but not nearly always (as with Crash the Superbowl, where the user needs a video camera and editing software in addition to the media platform). Whatever the case, these tools need to be defined in order to assess whether they should be built into the system, provided as a download, or trusted onto the participants to have as a prerequisite for participation. On the lightest level, if you are simply after well-articulated ideas, a simple discussion forum based on open source software will do, ideally coupled with rating/voting and filtering software plug-ins. However, if you wish customers to engage in-depth and actually create something, they need proper tools to do that. Web-based editors are a common choice when you want to solicit consumer-generated advertising.

The web editors can be used with a normal browser, and offer to the participant a set of tools (in the case of visual creations, canvas, graphical elements, typographical tools, etc.) to utilize in creating their works. In addition, the degree of freedom that the users will have in creating the work, can be adjusted with a web based editor, allowing just the right amount of freedom, and introducing the right constraints to induce maximum creativity and participation levels from the audience.

Downloadable clients are another form of software that can be used for enabling people to create and submit contributions. Lego's Factory invites everybody to design Lego models and kits, and all user-generated models are also on display on Lego's gallery, with the option to also buy the kits online (with only the pieces required for the kit shipped). For creating the models, Lego enthusiasts download and install the Lego Digital Designer, a piece of software which employs a sophisticated 3D user interface, and is also used to upload the models to be displayed in the gallery. The software itself is an example in collaborative product development, as it was first developed by Lego fans, and was taken into further development by the company after they spotted it at Lugnet (an online community for Lego enthusiasts).

Third party software (such as design software) and hardware (such as cameras) might be necessary for some forms of contribution, and it is necessary to assess whether the group you desire to engage is likely to have the equipment, and the associated skills needed. In some cases, you might need to think about other physical materials, too: Red Bull asked people to submit sculptures made from Red Bull cans for their 'Art of the Can' competition. Physical things that people already have can be used for co-creation, as the Japanese furniture seller NOyes has noted – they ask people to send in their old jeans, which the company then turns into customized, unique stools.

TOOLS FOR MONITORING AND LEVERAGING CONTRIBUTIONS

Tools for monitoring the contributions, such as administrative tools to moderate the influx of content and contributions, are needed for virtually any collaboration project. There needs to be a process in place to analyse and make sense of the contributions, in order to assess their value to the company or to the users, either manually (e.g. staff going through suggestions at Dell Ideastorm) or automatically (e.g. Amazon using people's buying behaviour to make automatic suggestions to drive sales).

As already observed, moderating contributions can be split into four methods: (1) community-level moderation, relying on human or software moderators to block or remove inappropriate or off-topic messages (Yahoo), (2) personalized moderation, in which different users get a different subset of messages matched to their interests, (3) collaborative moderation, in which members rate each others' messages (Digg), and (4) partitioning of the community, where the community is segmented into smaller, homogeneous sub-forums.[88]

Different kinds of analysis tools that can be used to make sense out of the moderated content and leverage it, realize value for either the contributors or the company, include tools such as: (1) cluster analysis (Platinum Blue Music Intelligence), (2) attributized Bayesian analysis (TiVo), (3) content-based filtering/decision trees (CNET), collaborative filtering (Amazon), prediction markets (Blue Shirt Nation), social network based recommendations (Last.fm), textual analysis (Google), and different forms of regression analysis.[89]

TOOLS FOR ACTING ON CONTRIBUTIONS

Tools for action involve the internal processes that the company needs to have in place in order take forward the contributions, ideas and suggestions that are deemed most interesting, and thus worthy of closer investigation. To realize the full potential from the collaboration you will need two capabilities: (1) appointed responsibilities and (2) scheduled forums.

---

88   Ren, Y. and Kraut, R.E. (Under review). *A Simulation for Designing Online Community: Member Motivation, Contribution, and Discussion Moderation.*

89   http://sloanreview.mit.edu/the-magazine/articles/2009/winter/50208/the-prediction-loverrs-handbook/

First, appointing people responsible for different areas of collaboration, setting up processes, building a pre-set criteria, screening the contributions against this criteria, and drafting decision point requirements, is key to having anything done.

Second, deciding on the internal forums that are used to present intermediate results, findings, insights, items to take forward within the company, etc., are absolutely crucial for anything to go forward beyond the person responsible for collaboration (e.g. the community manager). Usually people in the organization are interested in the process and results of collaboration, when these results are presented in well prepared presentations. But a few in the organization will come asking for this in the midst of busy everyday work. This is why you need *scheduled sessions* to spread the word and get people involved. Without addressing these last two issues, responsible people and scheduled forums, all the previous work developed for the intended collaboration is in danger of becoming useless, as nobody will have the incentive to take it forward, and nobody will be scheduled to hear about the results. Planning these carefully means you also have an incentive to measure, track and record performance.

9

Beyond Strategic Thinking: Strategy as Experienced and Embodied

JEANNE LIEDTKA

Jeanne Liedtka is a professor at the Darden Graduate School of Business Administration at the University of Virginia. Formerly the Executive Director of the School's Batten Institute, a foundation established to develop thought leadership in the fields of entrepreneurship and corporate innovation, Jeanne has also served as Chief Learning Officer for the United Technologies Corporation (UTC), headquartered in Hartford, Connecticut, and as the Associate Dean of the MBA Program at Darden. Jeanne's current teaching responsibilities focus on design thinking, innovation, and organic growth in the MBA and Executive Education Programs at Darden. She also teaches an elective course in Strategy Consulting, as well as a course focused on Strategy as a design process, conducted in Barcelona, Spain. She has consulted with a wide variety of organizations and their leaders, from museums to law firms to large corporations, on this topic. Her new book, *The Catalyst: How YOU Can Lead Extraordinary Growth*, co-authored with R. Rosen and R. Wiltbank, based on a three-year Batten Institute study of operating managers who excelled at producing revenue growth in mature organizations, was published in March, 2009. Jeanne received her DBA in Management Policy from Boston University and her MBA from the Harvard Business School. She has been involved in the corporate strategy field since beginning her career as a strategy consultant for the Boston Consulting Group.

Strategic thinking, no matter how well done, contained in mission statements, no matter how skillfully communicated, is rarely sufficient to motivate and sustain significant strategic change. That is the premise of Jeanne Liedtka's contribution. Drawing upon new developments across fields as diverse as cognitive science, philosophy, psychology, and the fine arts, Jeanne argues here that powerful strategies are driven by desire rather than by goals; they are experienced, rather than merely thought. Liedtka further elaborates on the differing aims, assumptions, and mechanisms that such a shift entails in practice, and concludes with how approaches to planning need to change to accommodate it.

Thinking versus Experiencing

The prescriptive ideal of strategy as 'thought' is pervasive, if often unarticulated, in the way we conceptualize strategy making – or, more accurately, in the way that we define the very notion of 'reason' itself.[1] Strategy as thought, grounded in a belief in rationality and objectivity, focuses on gaining employees' intellectual acceptance of a new strategy as an early milestone in successful strategy implementation. It emphasizes the value of effective strategic rhetoric that defines powerful core concepts, provides clear guidelines for action, and uses simple maxims to communicate vividly.[2] It urges strategic planning processes that utilize conscious forethought, commit aspirations and plans to paper, generally include a strong quantitative component, stress effective communication and carefully measure and monitor outcomes. In short, it makes a great deal of sense.

The problem that managers face is that it does not appear to be working very well in actual organizations today – the gap between strategy rhetoric and strategy action remains frustrating and recalcitrant. Study after study demonstrates that the 'knowing–doing gap'[3] is alive and well, and that many well-intentioned and carefully constructed strategies continue to be ignored, misunderstood, or just dismissed as relevant by the employees whose behaviours must change in order to make them work.

'Knowing' is clearly not enough, feeling must accompany it. What does it mean to feel strategy, to experience it in an emotional as well as cognitive way? It takes a change in our basic conception of what strategy is about. I urge for our consideration the notion that strategy as 'experienced' is grounded in an interpretive, socially constructed perspective, rather than an objectively rational one. It is focused on achieving a 'satisfying authenticity' that can only be accomplished through dialogue-based conversations and an emphasis on process rather than outcome. Taking literally the idea of strategy as 'crafted',[4] this perspective sees successful strategy as the product of human hands and hearts as well as minds, stressing notions of tangibility, vividness, and emergent feel.

The remainder of this chapter explores in more depth the differences entailed when viewing strategy as experienced rather than thought, and what these mean for planning processes. It concludes by questioning whether these differing conceptualizations of strategy are, in fact, mutually exclusive; arguing instead that they are potentially complementary, and taken together offer the best prospects for successful implementation. First, however, we review evidence supporting the need for a more enlightened approach to strategy making.

LOOKING FOR THE 'MISSING LINK' IN STRATEGY IMPLEMENTATION

Strategy's track record at translating its rhetoric into action fails to impress. A recent report by *The Economist* studied 197 companies and found that only about 63 per cent

1   Lakoff, G. and Johnson, M. 1999. *Philosophy in the Flesh: The Embodied Mind and its Challenge to Western Thought*. New York: Basic Books.

2   Eccles, R. and Nohria, N. 1992. *Beyond the Hype*. Boston: Harvard Business School Press.

3   Pfeffer, J. and Sutton, R. 1999. Knowing 'what' to do is not enough: turning knowledge into action. *California Management Review*. 42(1), 83–108.

4   Mintzberg, H. 1978. Strategy as craft. *Harvard Business Review*.

of new strategies' promised returns were actually delivered.[5] Consistent with these concerns, research on strategy practices as basic as the writing of mission statements – among the top-rated management tools employed over the last decade – continues to produce discouraging findings, including the lack of any substantial link between mission statements and organizational performance.[6] One researcher queried 356 managers in Europe, Asia, and Africa, and found that 82 per cent of their firms had mission statements but fully 60 per cent of managers interviewed did not believe that those statements reflected the reality of daily practices.[7]

One primary culprit blamed for these failures has been strategic planning processes.[8] Traditional approaches to planning are alleged to stifle innovation and favor incremental over substantive change; their emphasis on analytics and extrapolation to drive out creativity and invention. These processes, seemingly detached from the reality of a fast moving marketplace, produce plans that do not reliably lead in practice to successful, new strategic initiatives. Other critics look to the rhetoric itself as planting the seeds of its own demise. Eccles and Nohria,[9] in particular, argue for the centrality of rhetoric in creating the possibility for action, yet note that the torrent of verbiage directed at managers detracts from its effectiveness.

The adoption of strategic thinking as an alternative approach to traditional planning and top down rhetoric has been widely heralded. Emphasizing a systems-perspective, intelligent opportunism, and a hypothesis-driven approach, strategic thinking, it was hoped, would eliminate the 'knowing–doing gap' and produce superior results.[10] although little evidence exists that it has.[11]

As an advocate of the strategic thinking approach,[12] I have come to believe that an even more fundamental and seemingly obvious cause may underlie the long standing failure to align word and deed: that leaders must move beyond incorporating good strategic thinking and effective communication in order to succeed. Strategies must be felt to be vivid, personally meaningful, and compelling by the members of the organization who must adopt new behaviours in order to execute them. And thinking won't get you there.

Though this statement may appear self-evident, many well-accepted strategy practices, undertaken with good intentions in the name of better strategic thinking, may well work against accomplishing these outcomes.

5   Mankins, M. and Steele, R. 2005. Turning great strategy into great performance. *Harvard Business Review*, July/August, 65–72.

6   Bart C., Bontis, N., and Taggar, S. 2001. A model of the impact of mission statements on firm performance. *Management Decision*. 39(1): 19–35; David, F. and David F. 2003. It's time to redraft your mission statement. *Journal of Business Strategy*. 24(1), 11–15.

7   Wright, J. 2002. Mission and reality and why not? *Journal of Change Management*. 3(1), 30–45.

8   Mintzberg, H. 1994. *The Rise and Fall of Strategic Planning*. New York: The Free Press.

9   Eccles and Nohria, op. cit.

10   Liedtka, J. 1998. Strategic thinking: Can it be taught? *Long Range Planning*. February: 1–10.

11   Grundy, T. and Brown, L. 2005. Strategic thinking – has it any value? *Journal of Strategic Management Education*. 2(1),135–64.

12   Liedtka, op. cit.

THE PRIMACY OF STRATEGIC INTENT

In this contribution, I am primarily interested in strategic change, and accordingly, in that aspect of strategy that specifies an organization's aspirations for its future – its strategic intent. In Hamel and Prahalad's definition, such an intent 'envisions a desired leadership position and establishes the criteria the organization will use to chart its progress'.[13] This image of the future, and the extent to which it is both thought of and felt to be personally compelling by implementers, has long been seen as key to successfully implementing new strategies. The change management literature specifies that a clear and desirable future state is the cornerstone of successful change processes.[14] It is the tension between current reality and this desired intent that creates the energy for change – such a 'crystallizing intent' lies at the centre of organizational ability to create new futures.[15]

To talk about a strategic intent as experienced raises interesting issues. Perhaps most obvious, strategic intents are undeniably not tangibly real in any objective sense – they are images or ideas of future states that are imaginary and abstract, not sensate and concrete. How can they be experienced? It is the sense that the strategic intent is experienced that matters, and creates the impact on employee behaviours. As an example, consider the following quote from a manager at the New York Botanical Gardens, one of the oldest botanical gardens in the US, which had just completed a highly successful planning process aimed at rejuvenating the institution:

'At the time it was created, the plan was better than the institution. The plan was a view of what we wanted to be. As people came to understand and accept the plan, they came to embrace the Gardens that they saw through the plan, rather than the Gardens as it actually was, even though not much had actually been accomplished yet.'[16]

The pull of a powerful intent does not rest on delusion. The Gardens' stakeholders know that the future image specified in the plan does not reflect the current reality of the Gardens; they merely choose to act as though it did.

This willingness to treat as real, what we know is not, is prevalent in developed societies today. Consider the enormous popularity today of 'Reality TV'. This is not about reason and rationality. Viewers are fully aware that only some aspects of what they are watching are real, and that others are not. Rather than being disappointed or repelled by this, they find that it enhances the experience for them, making it more, rather than less, real.[17] Studies of the literary genre of 'historical fiction,' find that the 'vitality' added with the introduction of actual historical characters and settings to a novel – though patently 'false' in the sense that the events in which they are depicted never happened – enhances the reader's perception of the realness of the story and their enjoyment.[18] Similarly, sociologists studying the experiences of tourists note that 'pseudo-events' like battle re-enactments or re-created colonial villages complete with costumed guides, do

13   Hamel, G. and Prahalad, C. 1989. Strategic intent. *Harvard Business Review*. May/June, 63–76.

14   Fritz, R. 1989. The path of least resistance. New York: Fawcett Columbine; Hendry, C. 1996. Understanding and creating whole organizational change through learning theory. *Human Relations*. 49(5), 621–41.

15   Senge, P., Scharmer, O., Jaworski, J., and Flowers, B. 2004. *Presence*. Cambridge, MA: SoL Publishing.

16   Liedtka, J. 1999. *Strategic Planning at The New York Botanical Gardens (B)case*, Charlottesville, VA: Darden Publishing.

17   Rose, R., and Wood, S. 2005. Paradox and the consumption of authenticity through reality television. *Journal of Consumer Research*. 32(2), 284–97.

18   Hartman, J. 2002. *Scars of the Spirit: The Struggle against Inauthenticity*. New York: Palgrave Macmillan.

not dismay tourists. On the contrary, they are generally preferred to museum displays that merely exhibit a set of authenticated 'true' historical artifacts. As human beings, we seek out things that feel real to us – that combine reality and fantasy in a compelling way. Isn't that what strategic intent should be about?

Thus, my argument here is that strategy needs more costumed interpreters and re-enactors, rather than museum display space, because the more vivid and compelling the future image is – the more it is experienced as well as thought – the more effective it will be in facilitating the implementation of a new strategy. And you need to go beyond the faculty of reason and the power of slick communications to get there.

CONTRASTING THOUGHT AND EXPERIENCE

Exploring this idea in more depth, I want to differentiate between the notions of strategy as thought and strategy as experienced (see Figure 9.1) by examining their respective aims, assumptions, and attitudes and the differing outcomes they produce.

BEYOND INTELLECTUAL ACCEPTANCE: THE ROLE OF SATISFYING AUTHENTICITY

Strategy as thought aims for intellectual acceptance by its audience. Grounded in a rational perspective, the strategy itself is seen as independent, existing detached from its social context, and as objectively real and unproblematically knowable by those stakeholders to whom it is presented. Its important qualities are that it works – that is, be functional – and that it is cognitively comprehensible and understood. Strategy as thought rejects the old notion that employees should act on a strategy based solely on faith in their leaders. Employees' own ability to think strategically – to understand the broader strategic intent and to adapt it opportunistically – is seen as important.

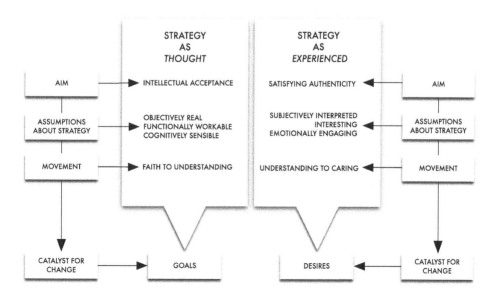

Figure 9.1   Strategy as Thought and Strategy as Experienced

Strategy as experienced, on the other hand, works from the perspective of social construction[19] – the idea that each of us interprets 'reality' through our own personal lens – and aims to achieve what researchers Rose and Wood have called a 'satisfying authenticity'.[20] In studying the enormous popularity of 'Reality TV', these researchers argue that what viewers seek is not 'truth' per se, but this 'satisfying authenticity'. Such authenticity, they argue, occurs at the intersection of the objectively real and the desirable.

Simultaneously grounded in the reality of current circumstances yet holding out promise of a better future, the idea of a strategic intent with satisfying authenticity is powerful and consistent with a view of strategy as narrative[21] – a story about an organization's desired future. If the story is perceived by constituents to have a 'satisfying authenticity' that combines reality and the desirable in a compelling way – rather than being merely intellectually accepted – its ability to motivate behavioural change increases dramatically. We can see this at play in the Garden employee for whom the 'story' contained in the plan is clearly personally desirable and therefore compelling – despite (or perhaps because of) the acknowledged reality that the Garden he sees before him today is a mess. If strategy as thought seeks to move employees beyond acting on faith in their leaders to understanding the strategy itself, strategy as experienced seeks to move them beyond such understanding to caring about whether it gets implemented. The catalyst that drives new strategic behaviours in the thought model is goals; in the experience model, it is desires.

Fundamental to discussions of understanding versus caring and goals versus desires are the ideological differences between the rational and constructivist perspectives on the nature of reality.

BEYOND THE OBJECTIVE: THE ROLE OF THE SUBJECTIVE

This debate between notions of the objectively real and the socially constructed – how human beings perceive reality – has been a central preoccupation of scholars since Plato offered his famous 'Allegory of the Cave'. The battle has been waged for centuries across a variety of different disciplines including philosophy, psychology, sociology and linguistics between objectivists who argue for a concrete and shared reality and social constructivists who see reality as constructed through social dynamics.[22] Not surprisingly, given the social nature of business organizations, the social constructivist perspective has been gaining influence in business theory.

What does the adoption of a social constructionist perspective mean for strategy? Specifically, how does a particular strategic intent become real to a given individual? Writing as early as 1890, psychologist William James posed a question of direct interest to the notion of strategy as experienced – 'Under what circumstances do we think things real?'

---

19   Berger, P. and Luckmann T. 1967. *The Social Construction of Reality*, New York: Doubleday.

20   Rose and Wood, op. cit.

21   Barry, D. and Elmes, M. 1997. Strategy retold: Towards a narrative view of strategic discourse. *Academy of Management Review*, 22, 429–52 (1997); Heracleous, L. and Barrett, M. 2001. Organizational change as discourse. *Academy of Management Journal*, 44, 755–78; Knights, D. and Mueller, F.. 2004. Strategy as a 'Project': overcoming dualisms in the strategy debate. *European Management Review*, 1, 55–61.

22   Anderson, W. 1990. *Reality isn't What it Used to be*. San Francisco: Harper and Row; Johnson, M. 1987. *The Body in the Mind*. Chicago: University of Chicago Press.

'The mere fact of appearing as an object is not enough to constitute reality ... it must appear both interesting and important ... reality means simply relation [sic] to our emotional and active life. Whatever excites and stimulates our interest is real ... whatever things have intimate and continuous connections with my life are things of whose reality I cannot doubt.'[23]

The mere creation and dissemination of a strategy – as embodied by the existence of a document or a slogan – does not assure its 'reality' to anybody but those who wrote them. Strategies are, by nature, abstractions. They begin to take on form and concreteness when translated into words or symbols. Yet, such translation is insufficient for them to be experienced as real by members of the organization not involved in their creation. The Garden employee does not see the new plan as reflective of a vivid future reality because he or she read it. Additional conditions must be met.

James suggests that progressing to the next step requires that the strategy win the competition for its audience's attention – it must avoid being ignored. What gives something the ability to draw such awareness? Decades of research by cognitive scientists demonstrate that the use of cognitive 'schemas' or 'scripts' dominate human sense making[24] – most of us, much of the time, operate on 'automatic pilot'. Getting someone to actively pay attention requires the interruption of schema-driven processing. Something must stand out among all the other messages competing for attention.

BEYOND FUNCTIONALITY: THE ROLE OF THE INTERESTING

If a strategy must attract attention, it must be more than functional or sensible. Recent research shows that the dominant characteristic of the winners of our attention are interesting to us, as James himself suggested. Sociologist Murray Davis demonstrated that the most attended-to theories in his field were valued because they were interesting, not because they were true. What made them interesting, he discovered, was that they combined the familiar with the novel.[25] They engaged audience interest, not by stating the obvious, but by offering the possibility of something not at all obvious. Researchers studying articles with impact in the business literature, found similar results – articles that readers found worth paying attention to were characterized as 'generating a particular balance of novelty and familiarity'.[26]

Translating this notion to business practice, consider the banality of much of the rhetoric of mission statements. Who sits up and takes notice of the exhortation to 'delight customers' any more? Contrast this with the example of a Swiss bank's avowed intent that all customers could say 'I know my banker'. This gets attention as it reverses the familiar 'we know our customer'.[27] Returning to the Garden example, its leader captured the attention of his employees at the start of the planning process with the statement,

23   James, W. 1952. *Principles of Psychology*. Chicago: University of Chicago Press.

24   Goffman, E. 1959. *The Presentation of Self in Everyday Life*. New York: Anchor Books Doubleday; Weick, K. 1979. *The Social Psychology of Organizing*. Random House.

25   Davis, M. 1971. That's interesting! Towards a phenomenology of sociology and a sociology of phenomenology. *Philosophy of Social Science*. 1(4), 308–44.

26   Golden-Biddle, K. and Locke, K. 1993. Appealing work: How ethnographic texts convince. *Organizational Science*. 4(4), 595–616.

27   Jacobs, C. and Heracleous, L. (forthcoming). Constructing shared understanding – the role of embodied metaphors in organizational development. *Journal of Applied Behavioural Science*.

'We are a museum of plants, not a park.' Both museums and parks were familiar concepts to employees – in fact, the Garden had been treated like a park for decades (complete with dogs, cars, and picnics) and so it was intriguing to be told that they were not one, after all. What was novel was the idea of becoming a 'museum of plants'.

The familiar, while 'true', rarely disrupts schema-driven processing. At the other extreme, the too radical message – one that contradicts too much accepted 'truth' – is likely to be rejected as false out of hand.

The artistry of the interesting is to find that point of optimal tension between the two that both engages attention and suspends disbelief. Tanner described great music as setting up expectations and then 'pleasurably defeating at least some of them'.[28] Studies of country music find that legends like Hank Williams were seen as both highly original and rooted in tradition.[29] In a similar vein, Frank Gehry, the noted architect, talks of the need to build 'conceptual handrails' into innovative designs – something stable to hold on to while you take in the new. Thus, strategies that engage at an experiential level combine novelty and familiarity to say something interesting. They are inevitably about change and also about what will not change.

BEYOND REASON AND UNDERSTANDING: THE ROLE OF EMOTION AND VALUING

Although attracting attention is an important precondition, it is rarely sufficient for motivating action. Understanding the message, as we have noted, is also key to successful strategy making. And understanding, according to constructivists, is always personal. As Johnson notes:

> *Objectivists treat understanding as transparent, as though the relation of sentences to truth conditions was mediated in a relatively unproblematic way. Between the symbols and the world there falls understanding. Grasping a meaning is an event of understanding … meaning is always a matter of relatedness. An event becomes meaningful by pointing beyond itself to prior event structures in experience or toward possible future structures.*[30]

Scholars exploring the process of understanding music discuss different levels of understanding. The first is appreciating its 'sense', getting the effect. A deeper level deals with understanding why it is as it is – understanding how the effect is achieved. This deeper level of understanding requires a level of knowledge and experience unavailable to many. This deeper understanding is the root of the ability to explain preferences in music. Without it, listening is likely to be bewildering as the listener 'cannot integrate aspects of the performance into a comprehensive understanding'.[31]

The risk in organizations is that executives, for whom the strategy is familiar, and understood at this deeper level, and whose background includes experiences that may differ

---

28   Tanner, M. 1999. Understanding music, in S. Kemal and I. Gaskell (eds), *Performance and Authenticity in the Arts*. Cambridge: Cambridge University Press. 97–113.

29   Peterson, R. 2005. In search of authenticity. *Journal of Management Studies*. 42(5), 1083–98.

30   Johnson, op. cit. 174–7.

31   Kemal, S. and Gaskell, I. 1999. *Performance and Authenticity in the Arts*. Cambridge: Cambridge University Press; Darey, N. 1999. Art, religion, and the hermeneutics of authenticity, in Kemal, S. and Gaskell, I. (eds). *Performance and Authenticity in the Arts*. Cambridge: Cambridge University Press.

markedly from many in the organization, will assume an employee level of understanding that does not exist. Senior managers, research has shown, consistently overestimate the extent to which subordinates share their view of the world.[32] A strategic intent capable of being experienced by all organizational members will need to carefully anticipate the differing experiences and frames of reference brought to its interpretation.

Moving from thought to experience, however, involves moving beyond even a deep understanding to caring or valuing, granting emotion a key role. James argued that the 'ability to arouse active impulses' – to excite pleasure or pain – was essential. In other words, compelling strategic intents need to engage emotions as well as reason. Emotions are the 'mainspring' of action: 'it is via awakened desires that emotions create tendencies to act'.[33]

BEYOND GOAL-DIRECTED: THE ROLE OF DESIRE

The ultimate catalyst for behavioural change as we move from the thought to the experience model shifts from goals to desires. Emotions play a key role in this shift – it is emotions that do the crucial work of translating goal-directedness into desire.

Desire, not goal-directedness, is the true driver of behavioural change. Helm argues that cognition and its attendant goal directedness drive a 'mind to world fit'. When confronted with a disconnect between our cognitions and the world, we are apt to change our mind to fit the 'facts' of the world. Our desires, however, drive a 'world to mind fit': when confronted with a disconnect here we are apt to try and change the world.[34]

Creating Experience in Practice

Thus far, the argument has been made that executing new strategy successfully is more likely when implementers are desire-driven, rather than merely goal-driven. Achieving this implies recognizing effective strategic intents as being subjectively interpreted, personally meaningful, and emotionally engaging, in contrast to merely objective, organization centric, and cognitive. Strategies with a satisfying authenticity, in other words, don't just reside in display cases in the British Museum, they feature costumed interpreters, like the Beefeaters at the Tower of London.

Moving strategies out of museum display cases and giving them life in day-to-day practice will require adapting different approaches to strategy making. Here, again, it is useful to contrast the kinds of mechanisms helpful for enacting strategy as thought versus those more suited for strategy as experience, as illustrated in Figure 9.2.

Strategy as thought emphasizes the effective communication of mission statements, plans, and pro formas; it utilizes conscious forethought to create these, and outcome metrics to monitor their implementation. Strategy as experienced, on the other hand, relies more heavily on dialogue-based strategic conversation as its foundation, with significant use of stories and metaphors, developed iteratively in an experimental approach. Rather

32   Bartunek, J., Lacey, C., and Wood, D. 1992. Social Cognition in Change. *Journal of Applied Behavioural Science*. 18(2), 204–23.

33   Pugmire, D. 1998. *Rediscovering Emotion*. Edinburgh University Press (1998).

34   Helm, B. 2001. *Emotional Reason*. Cambridge: Cambridge University Press (2001).

Figure 9.2   Enacting Strategy as Experienced

than relying on outcome metrics as a control device, it finds sustainability in the energy produced by the process itself. Again, we will turn to the New York Botanical Garden to better understand one story of how these elements might look in practice.

BEYOND THE PLAN: THE ROLE OF PARTICIPATION IN THE CONVERSATION

The strategy as thought perspective often argues for broader inclusion in strategy making processes as a good thing – helpful to improving the quality of the strategic choices made and the commitment to operationalizing them.[35] As strategy seeks to engage desire, as well as reason, however, the nature of the inclusion matters. Engagement that builds caring requires asking employees to bring more than just their data and opinions about strategy into the conversation – the opportunity is to bring a set of possibilities that energize them, into the search for the strategic intent, as well. Senge and his colleagues have argued recently that the future lies latent within the organization already – in the minds of managers awaiting the opportunity to emerge. Presencing is his term for creating an organizational conversation in which this latent future can emerge.[36]

The act of struggling with and coming to understand and value on one's own terms is critical. The role of audience is ill-suited for accomplishing this. The consumption of pre-packaged one-way communications, however well done, simply does not substitute for active participation in decision-making.[37] Studying the experiences of tourists, MacCannell notes that 'intimacy and closeness are more real than rationality and distance'.[38] Such closeness, he argues, means sharing the 'back region'. Creating desire necessitates inviting organizational members to be part of the back region, inviting them to be players, rather than audience. This back region has full transparency and is without

---

35   Liedtka, J. 2000. Strategic planning as a contributor to strategic change. *European Journal of Management.* 18(2), 195–206.

36   Senge et al., op. cit.

37   Hardt, H. 1993. Authenticity, Communication, and critical theory. *Critical Studies in Mass Communication.* 10, 49–69.

38   MacCannell, D. 1976, 1999. *The Tourist: A New Theory Of The Leisure Class.* Berkeley: University of California Press.

secrets; it is 'demystified'. The front region, conversely, is where the staged interaction between performers and audience occurs. To be 'one of them' is to be given access to the backstage – to be part of the production rather than the audience. Change theorists have long argued for such inclusion as beneficial to facilitating change,[39] strategy as experience demands it.

Inclusion can come in many forms – including the written. But as the emotional component becomes key to translating something that is understood into something that is cared about, the written word is less powerful than the spoken. Studies in the fine arts abound with discussions of the difference in emotional impact between reading a work and watching it performed, with the story of Alan Ginsberg's famous 1955 reading of Howl at San Francisco's City Lights bookstore emblematic of the extraordinary power of oral poetry.[40] Others decry the ambiguity and clumsiness of written language relative to the nuances available in spoken language.[41]

Certain types of speech, however, are better at evoking feeling. Metaphorical language, in particular, is seen as far more emotion-laden. Metaphor is not merely ornamental; it is central for sense making and understanding. To most, metaphors, analogies, and stories are more compelling than analytical logic and reasoning.[42] Yet, as troubling as words can be, numbers – the other language of business – can be even worse. David Boyle describes as prevalent in business the belief that only numbers are real; that 'any real knowledge is found in quantitative data, mathematical formulas and laws' and laments the illusion that what can't be measured is 'romantic tosh'.[43] Quite the contrary is true, he asserts – numbers are the ultimate abstraction and business' reliance on them to motivate and justify is a major cause of a strategy's failure to be seen as compelling. Boyle does not minimize the importance of quantitative measures and producing positive financial returns for business success. Instead, he highlights their limitations and, in particular, their lack of relevance to many in the organization who do not share executives' financial acumen and orientation. Conversations and stories cannot replace plans and pro formas – but they can make their content more compelling, more vivid.

The oral presentation format of the Garden's planning process matters to its outcome, as does the content of the questions asked. In this process, presenters don't talk about strategy, they speak for their dreams. The impact on the listeners is nearly as great as on the speakers.

BEYOND THE ABSTRACT: THE ROLE OF THE CONCRETE

The vividness necessary to strategy as experienced also lies in the particular, and one of the primary roles of strategy making processes is to give form to ideas, to render the abstract concrete. While strategy gains its power from ideas, these abstract ideas must be translated into something meaningful at the local level – something concrete to move from thought to experience. It is clear that strategies do not spring fully formed into being.

39   Liedtka, J. 2000. Strategic planning as a contributor to strategic change. *European Journal of Management*. 18(2), 195–206.

40   Kemal and Gaskell, op. cit.; Middleton, P. 1999. Poetry's oral stage in Kemal, S. and I. Gaskell (eds). *Performance and Authenticity in the Arts*. Cambridge: Cambridge University Press, 215–53.

41   Watzlawick, P. 1976. *How Real is Real?* London: Souvenir Press.

42   Pugmire, op. cit.; Eccles and Nohria, op. cit.

43   Boyle, D. 2003. *Authenticity*. London: Flamingo.

Similar to Pinocchio and the Velveteen Rabbit in the classic children's stories, strategies become more real over time and through interaction with them; they are not made that way. In the interplay between the abstract and the particular, the conceptual and the material, a strategy comes to have personal meaning and value. By making the abstract concrete in a believable way, strategic intention is linked to the details of daily practice. In the strategy field, three levels of strategy – corporate, business, and functional – are often discussed. A fourth level – the level of individual action in which grand strategies get translated into their practical implications for individuals in their day-to-day practice – has received far less attention.[44] Without success at this final stage, the other three levels are unlikely to produce new outcomes and the realization of the desired intent.

James points out that the opposite of believing something to be real is not disbelieving it – it is doubting it. Strategic intents specify a hypothetical future. As such, they can never be 'proven' to be true or false. What they must provide to be seen as real is not proof, but the absence of doubt. An interesting, meaningful, and valued intent may be doubted for many reasons – perceived underfunding, missing critical competencies, or a lack of specificity, among them. To pass beyond thought to experienced, a strategy must offer substantive evidence that achievement of the intent is possible; it must translate abstract intentions into concrete images that guide action.

In the Garden's case, the abstract notion of a 'museum, not a park' becomes more concrete as actions seen as aimed at protecting the 'works of art' – the plants – are taken. Fences are built, and dogs and cars are prohibited – all tough and unpopular (with neighbours) acts on the organization's part that both make the idea of museum more real and, at the same time, demonstrate that this time leadership really means to live their stated intentions.

BEYOND FORETHOUGHT: THE ROLE OF EXPERIMENTATION

Strategies move from the cognitive to the experienced through iteration, elucidation, and ultimately through hands-on engagement; the process of becoming requires experimentation, a kind of prototyping. Mintzberg's characterization of strategy as 'crafted'[45] ought to be taken as literal, not metaphorical – for strategy is embodied – the product of human hands as well as minds. Recent work in cognitive psychology[46] has demonstrated the fallacy of the commonplace view that reason is disembodied, that the human brain functions independently of its host, the human body. Experience is physical, as well as cognitive and emotional. Strategy must be made sensual, touchable, and viscerally accessible.

Strategy needs experiments – a way to iterate and manipulate strategies. This process of experimentation is considerably more challenging for ideas and images than it is for physical products. Architects build models; product designers build physical prototypes. How do strategies achieve similar vividness with images and ideas? This is one of the challenges experienced to achieve strategy.

---

44   Johnson, G., Melin, L., and Whittington, R. 2003. Micro Strategy and strategizing: Towards an activity-based view. *Journal of Management Studies*. 40(1), 1–22; Liedtka, J. and Rosenblum, J. 1996. Shaping conversations: Making strategy, managing change. *California Management Review*. 39(1), 141–57.

45   Mintzberg, op cit.

46   Lakoff and Johnson, op. cit.

Schon argues that expert practitioners across many fields use thought experiments as their basic method of solving problems.[47] The iterative processes of hypotheses generation and testing they use not only increase the likelihood of better solutions, they create opportunities for involvement that increases their tangibility as these hypotheses evolve into intentions. 'Serious play' has been offered as one approach for accomplishing this mental prototyping.[48] Michael Schrage observes:

> In order to have actionable meaning, the fuzzy mental models in top management minds must ultimately be externalized in representations the enterprise can grasp. Visionary speeches and mission statements embodying consultant-certified strategies don't cut it. Mental models become tangible and actionable only in the prototypes that management champions ... these models are not just tools for individual thought. They are inherently social media and mechanisms.[49]

Each idea that became part of the Garden's plan passed through four stages of review and reshaping – each time accompanied by tough questions on the part of the larger planning group. This process of continual revisiting in an iterative way spared the group from having to get it right the first time. They could play with the idea as the conversation progressed.

BEYOND OUTCOME METRICS: THE FLOW OF ENGAGEMENT IN PROCESS

One of the great truisms in management is that you 'manage what you measure'. Measurement occupies a critical role in the strategy as thought perspective, as it does in virtually any discussion of good management practice around the implementation of new strategies. Of late, however, the weakness of sole reliance on quantitative outcome measure as performance drivers is being recognized.[50] Creativity, energy, engagement in the process can all be stifled by too single-minded an emphasis on outcome goals.

Scholars who study the concept of 'flow'[51] – a 'subjective experience in which people report performing their best' – argue for the possibility of a more sophisticated approach that would value the intrinsic rewards of the process itself and allow participants to better utilize 'tacit goals, standards, and values to judge the quality of their work, consider the unique characteristics of a situation, adapt, and generate even goal-changing insights'.[52]

The idea of creating 'collective flow'[53] is especially intriguing for strategy making processes. The potential is for the act of engaging in compelling strategic conversations aimed at creating new futures to itself become a significant source of energy for sustaining the hard work of implementation. Such on-going and iterative conversations, utilizing storytelling and the language of possibilities to engage and particularize could do just

47   Schon, D. *The Reflective Practitioner*.

48   Heracleous, L. and Jacobs, C. 2005. The serious business of play. *Sloan Management Review*. 47(1), 19–20; Schrage, M. 2000. *Serious Play*. Boston: Harvard Business School Press.

49   Schrage, op. cit., 14.

50   Orlikowski, W. 2002. Knowing in practice: Enacting a collective capability in distributed organizing. *Organization Science*, 13, 249–73.

51   Czikszentmihalyi, M. 1990. *Flow: The Psychology of Optimal Experience*. New York: Harper Perennial.

52   Quinn, R. 2005. Flow in knowledge work: High performance experience in the design of national security technology. *Administrative Science Quarterly*. 50, 610–41.

53   Hatch, J. 1999. Exploring the empty spaces of organizing. *Organization Studies*. 20, 75–100.

that. Most studies of flow have focused on artists and athletes operating at world-class performance levels – is it possible to envision these kinds of peak experiences as part of strategy making processes in the work place? Designer Bruce Mau offers an intriguing insight:

'The process is more important than the outcome. When the outcome drives the process, we will only ever go to where we've already been. If process drives outcome, we may not know where we're going, but we will know we want to be there.'[54]

When the shift from desire-driven to goal-driven is successfully accomplished, attitudes shift along with it. 'Neglectful indifference' is replaced by 'passionate responsibility'. This is evident on the post-process reflection of a different Garden employee:

All of the good things that have happened here might have come out of a process where senior managers got together and made all of the decisions, but I don't think so. Even if they did, and even if the Gardens looked the same, it would feel a lot different. The ownership we feel – the investment that we all have in making the plan happen – that wouldn't be here. Neither would the patience that we developed in waiting for the things that my area has been promised in the plan.

Reconciling Thought and Experience

My ultimate goal here has been to suggest that rational prescriptions of strategy as thought are incomplete and would benefit from incorporating the insights that the socially constructed notion of strategy as experience offers. In contrasting these perspectives thus far, I have sought to highlight their differences; in this final section, I hope to point out how embracing these distinctions and accommodating both perspectives in both theory and practice has great merit. The idea of strategy as experienced, complemented by the traditional rational-analytic model of strategy as thought, offers a window into an approach to strategy making in which a series of long-standing tensions can be better understood and managed.[55]

THE TENSION BETWEEN FORETHOUGHT AND ACTION

This is perhaps the oldest battle in the strategy wars. Whether in the guise of designing versus doing, planned versus emergent, or analysis versus experimentation, the alternatives have been frequently presented as separate poles to be chosen between. Longitudinal studies of the successful strategy making processes in some of the world's largest firms have demonstrated, however, the fallacy of this dichotomy – both planning and acting, designing and doing, are evident.[56] Words are powerful and words are limiting. Consequently, finding the right words, while important, is never enough. Doing makes things vivid. And successful strategies require both.

---

54   Mau, B. '*An Incomplete Manifesto for Growth.*' Available at: http://www.brucemaudesign.com#112942 [accessed 1 September 2008].

55   Liedtka, J. and Mintzberg, H. (forthcoming). Time for Design. *Design Management Review.*

56   Grant, R. 2003. Strategic planning in a turbulent environment: Evidence from the oil majors. *Strategic Management Journal.* 24(6); Ocasio, W. and Joseph, J. (in draft). Strategic agenda management at General Electric: 1950–2004.

THE TENSION BETWEEN THE COGNITIVE AND THE AFFECTIVE

Disciplined reasoning, cause and effect, empirical demonstration, the underlying logic of economic models – all of these are critical components of strategy making processes and require non-judgemental observation of today's realities. But, as previously discussed, strategic intent is fundamentally about desire; emotion fuels change. Creating strategic intent that is experienced requires passionate imagining; yet emotions are infrequently acknowledged when we talk of strategy where the ideal of dispassionate 'rational' decision-making still dominates. Telling the truth about current reality and making the case for the plausibility of a new intent do indeed rely on a distanced, unbiased assessment of current corporate context and capabilities. Strategies, then, need to incorporate both.

THE TENSION BETWEEN THE ABSTRACT AND THE CONCRETE

Strategies have an important symbolic role. They are ideas and it is their indeterminacy that allows the emergence of new possibilities; their incompleteness invites engagement. Strategic intents, like unfinished cathedrals, are works-in-progress. Unlike their completed counterparts, they inspire engagement, rather than awe. Yet, it is at the level of the particular that ideas become real. It is in the translation from symbolic to something concrete that the sense of vividness emerges. Thus, strategies need to be both abstract and concrete simultaneously.

THE TENSION BETWEEN NOVELTY AND FAMILIARITY

Strategies exist to bring in the new (as well as to coordinate and control). As such, strategic intent is primarily concerned with tomorrow and the new possibilities resident there. Originality is a key attribute of the interesting – it also occupies a central role in strategy theory – finding a unique and differentiated position has been asserted to be the essence of competitive advantage.[57] At the same time, we have argued that familiarity – a connection to stability and rootedness – is also key. The future has no place to come from but the past. Finding the sweet spot with sufficient novelty to be innovative and sufficient familiarity to be experienced will be an on-going challenge in the creation of strategies.

Conclusion

This section has attempted to argue the case that an opportunity exits to enhance the likelihood of successful implementation of strategies in practice by moving beyond goal-driven approaches, to those *energized by desire* on the part of implementers. It has marshalled evidence from a wide variety of fields to support this hypothesis, and suggested how strategy making processes might be adapted to reflect it.

At one level, such a hypothesis appears self-evident – the power of emotional engagement and commitment is well-recognized. Its self-evidence, however, is belied by the fact that the majority of today's good practices and techniques operate on a far

---

57   Porter, M. 1980. *Competitive Strategy*. New York: The Free Press.

narrower set of assumptions grounded in rationality, objectivity, and functionality. Substituting pre-packaged communications, however expertly done, for participation, forfeits authentic engagement in strategy making processes and the possibilities inherent in this. The potential for creating both better strategic outcomes and increasing personal engagement on the part of employees argues for broadening our practices to include acknowledgement of the powerful role of subjective interpretation and experience in strategy making processes.

Such an extension brings with it new roles and challenges for executive leadership. Rather than acting as the organization's primary strategic thinkers themselves, they need to lead broadly inclusive strategic conversations among others. Such conversations are likely to be uncomfortably chaotic at times and call upon a willingness to cede the sense of control over process and content. What leaders cannot forfeit, however, is the responsibility to set the boundaries of the conversation, its rules of engagement, and the creation of a safe space in which genuine dialogue can take place.

Such a shift will require courage and patience – two qualities in short supply in organizations today. Its rewards, however, may be to finally locate the missing link between strategy's rhetoric and its execution and close the gap between knowing and doing.

Strategy Making at the New York Botanical Gardens

The New York Botanical Gardens, established in 1891 and modelled after London Kew Gardens, is one of the largest botanical gardens in the world, with both scientific and public use missions. For a period of several decades, it suffered a period of decline, with its horticultural and scientific mission eroding and its physical plant deteriorating due to use by picnickers, dogs, and cars. Throughout this time, the organization under different leaders had embarked on a number of strategic planning efforts intended to improve the Garden's position – both physically and financially. All had failed to halt the erosion. The last and most visible of these, led by a prestigious New York-based strategy consulting firm, had in particular left employees resigned and cynical.

In the early 1990s, under the leadership of a new president, the Gardens embarked on yet another extensive planning process, aimed at recapturing the Garden pre-eminence and restoring its original mission as a 'museum of plants' rather than a city park. The planning approach selected, however, was very different than previous ones – focusing on a high level of participation in what was to be a lengthy, all inclusive process. Input from all employees, at every level, was solicited during the two-year planning process. Central was the formation of the planning team, numbering about 85, which included all managers with programme responsibility and included previously ignored areas like security and food service. Each manager, beginning with those at the front-line, was asked to give a three-part oral presentation to the entire planning group that focused on three areas: (1) how their role contributed to the Garden achieving its mission; (2) the dreams they have for the future – the possibilities each of them perceived, individually in their own roles, to move the Garden forward over the next seven years; and (3) what resources they would need to accomplish this. Each presentation was followed by a question and answer period involving the group at large.

Not surprisingly, the total cost of the proposed plan when tallied exceeded even the most optimistic estimates of the fundraising capabilities of the institution. In the final step, the president, working with participating board members and senior leaders, synthesized and prioritized across all areas, and presented a proposed final plan for the larger group's discussion. Despite the need to cut back on the larger group's original dreams, there was almost complete consensus among all members of the extended planning group in support of the final plan. Realizing the aspirations the plan contained necessitated a 165 million dollar fundraising effort, three times larger than anything the Gardens had previously attempted.

A decade later, the results are impressive on many dimensions. 175 million dollars has been raised and virtually every aspect of the plan has been successfully achieved. The Garden's remarkable renaissance has been profiled in publications from the *New York Times* to *Architectural Digest*.

Senior management talked about the energy that the inclusive process created that sustained the on-going implementation of the plan, the increased understanding of the business issues the Garden faced that participation in the process generated, and the decrease in turf protection that resulted. The president described the rationale for his belief in inclusive planning processes:

> *We created the process based on the belief that the people in middle management know more about their work than we do. We respect their experiences and their opinions. We, as senior managers, had to filter it and integrate it and add our own ideas about priorities, but I believe that people have to be included. You need consensus – otherwise, a year or two later, people are shooting down the pieces that they didn't like in the first place.*

Afterword

'You have come so unpunctual into my life, that I decided to change my watches towards your possibility'

Leonardo Pardon

This book is a provocation; it aims to make you see things differently, to look at the world twice every time you read the daily headlines. It also aims to make you look at yourself and your organization in a new way, from a perspective of truth and openness. Truth and openness is to see life as an undeniable march towards its end, and that is important to face, because time is what we do not have. And if you understand this simple premise, then you understand why this book is focused on human desire as the cause of the economic system, as the reason why we build society, civilization and we create businesses. We desire Possibility. And when we let it fly away, Possibility as a Destination suffers, for all of us. What does it take to constantly try to meet yourself at your highest possibility?

To have the courage to change your watches?

The Nature of Innovation

Fifty-eight centimetres in diameter. 83.6 kilograms in weight. Sputnik 1. Launched on 5 October 1957. The launch of Sputnik spurred the development of technologies profoundly affecting our life today and changed the course of our culture. Technology was not the reason we went to space; the reason had to do with a larger theme. I started thinking about this in October 2007, 50 years after the launch of Sputnik. What was it all about? In 1968, the Apollo 8 astronauts completed the first circumnavigation of the Moon. What was on the Moon that so attracted humanity? We landed in Mare Tranquilitatis on 20 July 1969 and humans stepped on the surface at 04.17.42 pm. We abandoned the Moon just three years later, on 7 December 1972. The last crew: Gene Cernan, Ron Evans and Jack Schmitt.

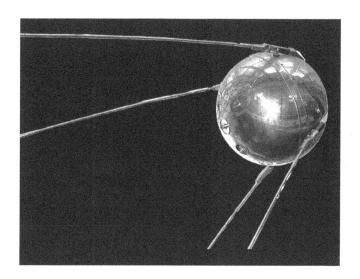

'I see something unbelievably beautiful'

'What is it?'

'Earth!'

'It IS beautiful!'

Earth; in all its uniqueness, solitude, and power.

We found what we came for; ourselves.

You and me. ***The ethos of innovation has little to do with technology; it has only to do with what we want of ourselves.***

Alexander Manu

Bibliography

Anderson, W. 1990. *Reality isn't What it Used to be*. San Francisco: Harper & Row.

Arendt, H. 1965. *The Human Condition*. Chicago and London: University of Chicago Press.

Ariely, D. 2008. *Predictably Irrational – The Hidden Forces that Shape Our Decisions*. HarperCollins.

Barry, D. and Elmes, M. 1997. Strategy retold: Towards a narrative view of strategic discourse. *Academy of Management Review*. 22, 429–52.

Bart C., Bontis, N., and Taggar, S. 2003. A model of the impact of mission statements on firm performance. *Management Decision*. 39(1), 19–35.

Bartunek, J., Lacey, C., and Wood, D. 1992. Social Cognition in Change. *Journal of Applied Behavioral Science*. 18(2), 204–23.

Bellis. M. *History of Pens and Writing Instruments*. Available at: http://inventors.about.com/library/inventors/blpen.htm [accessed: 13 August 2009].

Berger, P. and Luckmann, T. 1967. *The Social Construction of Reality*. New York: Doubleday.

Boyle, D. 2003. *Authenticity*. London: Flamingo.

Charron, C., Favier, J., and Li, C. 2006. *Social Computing: How Networks Erode Institutional Power, And What to Do About It*. Forrester Big Idea.

Czikszentmihalyi, M. 1990. *Flow: The Psychology of Optimal Experience*. New York: Harper Perennial.

Darey, N. 1999. Art, religion, and the hermeneutics of authenticity, in Kemal, S. and Gaskell, I. (eds). *Performance and Authenticity in the Arts*. Cambridge: Cambridge University Press.

David, F. and David, F. 2003. It's time to redraft your mission statement. *Journal of Business Strategy*. 24(1), 11–15.

Davis, M. 1971. That's interesting! Towards a phenomenology of sociology and a sociology of phenomenology. *Philosophy of Social Science*. 1(4), 308–44.

Deci, E. 1972. Intrinsic motivation, extrinsic reinforcement, and inequity. *Journal of Personality and Social Psychology*. 22(1), 113–20.

Eccles, R. and Nohria, N. 1992. *Beyond the Hype*. Boston: Harvard Business School Press.

Franke, N. and Shah, S. 2003. How communities support innovative activities: An exploration of assistance and sharing among end-users. *Research Policy*. 32, 157–78 Selection. PasteAndFormat (wdFormatPlainText).

Fritz, R. 1989. *The Path of Least Resistance*. New York: Fawcett Columbine.

Füller, J., Bartl, M., Ernst, H., and Mühlbacher, H. 2006. Community based innovation: How to integrate members of virtual communities into new product development. *Electronic Commerce Research*. 6, 57–73.

Gao, G., Gu, B., and Lin, M. 2006. The Dynamics of Online Consumer Reviews. *Workshop on Information Systems and Economics* (WISE).

Gladwell, M. 2000. *The Tipping Point: How Little Things Can Make a Big Difference*. Little Brown. 33.

Goffman, E. 1959. *The Presentation of Self in Everyday Life*. New York: Anchor Books Doubleday.

Golden-Biddle, K. and Locke, K. 1993. Appealing work: How ethnographic texts convince. *Organizational Science*. 4(4), 595–616.

Grant, R. 2003. Strategic planning in a turbulent environment: Evidence from the oil majors. *Strategic Management Journal*. 24(6).

Grundy, T. and Brown, L. 2005. Strategic thinking – has it any value? *Journal of Strategic Management Education*. 2(1),135–64.

Hamel, G. and Prahalad, C. 1989. Strategic intent. *Harvard Business Review*. May/June, 63–76.

Hardt, H. 1993. Authenticity, communication and critical theory. *Critical Studies in Mass Communication*. 10, 49–69.

Harhoff, D., Henkel, J., and von Hippel, E. 2003. Profiting from voluntary information spillovers: How users benefit by freely revealing their innovations. *Research Policy*. 32, 1753–69.

Hartman, J. 2002. *Scars of the Spirit: The Struggle against Inauthenticity*. New York: Palgrave Macmillan.

Hatch, J. 1999. Exploring the empty spaces of organizing. *Organization Studies*. 20, 75–100.

Helm, B. 2001. *Emotional Reason*. Cambridge: Cambridge University Press.

Hendry, C. 1996. Understanding and creating whole organizational change through learning theory. *Human Relations*. 49(5), 621–41.

Heracleous, L. and Jacobs, C. 2000. The serious business of play. *Sloan Management Review*. 47(1), 19–20; Schrage, M. 2000. *Serious Play*. Boston: Harvard Business School Press.

Heracleous, L. and Barrett, M. 2001. Organizational change as discourse. *Academy of Management Journal*, 44, 755–78.

von Hippel, E. 2001. Innovation by user communities: Learning from open-source software. *MIT Sloan Management Review*. Summer.

von Hippel, E. and von Krogh, G. 2003. Open source software and the 'private-collective' innovation model: issues for organization science. *Organization Science*. 14(2), 209–23.

Hume, D. 1888. *A Treatise of Human Nature*. Oxford: Clarendon Press, 134.

Jacobs, C. and Heracleous, L. (forthcoming). Constructing shared understanding – the role of embodied metaphors in organizational development. *Journal of Applied Behavioral Science*

James, W. 1952. *Principles of Psychology*. Chicago: University of Chicago Press.

Jeppesen, L.B. and Fredriksen, L. 2006. Why do users contribute to firm-hosted user communities? The case of computer-controlled music instruments. *Organization Science*. 17(1), 45–63.

Johnson, G., Melin, L., and Whittington, R. 2003. Micro Strategy and strategizing: Towards an activity-based view. *Journal of Management Studies*. 40(1), 1–22.

Johnson, M. 1987. *The Body in the Mind*. Chicago: University of Chicago Press.

Katz, E. and Lazarsfeld, P.F. 1955. *Personal Influence – The Part Played by People in the Flow of Mass Communications*. Free Press.

Kemal, S. and Gaskell, I. 1999. *Performance and Authenticity in the Arts*. Cambridge: Cambridge University Press.

Knights, D. and Mueller, F. 2004. Strategy as a 'project': Overcoming dualisms in the strategy debate. *European Management Review*. 1, 55–61.

Lakhani, K.R. and von Hippel, E. 2003. How open source software works: 'Free' user-to-user assistance. *Research Policy*. 32, 923–43.

Lakhani, K.R. and Jeppesen, L.B. 2007. Getting unusual suspects to solve R&D puzzles. *Harvard Business Review*. May, 30–32.

Lakoff, G. and Johnson, M. 1999. *Philosophy in the Flesh: The Embodied Mind and its Challenge to Western Thought*. New York: Basic Books.

Liedtka, J. 1998. Strategic thinking: Can it be taught? *Long Range Planning*. February: 1–10.

Liedtka, J. 1999. *Strategic Planning at The New York Botanical Gardens (B)case*, Charlottesville, VA: Darden Publishing.

Liedtka, J. 2000. Strategic planning as a contributor to strategic change. *European Journal of Management*. 18(2), 195–206.

Liedtka, J. and Mintzberg, H. (forthcoming). Time for design. *Design Management Review*.

Liedtka, J. and Rosenblum, J. 1996. Shaping conversations: Making strategy, managing change. *California Management Review*. 39(1),141–57.

MacCannell, D. 1976, 1999. *The Tourist: A New Theory of the Leisure Class*. Berkeley: University of California Press.

Mankins, M. and Steele, R. 2005. Turning great strategy into great performance. *Harvard Business Review*, July/August.

Manu, A. 1998. *The Big Idea of Design*. Copenhagen: Dansk Design Center.

Manu, A. 2007. *The Imagination Challenge: Strategic Foresight and Innovation in the Global Economy*. Berkeley: New Riders.

Manu, A. 2008. *Everything 2.0: Redesign your Business Through Foresight and Brand Innovation, DVD Video*. New Riders. Part of the 'Voices That Matter' series. First Edition.

Marsden, P. 2006. Consumer advisory panels – The next big thing in word-of-mouth marketing? *Market Leader*. Summer, 33, 45–7.

Maslow, A.H. 1943. A theory of human motivation. Originally Published in *Psychological Review*. 50, 370–96.

Mau, B. '*An Incomplete Manifesto for Growth.*' Available at: http://www.brucemaudesign.com#112942 [accessed 1 September 2008].

Middleton, P. 1999. Poetry's oral stage in Kemal, S. and I. Gaskell (eds). *Performance and Authenticity in the Arts*. Cambridge: Cambridge University Press, 215–53.

Mintzberg, H. 1987. Strategy as Craft. *Harvard Business Review*.

Mintzberg, H. 1994. *The Rise and Fall of Strategic Planning*. New York: The Free Press.

Ocasio, W. and Joseph, J. (In draft). *Strategic Agenda Management at General Electric: 1950–2004*.

Ogawa, S. and Piller, F.T. 2006. Reducing the risks of new product development. *MIT Sloan Management Review*, 47(2).

Orava, J. and Perttula, M. 2005. Digitaaliset yhteisöt B2C – markkinointiviestinnässä. DiViA.

Orlikowski, W. 2002. Knowing in practice: Enacting a collective capability in distributed organizing. *Organization Science*. 13, 249–73.

Palmisano, J.S. 2006. Foreign affairs. *Foreign Affairs*. 85(3), 132.

Peterson, R. 2005. In search of authenticity. *Journal of Management Studies*. 42(5), 1083–98.

Pfeffer, J. and Sutton, R. 1999. Knowing 'what' to do is not enough: Turning knowledge into action. *California Management Review*. 42(1), 83–108.

Porter, M. 1980. *Competitive Strategy*. New York: The Free Press.

Pugmire, D. 1998. *Rediscovering Emotion*. Edinburgh University Press.

Quinn, R. 2006. Flow in knowledge work: High performance experience in the design of national security technology. *Administrative Science Quarterly*. 50(4), 610–41.

Ren, Y. and Kraut, R.E. (Under review). *A Simulation for Designing Online Community: Member Motivation, Contribution, and Discussion Moderation*.

Rose, R. and Wood, S. 2005. Paradox and the consumption of authenticity through reality television. *Journal of Consumer Research*. 32(2), 284–97.

Sansone, C. and Smith, J.L. 2000. Interest and self-regulation: The relation between having to and wanting to. Intrinsic and extrinsic motivation: The search for optimal motivation and performance. San Diego, CA, Academic Press: 341–72.

Senge, P., Scharmer, O., Jaworski, J., and Flowers, J.B. 2004. *Presence*. Cambridge, MA. SoL Publishing.

Surowiecki, J. 2004. *The Wisdom of Crowds – Why the Many are Smarter than the Few*. Abacus.

Tanner, M. 1999. Understanding Music, in S. Kemal and I. Gaskell, (eds), *Performance and Authenticity in the Arts*. Cambridge: Cambridge University Press, 97–113.

The Internet of Things: Executive Summary. (November 2005) ITU Internet Reports 2005. Geneva: International Telecommunications Union.

Vargo, S.L. and Lusch, R.F. 2004. Evolving to a new dominant logic for marketing. *Journal of Marketing*. 68(1), 1–17.

Viitamäki, S. 2008. *The FLIRT Model of Crowdsourcing – Planning and Executing Collective Customer Collaboration*. HSE Print, Helsinki School of Economics Master's Thesis.

Wang, Y. and Fesenmaier, D.R. 2003. Towards understanding members' general participation in and active contribution to an online travel community. *Tourism Management*. 25(6), 709–22.

Watzlawick, P. 1976. *How Real is Real?* London: Souvenir Press.

Weick, K. 1979. *The Social Psychology of Organizing*. Random House.

Weill, P., Malone, T.W., D'Urso V.T., Herman, G., and Woerner, S. 2004. Do some business models perform better than others? A study of the 1000 Largest US Firms. *MIT*. 5.

Wenger, E., McDermott, R., and Snyder, W.M. 2002. *Cultivating Communities of Practice*. Harvard Business School Press.

Whitla, P. 2009. Crowdsourcing and its application in marketing activities. *Contemporary Management Research*. 5(1), 15–28.

Wright, J. 2002. Mission and reality and why not? *Journal of Change Management*. 3(1), 30–45.

Index